A PRIMER FOR
WRITING
TEACHERS

A PRIMER FOR WRITING TEACHERS

Theories, Theorists, Issues, Problems

SECOND EDITION

David Foster

Boynton/Cook
HEINEMANN
Portsmouth, NH

BOYNTON/COOK PUBLISHERS
A Division of
HEINEMANN EDUCATIONAL BOOKS, INC.
361 Hanover Street   Portsmouth, NH 03801-3959
Offices and agents throughout the world

Library of Congress Cataloging-in-Publication Data

Foster, David, 1938 August 17-
      A primer for writing teachers : theories, theorists, issues,
   problems / David Foster. -- 2nd ed.
            p.   cm.
      Includes bibliographical references and index.
      ISBN 0-86709-302-1 : $23.50
      1. English language--Rhetoric--Study and Teaching.   I. Title.
   PE1404.F67   1992
   808' .042'071--dc20   92-7941
                                                                                   CIP

Printed in the United States of America
92 93 94 95 96   9 8 7 6 5 4 3 2 1

Contents

Preface
vii

Chapter One
Teaching Writing
Tradition and Change
1

Chapter Two
**Writing and Reading,
Writers and Readers**
44

Chapter Three
Discourse Systems
What They Offer Writing Teachers
82

Chapter Four
Pressure Points
Literacy, Writing Evaluation, Basic Writing
123

Chapter Five
Planning the Course
Six Key Questions
166

Chapter Six
Teaching the Course
193

Appendix A
Teaching Composition
A Position Statement
223

Appendix B
**Partial Text of "Students' Right to
Their Own Language"***
226

Further Readings
234

Index
244

Preface to the Second Edition

Since the first edition of this book appeared at least two movements in the field of writing pedagogy have gathered momentum. One is the growth in the number of graduate programs in writing pedagogy and the consequent rise in expectations on the part of schools, colleges, and universities seeking fully trained and professionally committed teachers of writing. Gone for the most part are the days when graduate students were thrust into introductory writing classrooms innocent of any preparation, and hired as full-time teachers ignorant of the issues, problems, and strategies deriving from a serious study of fields bearing on writing pedagogy. The majority of graduate programs in English now offer a structured teaching apprenticeship which includes a range of courses in those fields related to the teaching of writing and literature; many offer specializations in composition, and even students concentrating on literary studies usually study some writing pedagogy. English Education programs in many universities, seedbeds of both theoretical and practical innovations in the teaching of writing, have influenced programs in secondary and elementary schools as well, though limited both by the inherent conservatism of state and local educational bureaucracies and by the massive social and financial problems many school districts face.

The other change, now accelerating in pace, is the increasing impact upon writing pedagogy of social, cultural, and political models of language and writing. In 1960s and 1970s, the dominant theoretical paradigm in composition was individualist, with most research focusing on the rhetoric and psychology of the individual writer. In the same decades, however, structuralist thought began to influence discourse theory, linguistics, and anthropology, gradually intensifying its impact as it was extended and modified by various poststructuralist initiatives. In the 1980s and 1990s these influences have come to affect writing theory and instruction very strongly. My primary goal in this new edition is to attempt to show how these influences have come to bear upon writing theory and pedagogy, with their emphases upon the role of community, situation, and context in writing.

I owe much to others in preparing this new edition, which features a new chapter and very considerable rewriting and reorganization-tion of material from the first edition. Gary Olson has provided continuous encouragement and gave an early version of the manuscript a keen and most helpful reading. Colleagues Bruce Campbell and Susan Wright read portions of the manuscript and made helpful suggestions. Lisa Ede furnished me with materials that helped me better understand the history of rhetoric. Perhaps needless to mention, most of us who write about teaching writing benefit richly from the constant flow of ideas and information at 4C's meetings, whose spectacular growth attests to their importance in our professional lives. And of course, Bob Boynton's support and encouragement gave this new edition its crucial impetus; his influence on teachers of writing is plain for all to see.

Chapter One

Teaching Writing
Tradition and Change

Once upon a time, several decades past, it was rumored that a student named Johnny couldn't read or write, and that this was mainly the fault of schools and colleges. Though in the years since then Johnny's (and Jill's) reading and writing have not improved much by most standard measurements, the teaching of writing has nevertheless gained a new sense of political and intellectual purpose. Language test scores have become a public issue as schools, communities, and governments vie in proclaiming their devotion to literacy education, while English teachers remain in demand in the marketplace. The teaching of writing has gained public recognition, as mandatory competency testing in many states forces students in schools and colleges to demonstrate testable writing skills. Writing-across-the-curriculum programs have gained visibility in schools and colleges around the country. These developments have stimulated the growth of graduate programs in composition in many universities and provided encouragement to graduate students to specialize in the teaching and studying of writing. Teachers of writing increasingly receive recognition and encouragement as they learn and practice their profession.

Throughout this book the term "composition" will be used to denote the teaching and studying of writing. While this term carries considerable historical baggage (which for our purposes here doesn't need opening), it is for now the most generally accepted term for writing pedagogy. Actually, some scholars and teachers of writing would argue that composition is less an academic discipline than a collection of separate theories and interests held together by a

1

common interest in the practice of teaching writing (the Greek term "praxis" has recently been used by some to describe the active, pedagogical dimension of composition). Indeed, such strong new influences have affected composition in the last two decades as to constitute what some have termed a "paradigm shift," a term coined by science philosopher Thomas Kuhn to describe how scientific theories change as scientists' attitudes alter, and first applied to composition by Richard Young.

Whether or not composition is a discipline or can be said to have one governing paradigm, it has certainly enjoyed a massive infusion of intellectual energy from such sources as cognitive-developmental psychology, structural and poststructuralist literary theory, linguistics, theories of social construction, and ethnology. Later in this chapter we will consider a major example of this influence—the impact of cognitive psychology upon our understanding of writing as a psychological process. In the later 1970's and early 1980's, partly in response to theories of cognitive process, "the writing process" became a universal for writing teachers. Courses, textbooks, and research results increasingly explored and multiplied notions of writing process, activity which was said to signal a massive shift from "product" to "process" in understanding writing. No sooner had the paradigm shift been comfortably identified with process, however, than the shift itself began to shift. In recent years process-oriented research has been criticized, while theorists from various fields have broadened the writer-centered notion of process itself into a wider social view of writing—one which we will explore in Chapter Two.

Knowledge, Power, and the Teaching of Writing

Though our understandings of the relationship between language and thought have altered as its cultural premises change, there are some constants underlying the process view of writing. The current cognitive-process emphasis relies to some extent on the same faith in the connection between reasoning and language shown almost a century ago in the Report of the Committee of Ten, which argued that "if the pupil is to secure control over the language as an instrument for the expression of his thoughts, it is necessary . . . that every thought which he expresses, whether orally or on paper, should be regarded as a proper subject for criticism as to the language" (Wright 329). The difficulty in this view is its implication that language is merely the articulation of something "behind" and psychologically prior to it—"thought"—where meaning is actually created to be dressed in words. Such a view reflects that "ornate" interpretation of rhetoric which, invoked by Plato, gave him grounds for rejecting all rhetoric as uninterested in truth. It allowed him and those in his sceptical tradition to argue that since skill in discourse consists in being able to decorate thoughts attractively, rhetoricians were at best schooled in the trivial and at worst skilled in disguising untruths. To see language as a means of expressing thought and meaning is to construe it as a tool.

This instrumental view of language is countered today by two kinds of *constructionist* views, each arguing in its own way that language is constitutive, a way not merely to express but to make meaning. We will examine both kinds more fully in Chapter Two. One view—I will call it *cognitive construction*—is that thinking and language are embedded in one another as processes of the individual mind. This view proposes that what we hold as knowledge are mental "constructs" or ways of seeing which shape our sense of the "real." In this perspective, writing and reading are constructive activities of the individual mind, writers making texts and readers (re)constructing their versions or representations of it. Communication is a matter of reciprocal meaning-making between writer and reader, speaker and audience.

Another version of constructionist theory is widely termed *social construction*—the view that self, community, and even "meaning" itself are "social constructs" emerging from the collective processes of social discourse. In this view, composing—writing and reading—are functions of the relationship among writers, readers, and their social contexts. The "relational" or "contextual" view of composition arises from this emphasis upon the social dimensions of language. From this perspective, for example, so-called "discourse communities" are said to be the real determiners of individual composing and meaning-making. A call for collaborative groups in writing classrooms is one practical result of this perspective.

While it continues to gain institutional power, composition is still shaping and defining itself intellectually under the influence of various streams of thought. While linguistics, psychology, and rhetoric continue to contribute to the theory and practice of writing pedagogy, recent poststructuralist and "anti-foundationalist" views of discourse are also making themselves felt. Several new general terms for a governing perspective in composition have been offered: "relational," "contextual," "ecological"—all suggesting that writing is a dynamic interaction among writers, readers and texts. Yet the general shiftiness in composition in recent years should make us wary of convenient labels. Perhaps we ought instead to admit that the more we understand about writing from various sources—empirical research, rhetorical inquiry, discourse modeling, hermeneutics—the more we realize how complex it really is, and the less we can tolerate its encapsulation in any particular phrase. Given the inherent ambiguity of most measures of writing achievement, it is often difficult to establish or analyze the results of writing instruction. It is far easier to discover whether students have learned the muscles of a cat or an algebraic function than to determine whether a student's writing has really improved.

If we cannot adequately measure the results of writing instruction, and if we cannot comfortably identify a unified theory to explain writing itself, how can we talk sensibly about the teaching of composition? It is an important question with no easy answer, a fact which should encourage us to be cautious and and yet open in our assessments of current writing theory and practice. Writing teachers are tempted to envy math, history, or physical education teachers, who can at least measure their teaching success by the number of equations solved, dates remembered, or chin-ups counted. Despairing at the lack of measurable results often appearing at post-test time, writing teachers may resort to the psychotherapist's excuse: the patient didn't want to change after all. And the writing problems students still have after finishing composition courses make writing teachers vulnerable to criticism from colleagues in other disciplines. An inability to focus and organize a paper, a difficulty in constructing coherent paragraphs and sentences, or, particularly, editing and proofreading failures mark students in the public eye as victims of English department malpractice.

Teaching writing often seems a uniquely thankless job. Indeed, writing teachers may be excused for thinking their job today is even harder than it used to be because they are assailed by so many competing ideas and goals. Theories of language, various ideologies, rhetorical systems and thorny epistemological tangles confront teachers in texts and journals, even as they face the daily practicalities of freshman composition, business and technical writing, and myriad other academic writing purposes. Writing teachers are prone to feel nostalgic over the popular image of the nineteenth century English teacher single-mindedly shaking out of her pupils all the rude differences of language inevitable in an immigrant society, in favor of the formal idioms of McGuffey's reader. Yet the history of English education in America reveals educators at different periods defining the purposes of writing instruction in oddly familiar terms. At least three major concerns recur in English educational policy: the value of writing as a form of power, the primary importance of literacy instruction in the English teacher's job, and changing perceptions of the relationship between language and thought.

Writing has often been justified as an instrument of both personal and social power. One nineteenth century headmaster, using the code words of the Protestant work ethic, associated language learning with character-forming labor: "the earnest, laborious student of language develops a power which no other training could possibly give him, and in comparison with which all his acquisitions of mere knowledge sink into utter insignificance" (Applebee xii). The kind of power conferred by language mastery was spelled out nearly a hundred years later by the Commission on the English Curriculum, which asserted that the "power to use words orally and in writing" allows the student to "achieve adequate adjustment for himself and his teen-age friends" (Applebee 138). The emphasis on language's life-adjustment power reflects the impact of progressive education upon language goals, and foreshadows the more recent emphasis upon language play as a means of personal discovery and growth, the "expressive" attitude that "writing development can aid personal development" in producing "better psychologically integrated people" (Faigley 531). Rooted in the Romantic virtues of imaginative freedom and spontaneity, the expressive view sees writing as a valuable form of language play by means of which individual discovery and resistance to convention is nurtured. As we will see in later chapters, the expressive position has strongly influenced both student roles and teaching strategies in writing classes.

But interest in the kind of power language confers upon students is not the only link between traditional and contemporary writing pedagogy. The place of writing instruction in the English department is another subject of longstanding debate in American education. Arguments over the relative importance of teaching writing, as opposed to literature, have heated teachers' lounges for at least a hundred years. In the later nineteenth and early twentieth centuries, "composition" was a general term for instruction in rhetoric, usage, and correctness, with particular attention in schools to correcting the nonstandardisms of an increasingly diverse population. Arthur Applebee argues that pressure from the Committee of Ten Report and other efforts to standardize college and preparatory studies enhanced the stature of literary instruction until, by the early twentieth century, school and college writing was taught as an element of, and a tool for, the study of literary culture (38). Rhetoric gravitated to speech departments, in the wake of the split between English departments (which took over literature and composition) and speech departments (which appropriated, by default, "oratory," or "public speaking," and the rhetorical tradition behind it). Later, composition in the schools began to receive a different emphasis with the coming of progressivism: "Our major task in the ordinary school is to teach all our pupils to read ordinary matters with ordinary intelligence and to express ordinary thoughts with reasonable clarity," remarked an NCTE president in the mid-1930s (Applebee 106). Following Dewey's insistence that the business of education was designing proper experiences for students, English curriculum planners emphasized the role of writing in students' self-development. Advocacy by participants in the 1966 Dartmouth conference of developmental goals for the English curriculum—e.g., the self-awareness gained from increased mastery of language skills—reinforced the expressive perspective and antagonized tradition-oriented conservatives in English departments. As a result of such shifting emphases, tension persists today within English departments not only between those who teach literature and those who teach writing, but also between writing teachers attracted to current (and still evolving) pedagogical ideas and those who continue to rely on traditional teaching methods. As we will see in later chapters, such tensions can strongly influence teaching approaches and methods.

Rather than attempting to reconcile the rich diversity of competing ideas in composition today, we need to explore their sources, their interactions, and their potential for our teaching. In the following chapters, we will consider many of the influences upon composition mentioned above, in order to better understand how they underlie our thinking as teachers of writing. Various approaches to teaching writing will be studied, in order to distinguish what seems more effective from what seems less. We will examine why some traditional aspects of writing instruction are ineffective and counterproductive, which traditional and current theories seem most useful and how they might affect our teaching, and how to plan and run an effective writing course.

Talking About Teaching Writing

What do we think we're doing when we teach writing?

Needless to say, divergent views of the relationship between thought and language have generated rivalry among traditional and new pedagogical methods. For example, sentence combining, emerging at the height of transformational linguistics's dominance, has diminished in popularity as teachers discovered that its focus on syntax tends to downplay other aspects of composing—structure, writers' intentions, and readers' expectations. The concept of "persona," the attitudes and sensibilities identified with the writer, has also been traditionally popular as a way of expressing the writer's presentation of self in language. But more recent perspectives on the interactive relationship between writer and reader have led to a redefinition of personal authority in writing as a transaction between writer and hypothetical or imagined reader—not just the presentation of the writer's identity. Such recent shifts suggest a discipline (remember, we are using "discipline" by agreement as a convenient term of reference only) still seeking its roots, or to wrench the metaphor a bit, still putting out main branches in different directions.

Ambivalence and shifting emphases characterize writing pedagogy because writing is a complex blend of abilities and learned skills. Writing is—to borrow from the vocabulary of education philosophy —both an "open" and a "closed" capacity. As John Passmore points out, a closed capacity is one that eventually "allows of total mastery," while an open capacity is "never fully mastered to perfection. . . . Somebody else—or ourselves at some other time—could do it better" (40). Examples of closed capacities, he suggests, are adding and subtracting, playing tic-tac-toe, performing an assembly-line operation, solving equations, or operating a complex machine. All these tasks may in time be mastered completely and accomplished at a speed only surpassed by machines or computers programmed for the same tasks. Open capacities, on the other hand, are never completely mastered; there is always more to be learned about improving chess skills, suggests Passmore, in contrast to tic-tac-toe (41). Any task that requires imagination, judgment, or creativity involves open capacities, whether manual or mental, in trades, management, or the professions. An open capacity may depend upon a closed capacity. Determining the effectiveness of a drug or a teaching method may depend upon skill in applying measurement statistics and drawing the proper inferences from them. Such a determination requires the closed capacity to work statistical procedures in order to produce data; drawing conclusions from the project requires the open capacity (a combination of imagination and judgment) to interpret the data and make decisions from such interpretations.

Writing, and teaching writing, are open capacities. Yet some of the actions and skills contributing to their success are closed, needing only to be mastered to fill their place in the larger effort. Successful writing instruction depends upon the instructor's understanding which elements of writing depend upon closed capacities, at what point writing must be treated as an open capacity, and what attitudes and methods are appropriate to each kind of capacity. Teaching an open capacity as though it were a closed capacity may be profoundly counterproductive, yet perhaps no more so than attempting to treat some of the closed capacities in writing as though they were actually open.

The act of writing depends upon many closed capacities. Most obvious is the skill in editing mechanics: spelling, punctuation, error-avoidance, and the correcting of typographical errors. The application of such skills is often what people—even some writing teachers—mean by writing "correctly," and writing handbooks enforce the view that teaching such skills is a primary mission of composition instruction. The detailed elaboration of grammar rules and the etiquette of documentation, for example, imply that these elements of the written product ought to be supremely important to student writers. But documentation, for example, is a closed capacity governed by formulas. A perfect footnote is possible for careful students to achieve. Insisting on accurate spelling often draws much of the writing teacher's energy, because it's the most visible evidence of "literacy" to many readers. Yet spelling correctly is a closed capacity that can be taught to most students. Finally, the error-orientation that underlies many handbooks' emphasis upon rules suggests that error-free writing should be the writing teacher's main goal. But error-free writing can easily enough be achieved and is not necessarily effective writing. Learning the conventions of standard written English requires detailed, painstaking labor; it does not require imagination, inventiveness, or reasoning power.

Even activities requiring these abilities may involve closed capacities. "Heuristic" or exploratory methods, for example, can become sterile exercises for students who, having learned the basic heuristic steps, satisfy themselves with applying them routinely without real insight or discovery. Some traditional ways of imposing structure upon paragraphs may also inculcate closed capacities in students. For example, the notion of a topic sentence in paragraphs has been maligned frequently on the grounds that pedagogical insistence upon a topic sentence ignores the infinite number of possible paragraph arrangements that do not have one. Yet the very attempt to "teach" students paragraph patterns, with or without topic sentences, may itself develop into a closed, limiting exercise. Paragraph models themselves derive from completed writings, the visible results of global acts of composing specific to a particular writer addressing a particular audience in a particular situation. Teaching students to generate paragraphs according to sanctioned models may encourage students to practice what must be an open-ended capacity as a closed, form-bound skill. The same danger lurks in other strategies as well: teaching expository discourse by the five-paragraph model, teaching organization by means of outlining, or teaching sentence-making as an exercise in combining coordinate clauses into more "efficient" syntactical structures.

Another way to think about how and what we know as writers is to consider what philosopher Michael Polanyi calls "personal knowlege," part of which, he says, is "tacit knowledge, an "obscure" and inarticulate awareness of things. While "focused" knowledge is conscious, rationalized formulation of what we think we know, "we know more than we can tell" and that "more" which resists articulation is tacit knowledge (*The Tacit Dimension* 4). In Polanyi's view using language is just such a form of knowledge: "to learn a language or to modify its meaning is a tacit, irreversible . . . feat" (*Personal Knowledge* 106). Attempting to turn tacit knowledge into focused knowledge is "self-defeating": for example, "the skill of a driver cannot be replaced by a thorough schooling in the theory of the motorcar . . . and the rules of rhyming and prosody do not tell me what a poem told me, without any knowledge of its rules" (*The Tacit Dimension* 20). When our knowledge is intuitive and a priori, attempts to formalize rules about it are inevitably reductive and rigidifying.

The surprising power of "tacit" knowledge in writing exemplifies what Passmore means when he suggests that an open capacity makes it possible for the student

> to take steps which he has not been taught to take, which in some measure surprise the instructor, not necessarily in the sense that no other pupil has ever done such a thing . . . but in the sense that the teacher has not taught his pupil to take precisely that step and his taking it does not necessarily follow as an application of a principle in which the teacher has instructed him (42).

To effectively nurture our students as writers, we must distinguish in our teaching between those elements of our students' writing which will remain personal and tacit, and those which must be subjected to external conventions. Adhering to the editing codes of standard written English requires students to learn precise, rule-governed behavior which, though contributing to good writing, does not constitute it. Composing must be taught as an open capacity responsive to each writer's unique way of working. Some students like to organize ideas before they write; some discover what they want to say by writing a first sentence and building on it, without any elaborate prewriting labor. Requiring students to make outlines before writing may encourage them to think they have the entire discourse under control, or that any ideas that come in the process of composing must be fitted into the pre-established organization or excluded. Experienced writers know how often an early intention vanishes under the pressure of a clearer, firmer direction emerging during writing itself. Only when students understand that discovering and developing what they wish to say may occur at any point in writing, will they be able to exploit these capacities in a truly open way. And only if they see every draft as an incomplete intention, open to further development, will they be able to exploit writing as an open capacity.

This flexibility, an intuitive awareness of the incompleteness of any text, is at the heart of all good writing behavior. It is this uncomfortable tension between what is done and what is still unrealized intention, so familiar to practiced writers, that makes the act of writing and its teaching so difficult. And it is just this relativity of "completed" intention that dismays students. For they can finish the math problem and find that they have the right answer, or absorb the sociology text and score well on a multiple-choice test, or perform the lab experiment and fill in the worksheet correctly. But never, it seems, can they fully please their writing teacher—or even their peers—who always manage to find some ways in which they might have written a piece more effectively. When students find it more expedient to blame their teachers and peers for unanticipated responses, it may be because they have not grasped the probationary condition of even the best of writing intentions. Only continuous exposure to this principle will bring home to inexperienced writers the complex, humane effort that is writing. Unfortunately, schools and colleges are generally not adapted to such teaching. Instead, they feel pressured to seek the obvious remedy for what they take to be writing's obvious ill: its failure to obey rules. For such a problem, the manifest solution is to teach students rules so that they can write more "correctly."

The Handbook Tradition

The best way to understand this popular tendency to value the teaching of rules in composition is to examine a major tool of that teaching —the composition handbook. Nearly every trade publisher of school and college texts offers one or more versions of what has become popularly known as the "current-traditional" writing handbook competing directly with one another. Because the most popular of them sell in huge numbers, appearing in writing courses in schools and colleges everywhere, they inevitably influence what and how writing teachers teach. Printed on heavy-grade, glossy paper and securely bound to withstand a life of eternal recycling between bookstore and dorm room or school locker, many of these texts urge the making of outlines, the writing of thesis sentences, and careful editing.

Texts used in high school writing courses are especially prone to this format. The uninitiated writing teacher, charged with selecting a text and correlating a course syllabus with its contents, might conclude that in its few hundred pages live all that a student needs to know about writing. Their content and organization are formulaic. Early chapters focus on how students should begin their writing assignments: they are often urged to formulate thesis statements, build clear beginnings, middles and endings, and develop support for generalizations. This standard advice only takes a few chapters to impart, however; much of the rest of the typical handbook is given over to mechanics, usage, spelling, diction, and common errors in syntax and idiom. Handbooks, that is, tend to focus on the form of the written product. The bulkiest texts are the ones with the most thorough collation of rules. They signal the unmistakable message that format and editing codes are the student writer's most important goals.

But most writing teachers and researchers have long since become convinced that language-fact exercises do not influence writing ability. Patrick Hartwell puts it bluntly: "the advice given in 'the common school grammars' is unconnected with anything remotely resembling literate adult behavior" (120). Students' ability to recognize "compound-complex sentences" or "participial phrases" does not enhance their ability to make sentences. Mastering the notorious "five-paragraph theme" does not help them compose a coherent piece of writing appropriate to a particular situation and set of readers. "We need to attempt some massive dislocation of our traditional thinking," continues Hartwell, referring implicitly to the concept of tacit knowledge, "to shuck off our hyperliterate perception of the value of formal rules, and to regain the confidence in the tacit power of unconscious knowledge" about language (121). It is for just this reason that writing measurement is shielded by warnings about intangibles and hidden variables. If writing skill were responsive to the writer's knowledge of language facts, then teaching and measuring writing would be far easier than they are. Writing is often taught as though it were a matter of learning *that* certain facts of English syntax exist: that a clause has a noun and a verb, that adverbs are those words modifying verbs and modifiers, that parallel structures must be consistent. "Correct" writing is cited as the students' goal in learning that certain words, phrases, inflections and punctuation marks are "wrong," and that certain others are "right."

In writing handbooks, the presentation of sentence patterns and errors is sometimes based on traditional word-grammar analysis, in which parts of speech and their structures are the basis of stylistic discussions and error analysis. Today's handbooks are more likely to reflect the terminology of transformational grammar, though with the same intent. The ill-fated enthusiasm given early transformational theory by curriculum planners in the 1960s exemplifies this misguided emphasis. When transformational grammar first became known to educators, it was welcomed as a way of revolutionizing the teaching of syntax. Many text-makers and teachers felt that for the first time a grammar theory had emerged that if taught to students could help them generate good sentences. But first the new theory had to be taught; and students were confronted with the spectacle of apparently simple sentences fragmented into baffling branching-tree diagrams. Many classrooms became battlefields in which both sides, teachers and students, surrendered in the face of their common enemy, leaving transformational grammar in possession of the field.

Many studies have shown that knowing grammar theory does not lead to increased writing competence; Frank O'Hare's work provides the fullest summary of such studies. Yet despite its proven inappropriateness to learning to write, grammar instruction still has its advocates. Handbook authors defend their approach to teaching writing as essential to preserve the normative function of written language. Indeed, the written form of a language changes much more slowly than its oral form, as E. D. Hirsch points out: "the conservatism of written speech has . . . been the foundation of a genuine *lingua franca* within every large literate community in the world" (40). This linguistic justification underlies the implicit agreement among handbook writers and publishers that writing teachers' main task is to teach students the editing codes of standard written English.

Debate over written language's normative function is widespread today. Opponents of the normative position say that it is both invalid and culturally insensitive. It is invalid because modern language theory deems any standard dialect a function of what the majority actually speak and write, not the result of grammatical "laws" formulated by the harmless drudges who make dictionaries and textbooks. The "prescriptiveness" of modern handbooks, argue critics, is a vestige of earlier days when the established rules of Latin grammar were taught to youthful and recalcitrant speakers of a living language like English. Moreover, an insistence on the necessity for a standard form of the language is intolerably authoritarian, because dialectal variation represents cultural variety. To insist on an "official" dialect is to encourage social and cultural leveling. "Traditional grammatical nitpicking," says linguist James Sledd, "survives because . . . it teaches respect for 'proper' English and its users, contempt for speech and speakers branded as *improper*, and unquestioning obedience to even irrational commands" (175). By requiring all students to submit to the language patterns of the dominant standard dialect, the educational establishment denies those from different ethnic and dialect traditions the right to flourish in a society that supposedly welcomes diversity.

The text-makers counter that such an argument overlooks the basic function of language in a diverse society: to make communication possible amid cultural and ethnic variety. There are many countries of the world claiming to be nations which are, in fact, separate regions kept separate by different languages or dialects too dissimilar to allow communication. It has been the standard written English taught in schools and colleges, argue the text-makers, which has been a major contributor to the geographical and political unity of the United States. And to maintain the normative power of standard English, they persist, educators must insist on its primacy in schools and colleges. The key element in teaching standard English is the codification of its rules of "etiquette"—its idioms, usages, mechanics and spellings—summarized in universally available handbooks. Without firmly established rules, there can be no standard dialect, and without handbooks to purvey them, codes cannot remain firmly established.

This circularity offers theoretical justification for either position. For teachers in practical situations, however, the normative, handbook-aided approach often confuses technique with technicality. As we have already seen, writing is a complex, amorphous activity whose openness eludes confident systematizing. Handbooks that emphasize editing codes misrepresent writing, just as do teachers who emphasize spelling and punctuation over other elements of the process, by forcing a false equation between the open-ended process called "writing" and the rule-bound activity called "editing." Developing something to say requires numberless choices big and small, with the writer's shaping purpose the only reference—a purpose which may itself alter as writing proceeds. Inventing, organizing, developing—these processes are difficult to teach precisely because they have no norms of right or wrong, but only the measure of integration with respect to the evolving purpose. Editing is much easier to teach just because it is controlled by rules. Thus, writing handbooks seize on the pedagogically easier aspects of writing, giving them disproportionate attention at the expense of other aspects of composing. In thinking out their courses, teachers of writing must begin by realizing just how limitedly useful handbooks are, nearly in inverse proportion to their availability.

The Rhetorical Tradition

Handbooks' disproportionate attention to editing rules suggests, in the terms of classical rhetoric, the sway of style over invention and arrangement in the classroom. We need now to consider briefly the importance of the rhetorical tradition for teaching writing today. The story of rhetoric from its classical origins to its modern forms has been well and frequently told, and requires no recounting here. The

elements of classical rhetoric are deeply embedded in the way
Western culture regards discourse; until modern times rhetoric
formed a major part of school and university curricula in Europe and
America. Derived from the Greek word *rhetor* ("orator"), rhetoric in
the classical period centered on spoken discourse, and by the end of
the Roman period had become formalized in categories: invention
(the discovery and development of content), arrangement (the organization of the discourse), style (e.g., figurative language, sentence
patterns), memory, and delivery. The first three of these categories—
invention, arrangement, and style—continued to influence speaking and writing in the Renaissance and Enlightenment periods of
Western culture, and to develop a psychological grounding which
became influential by the end of the eighteenth century. Throughout
the nineteenth century, European and American schools and universities emphasized training in rhetoric for both speaking and writing.
In America, however, the early twentieth-century split between the
disciplines of English and speech allowed rhetoric thereafter to be
identified primarily with speaking. While speech departments carried rhetoric into their camp, viewing it as their birthright, English
departments claimed only that part of rhetoric applicable to the study
of prose composition. As a result, English department "rhetoric"—
focused on writing—inherits a vulnerability to being limited to
matters of style and form, the study of discourse forms, sentences,
diction, and usage.

While the "handbook" tradition discussed above keeps this
reductive view of rhetoric alive and well in writing pedagogy, in the
last two decades a rhetoric "revival" of sorts has brought the true
range of rhetoric renewed attention from teachers of writing. Certain
elements of traditional rhetoric have taken particularly noteworthy
contemporary form. As we will see below, those strategies traditionally labeled "invention" have manifested themselves in recent years
as "composing," usually represented as a complex network of cognitive processes. Another contemporary manifestation of traditional
rhetoric's concerns can be found in the ways in which "rhetorical
situation" may be defined. As we will see in Chapter Two, for example, the situational emphasis in rhetoric is strongly linked to recent
social and collectivist emphases in poststructuralist reading theory.
Although the study of rhetoric has traditionally covered the relationship among the rhetor's purposes, audiences, and contexts, recent
rhetorical theorists have accentuated the relational or interactive
dimension of rhetoric. For example, Lloyd Bitzer spurred debate by
arguing that "rhetorical" discourse is always situational, generated
not by a speaker's (or writer's) purpose so much as by the situation
in which the speaker and the audience find themselves. Other

rhetoricians—notably Chaim Perelman—have also made a case for the power of audience and situation to shape discourse. Increasingly, writing teachers are finding in rhetorical inquiry the same concern for the interaction of writers and readers, and the reciprocal power of each to shape writing, that is characteristic of recent literary theory.

Though its emphases change with time, rhetoric—as an art and as a set of strategies—continues to exert a powerful influence on the teaching of writing. This influence manifests itself primarily in the enduring fruitfulness of rhetoric's traditional concern with the interaction among intention, audience, and structure. Though we tend to talk about composing rather than "inventing," even much of the language of classical rhetoric still finds a place in the way we analyze writers' purposes, readers' expectations, and textual style. It is as appropriate now as in the past to say that rhetoric teaches us to account for the situational variables which come into play when we are trying to inform and persuade listeners or readers.

The Influence of Cognitive Psychology

Though its views of writing—and language behavior generally—have been challenged in recent years, cognitive or developmental psychology has provided crucial insights into the ways writers work. These insights have profoundly altered the way compositionists understand writers and writing. In this chapter, we will examine the major cognitive theorists whose views created the basis for psychology's dominance in composition; we will also examine critiques of the cognitive approach to writing. We will then study some of the pedagogical outcomes of the psychology of composing. Later, in Chapter Two, we will study the psychology of composing from a different perspective, comparing its individualistic tendencies with the social emphases of other recent kinds of discourse theory.

Piaget, Vygotsky, and Bruner

Jean Piaget has presented a seminal interpretation of language as an activity of mind. As the originator of what he termed "genetic epistemology," the study of how the developing mind structures knowledge in systematic ways, he studied the stages of learning through which children pass from birth to late adolescence. His method was both speculative and empirical. He observed individual children or small samples of a particular age group, wrote descriptions of their learning behavior, and built theoretical constructs of the learning process. Because this methodology differed radically from the controlled experiments of the behaviorist school, his influence did not begin to spread until after World War II, two decades after he began publishing his work. In the composition field, his influence has appeared relatively recently, long after it came to dominate cognitive psychology and educational theory. His description of the cognitive stages of childhood, the core of Piaget's theories, is a useful starting point for a consideration of his influence upon the teaching of writing.

The periods of cognitive growth, each consisting of certain "operations" which the child becomes capable of, are in Piaget's view successive but not linear. They overlay one another, the capabilities typical of each period synthesized in the development of the succeeding period, and integrated in the mature individual. The first period Piaget terms "sensory-motor," the phase of growth before language when the infant learns to respond to its environment in nonlinguistic ways. Language has a central place in Piaget's theory of learning, but this first period reveals "that the rudiments of intelligent behavior evolve before language develops" (Wadsworth 67). Infant behavior demonstrates that human learning depends not on the ability to generate language, but upon a more basic ability of which language is a manifestation. This capacity Piaget terms "semiotic ability"—the human capacity to communicate with symbols. During the "sensory-motor" period, the child gradually learns to represent experience internally—to think, in other words. "From an organism whose most intelligent functions are sensory-motor, overt acts," the child alters after the second year into one "whose upper-limit cognitions are inner, symbolic manipulations of reality" (Flavell 151).

This transition marks the child's entry into the second learning stage, the "period of preoperational thought," during which the child extends the ability to symbolize experience in various ways. "Individual semiosis," says Piaget, includes "imitation, symbolic play, and the [mental] image"; language is the most articulate form of "semiotic thought" (*The Psychology of the Child* 84). By the third year, the child is making sentences, revealing an innate capacity to articulate thoughts according to syntactical rules that cannot be attributed merely to imitation of other speakers. Once the child begins to use language, the rate of learning increases because the child can assimilate experience in an increasingly complex and efficient fashion. The progress from the "preoperational" to the period of "concrete operations" (which begins about the eighth year) is made possible largely by an increasing ability to represent reality abstractly. The "concrete logical operations," which involve such things as the ability to perceive quantities and relationships, are products of the growing capacity for symbolic manipulation of reality.

The last stage of cognitive growth, the period of "formal opera-tions," reveals the child's enhanced ability to deal not just with con-crete elements of reality, but with abstract verbal issues and complex logical problems. The child begins to deal with the possible as well as the real, with the past and future as well as the present. "Language is indispensable to the elaboration of thought" in this period, says Piaget (*Six Psychological Studies* 98). The process of abstraction, he argues, "detaches thought from action and is the source of represen-tation. Language plays a particularly important role in the formative process," for it is "elaborated socially and contains a notation for the entire system" of cognitive functions (*The Psychology of the Child* 86–7). For Piaget, then, language has two major functions in the child's intellectual growth: it permits the development of an increas-ingly complex awareness of experience, and through a process Piaget calls "decentering" it enhances the child's ability to understand other perspectives and distinguish them from her own. Decentering is the process by which he escapes from the "cognitive egocentri-cism" characterizing the early years of growth. In these years, says Piaget, the child's awareness "is marked by unconscious preferential focusing," a "lack of differentiation between one's own point of view and the other possible ones" ("Comments" 4–5). That is, he begins by perceiving the world as continuous with his own understanding. He is unable to grasp people or events as "outside" his own world and different from the way he sees them or thinks them to be. He attempts to communicate by means of "egocentric speech," whereby he "talks for himself," although he "thinks he is talking for others and is mak-ing himself understood" (Comments, 8). Decentering is the child's gradual liberation from egocentricism through the ability to under-stand experience from more than a single perspective. "The progress of knowledge," says Piaget, is "a perpetual reformulation of previ-ous points of view by a process which moves backwards as well as forward ... this corrective process ... [obeys] the law of decen-tering" (Comments, 3). Decentering is essential to the maturing pro-cess, and language is essential to decentering, by permitting the child to interact with others. As language enhances the ability to "see" var-ious perspectives on experience, it also greatly increases the capacity to develop concepts about the relationship between self and world.

The influence of Piaget's theories has been paralleled by the wide recognition given to the work of L. S. Vygotsky, a Soviet psychologist whose work both extends and challenges Piaget's early theorizing. Vygotsky's provocative studies of the relationship between thought and language, and of the power of social development to shape indi-vidual psychological growth, have gained important influence in composition. In *Thought and Language*, the first of his works to become available in English (in 1962), Vygotsky emphasizes that language is not merely the expression of thought, but provides "reality and form" (126) for thought.

Vygotsky insists on an integral relation between language and thought. Piaget (says Vygotsky) defines egocentric speech as an expression of the child's self-centered understandings, so that when decentering occurs egocentric speech vanishes. Vygotsky agrees that egocentric speech does decrease as the child matures; but he also maintains that this decrease signals the child's developing ability to think in language—to use what he calls "inner speech," "a dynamic, shifting . . . thing, fluttering between word and thought," a "thinking in pure meanings" (*Thought and Language* 149). The decrease in egocentric speech, he says, "denotes a developing abstraction from sound, the child's new faculty to 'think words' instead of pronouncing them" (*Thought and Language* 135). He identifies that verbal play which provides a transition from egocentric to inner speech as "self-directed speech," which is partly social, in that it may be responding to others' talk, and partly inner-directed, in that it is often a thinking aloud. Vygotsky does not reject the concept of egocentric speech as the child's earliest form of language; what is important, he insists, is that—contrary to Piaget's belief in the self-centeredness of early speech—"the initial function of speech [for young children] is . . . communication, social connection, influencing others" ("Psychological investigations" quoted in Kohlberg 197).

Thus "the true direction of the development of thinking is . . . from the social to the individual" (*Thought and Language* 20). A young child's speech is largely "preintellectual," while that child's thought is largely nonverbal or "prespeech." "At a certain point," says Vygotsky, "the two lines meet, whereupon thought *becomes* verbal, and speech *becomes* intellectual" ("Psychological investigations" [1956] quoted in Kohlberg 194). Self-directed speech disappears as the "self-regulative" power of inner speech increases—that is, as "thought becomes verbal." As the child matures, this inner speech, characterized by the dominance of predication, simplified sentence structures, and shifting, flexible word meanings, shapes the child's thinking. Meanwhile, the capacity for truly "socialized" speech—purposively communcative speech—also evolves, paralleling the development of inner speech. Language capacities thus develop in two directions: inwardly as inner speech or thinking in language, and outwardly as increasingly socialized, communicative speech.

The mind of the mature individual thus depends upon language in two ways: language as inner speech is part of the thinking process, while language as external speech is necessary for communication.

"Speech structures mastered by the child become the basic structures of his thinking," while "intellectual growth" in turn depends upon the child's "mastering the social means of thought, that is, language" (*Thought and Language* 52). Inner and outer speech are reciprocal processes, both essential to the maturity of the individual. Vygotsky's insistence upon the social origins of thought and language results in a noteworthy attitude toward writing. Writing is not inscribed speech, a written-down version of talk. Rather, he maintains, it is the fully developed offspring of inner speech, whose predication and condensation in its thought-form gives way in writing (its external form) to fully developed syntax and word specificity. Vygotsky suggests that the composing process itself—the movement from "mental draft" to written draft—reflects a reformulation and redirection of inner speech into communicative discourse. In his view, composing writing is not a matter of turning speech into written syntax, not a matter of a direct "talk-write" connection, as some behavioral psychologists have proposed. It is a complex interaction of verbal thinking—inner speech—and the lexical and syntactical demands of written language.

Vygotsky and Piaget, however, carefully avoid saying that language-making and thinking are identical, despite their interconnectedness. Rather, thought and language are seen as two intersecting circles, with verbal thought the crucial ability emerging from the interaction of both. For Vygotsky "there is no rigid correspondence between the units of thought and speech"; "just as one sentence may express different thoughts, one thought may be expressed in different sentences" (*Thought and Language* 149). However, both Piaget and Vygotsky subscribe to what has been called the "constructionist" view of language. That is, they maintain that language is more than merely an expression of some prior process we might call "thinking"; language is a form of thinking or constructing experience. In the cognitive view, language is essential to the development of intelligence because grammatical structures express logical relationships similar to those expressed in nonverbal forms of thought. Piaget sees language as a crucial form of cognition, but not its only form: "the roots of logical operations lie deeper than the linguistic connections," he suggests; "language is thus a necessary but not sufficient condition for the construction of logical operations" (SPS, 98). The development of intelligence in the child is catalyzed by the growth of language, but language is not "the source of all logic for the whole of humanity" (PC, 87). For logic is not, in Piaget's views, simply "generalized syntax." Mathematical logic is an important mode of thought, as are imagemaking and other nonverbal processes. Language is a crucial but not an exclusive form of intelligence.

Another noted spokesman for the discipline of cognitive psychology, Jerome Bruner, follows Piaget and Vygotsky in arguing that language is "at the center of the stage" in intellectual development. He maintains that language is an "instrument of thought" because the syntax of language organizes human experience into "hierarchical categories" which underlie all human experience (*Toward a Theory of Instruction* 20). These categories, which he terms "causation, predication and modification," make possible the child's ordering of his world (*Studies in Cognitive Growth* 47). "The medium of language ... [is] the instrument that the learner can use himself in bringing order into the environment" (TTI, 6), says Bruner. But he is not suggesting that language constitutes reality, or that thought is made up of language. In saying that language is "a tool for organizing thoughts about things" (TTI, 105), Bruner means that language expresses the mind's drive to categorize experience, and provides a method by which thought can deal with experience. Bruner reaffirms Piaget's principle that language enables the developing mind to objectify experience by abstracting from it and communicating about it. Ultimately language expresses the quality of the intelligence which uses it: "the shape and style of a mind is, in some measure, the outcome of internalizing the functions inherent in the language we use" (TTI, 107). Like Piaget and Vygotsky, Bruner insists on language's crucial ability to make learning possible.

Some Cognitive Process Models and Their Critiques

From cognitive psychology comes our view of writing as "cognitive process." In this view, writing is an activity of mind, an individual mental process which exhibits certain general features manifested in the behavior of all writers. Through "protocols"—the individual records of writers asked to document their thoughts and behavior as they write—writing researchers have observed the ways writers work, and from these observations have made general models of what writers do. They have devised "cognitive process models" of writing as ways of visualizing the complex interrelations of language and thought in composing.

In composing research's early years, such models tended to be linear, dividing composing into three parts: the preparatory or conceptual stage, the developmental or incubation stage, and the production stage. This third stage was seen to include the actual writing, revising, and editing upon which most textbooks focus. One of the earliest and best-known of these models identifies "conception" as the beginning point of writing, saying that "writing is a deliberate act; one has to make up one's mind to do it" (Britton). In this model writing is identified with intention and choice; an act of will initiates a process of choices which move in a linear fashion from an intention through various discovery stages, then through the process by which thoughts are put into words into the "final" editing phase.

Conception	Incubation	Production
Begins with the decision to write. This may be initiated by an external or mental event.	Activities: Exhausting the topic—getting the facts and finding what is known about the topic. Satisfying the self—squaring the topic with one's own experience and one's own sense of how it should be presented.	Activities: Getting a start—finding the way into the topic and finding the right way to express it. Writing (includes many pauses). Editing

Britton's model implies the "instrumental" view of language mentioned earlier: the view that words are the means of expressing thought, which is "prior" to language. More recent process models have inclined to the constructivist view that language "translates" other thought-forms, so that thinking in words and writing words are interactive and reciprocating cognitive stages. Though protocol research and process modeling continue to be popular modes of composition study, its models have become more complex. Increasingly researchers insist that the "stages" of composing interact continuously, so that the process itself is not at all linear, but manifold and reciprocal, with various phases continuously interacting with one another. The term "recursive" has become the common term for this circular, interactive view of writing. Flower and Hayes' diagram on page 22 exemplifies such a model.

Such models are troubling, however, in terms of the kind of validity they may be said to have—one of composition's more controversial issues. Cognitive theorists believe that observed behavior permits inferences to be drawn about the mind's activities. Models of composing are drawn by researchers who conscientiously observe actual writers describing their thoughts as they write; empirical observations furnish the basis for the schematic models. But as with any attempt to visualize the unknown, such models must flatten, simplify, and distort whatever it is that happens in the consciousness of a writer. Thus, models of composing offer analogical rather than empirically verifiable truth; each model represents a "metaphor of

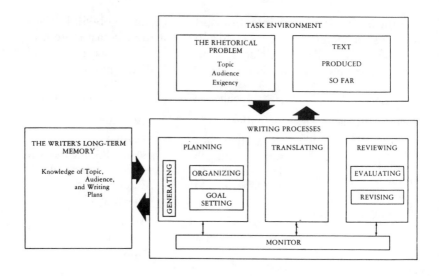

mind" with its own distinct bias of origin. Those who devise such models, though usually offering them cautiously as conditional and subject to revision, nevertheless remain confident of their cognitive framework: "composition scholars agree that the composing process exists or, rather, that there is a complex of activities out of which all writing emerges" (Bizzell, 49).

Those who believe that each individual writer's composing reflects universal structures of mind accept protocol research and process models as useful ways of understanding writing. But to its critics the weakness of the cognitive-process approach is just this underlying assumption that there *is* something called "mind" which has inherent "processes" we can know and make models of. Some composition theorists do not view "mind" as an entity in itself, a "black box" which if opened can reveal the basic principles of its functioning. Instead, they argue that the term "mind" is simply a social construct—a culturally-shared way of speaking—by means of which we talk about that which we really cannot "know" objectively. For them, process models are not useful even as metaphors, for they can't be said to refer to anything universally valid.

One influential and often-cited source of opposition to the cognitive-process view of writing is Vygotsky's emphasis on the social origins of thought and language. Though he shares Piaget's focus on individual psychological development, particularly in *Thought and Language*, Vygotsky's more recently available work makes clear how deeply convinced he was of the social origins of individual development. Influenced by his readings of Marxist dialectic, Vygotsky came to believe that "all higher mental functions are internalized social relationships. . . . their whole nature . . . is social" (Wertsch 66). His theory of the social origins of "egocentric speech" is one consequence of his social perspective on individual development. Another is his theory of the "zone of proximal development," which he formulates in *Mind and Society*. Children will not reach their full potential unless their development is social and interactive: the "zone" is the "distance between the [individual] developmental level . . . and the level of potential development . . . [gained] under adult supervision or in collaboration with more capable peers" (*Mind in Society* 86). All human learning, he adds, "presupposes a specific social nature and a process by which children grow into the intellectual life of those around them" (*Mind in Society* 88). Vygotsky's social view of language development suggests why his theories have gained so much currency in recent years: they reinforce that "relational" or "ecological" paradigm emergent in composition studies. In Chapter Two we will explore this paradigm and its focus on the social and relational aspects of writing. It is also worth noting that Vygotsky, despite his and others' researches, regarded the psychological processes of writing as largely mysterious; his caution should guide us as we explore various theories of composing.

Invention Strategies

It is just this mysteriousness about writing—its way of eluding definition even by the most careful and confident scrutiny—that continues to promote controversy among its scholars. But despite misgivings by some, the cognitive-process view of writing has powerfully influenced the way writing teachers view their responsibilities. One of cognitive-process theory's most visible effects on the teaching of writing has come in the area of "invention" or "discovery," that element of rhetoric concerned with finding something to say. In classical rhetoric, invention means developing proofs for an argument, using "topoi" or "topics" which help the speaker think up and marshal the elements of proof. Aristotle and other classical rhetoricians viewed "topoi" as "places" of thought to which any speaker could turn for help in developing proofs; thus they came to be called "common places" available to all speakers. Aristotle lists four "universal" or "common" topics which are to apply to any matter: the possible and the impossible, past fact, future possibilities, and degree, or relative magnitude. He also developed a number of special topics (division, classification, analysis of consequences, etc.) which have application to a narrower range of subjects than the common topics.

Later classical and Renaissance rhetoricians expanded the study of topics or commonplaces to include a very wide range of possibilities for argument, so that orators could find something to say about nearly any subject that might confront them. Thus, within the rhetorical tradition, "invention" has not generally meant finding new and unique truth about a given subject; it has meant producing persuasively organized arguments from time-tested ideas, issues, and attitudes already familiar to the speaker and, to some extent, to the audience as well. Following Aristotle, classical rhetoricians generally identified oratory appropriate to three situations: deliberative oratory, concerned with persuading hearers to believe or act in a certain way; forensic, concerned with judicial questions of right and wrong; and epideictic, concerned with celebrating an event, person or public institution. Thus, the purpose of a discourse is fixed by circumstance and context; invention is "discovering" or finding out the proofs which might put across the purpose most effectively.

The concept of invention has undergone something of a sea change in recent decades. As with other aspects of composition, it has been influenced by the cognitive-process approach to writing, which views invention as much a psychological activity as a rhetorical method. The models of the composing process discussed below show the extent to which invention has recently been defined as a self-fulfilling activity of mind. Implicit in them is Piaget's definition of learning as a constant search for the resolution of "disequilibrium," a condition "in which our ways of thinking and acting become inadequate to deal with a change that has taken place within or outside ourselves" (Odell 36). Psychological "disequilibrium" occurs when the mind confronts an experience it cannot categorize or put adequately into perspective. Because, in Jerome Bruner's words, language is "a powerful instrument for combining experiences" (TTI, 105), it is the primary means by which the individual reconciles the unfamiliar with the familiar. Bruner argues that "the combinatorial or productive property of language" is an invitation "to take experience apart and put it together again in new ways" (TTI 105).

Thus, the basis for defining invention has shifted from rhetoric to psychology. In the perspective of cognitive psychology, all acts of composing begin as explorations of new ways to understand experience; the urge to write begins in the hope of discovery. This definition of writing's beginning point underlies several contemporary systems of discovery, of which we will study four: problem-solving, dramatism, tagmemics, and prewriting. All are worth considering as ways of seeing the influence of cognitive-process thought upon an originally rhetorical function.

The problem-solving approach to discovery begins with the cognitive-process view that we continuously encounter and are changed by new experiences—and that when we have not accommodated such experiences, a disequilibrium or "cognitive dissonance" exists. Dissonance generates cognitive activity to eliminate it, according to this view, in a psychological parallel to the body's drive to maintain physiological balance. Although this potentially reductive analogy between mind and body poses some difficulties for problem-solving as a writing strategy, it does offer some ways of developing ideas and perspectives for writers. The phrase itself implies a situation whose boundaries are known (the problem) and which can therefore be understood and resolved (the solution). All formal problem-solving techniques or "heuristics"—in science, engineering, or business, for example—suggest understanding and mastery as primary goals. Indeed, Webster's New Collegiate Dictionary defines a heuristic as a technique for "providing aid or direction in the solution of a problem but otherwise unjustified or incapable of justification." A heuristic may be a set of questions, analytic categories, or, in the sciences, formulas which help define the issues involved in a problem or "dissonance." The heuristics posed as algorithms in the sciences—closed systems of answer-finding—parallel the rule-based quality of problem-solving approaches in writing; students are given a set of guidelines (or rules) which will be said to reduce the writing problem—"what to say?"—to its solution—"what is said," a text.

One advocate of problem-solving as a writing strategy, citing Piaget and Bruner, asserts that "the ability to read and write sensitively, thoughtfully, and independently presupposes the ability to formulate and solve problems" (Odell 37). Effective problem-solving techniques, argues another advocate, may be judged by the criteria of "transcendence" and "flexibility" (Lauer 268–9`). If a problem-solving writer is to take the trouble to master a heuristic strategy, it must hold promise of usefulness for most writing situations by containing within itself points of appropriateness for each situation. It must be comprehensive or "transcendent" rather than dependent on particular situations. It must also be flexible so that the writer can utilize any part of it that seems useful to the situation, without having to work through the entire strategy, particularly if it has complex "steps" to follow. If it is limited in its appropriateness, the writer is forced to improvise when confronted with a problem beyond its range. The heuristic itself becomes a "problem" requiring a solution, rather than a way of providing one.

A problem-solving heuristic that is genuinely comprehensive ("transcendent") and flexible can be useful for writers whose composing requires a certain amount of extrinsic structuring. It implies that some given topic or interest already exists, so that the nature of the "problem" to be "solved" has at least an initial focus. But the implications of problem-solving as a concept require that writing teachers be cautious in relying on it. Earlier we saw that writing appears to be both an "open" and a largely "tacit" process, variable and rule-resistant. Thus, if as writers we begin writing not with a particular focus in mind, but in order to explore and develop a focus, then there is no goal other than to find out what can be written and how to write it. That is, we are not really "solving problems" because we are articulating the "problem" even as we develop its "solution"; discovering how to ask in language what we wish to know carries its own "resolution." To say what we want to discover is to take a long step towards finding it. The problem-solving strategies that work well in science and technology, where most "problems" are defined by their place in a larger hierarchy of functions and goals, may be reductive when applied to writing, which often begins with no specified goal or end-point. It is the "creative imagination," says Ann Berthoff, which writing teachers must nurture in their students. "For creativity is not an area" or a tool for doing a job, she points out, but "the heart of the matter," and writing "conceived as the expression of thinking about experience" is the proper way to describe what the process of discovery serves (102–3). Problem-solving strategies may confuse or blur the complex and elusive processes of composing, if such strategies are not employed guardedly and carefully.

Another discovery method with the limitations of a rule-bound methodology is tagmemics. Tagmemics began as a system of language analysis developed by Kenneth Pike, whose purpose was to formulate a heuristic which could aid in the discovery of the grammatical structure of a language. Influenced by the problem-solving approach to invention, tagmemics's developers intended their heuristic to aid in the "retrieval of relevant information already known, analysis of problematic data, and discovery of ordering principles" (Young 42). Its proponents maintained that the tagmemic system's universal applicability derives from its grounding in hierarchical structures of thought inherent in all language. In this view, the structure of syntax is echoed at other levels of discourse, including the paragraph and even larger units.

The tagmemic heuristic rests on two "maxims" that form the basis of a "nine cell" grid of perspectives. The first is that any experience "can be adequately understood only if three aspects of the unit are known: (1) its contrastive features, (2) its range of variation, and (3) its distribution in larger contexts" (Young, Becker, Pike 56). The second is that "a unit of experience can be viewed as a particle, or as a wave, or as a field" (122). The resulting grid requires the problem-solving writer to analyze an object, event, or experience by asking nine questions about it that emerge from the conjunction of these perspectives. A topic "processed" through this system will presumably be developed in a variety of perspectives available to the writer.

	Contrast	Variation	Distribution
Particle	1. View unit as isolated, static entity. What are its contrastive features?	4. View unit as an instance of a concept. What is range of physical variation of concept?	7. View unit as part of larger context. What is unit's position in a class? temporal sequence? space?
Wave	2. View unit as dynamic object or event. What physical features distinguish it?	5. View unit as dynamic process. How is it changing?	8. View unit as part of larger dynamic context. How does it interact with environment?
Field	3. View unit as abstract, multi-dimensional system. How are components interrelated?	6. View unit as physical system. How do instances of the system vary?	9. View unit as abstract system within larger system. What is its position in the system?

One critic of discovery strategies argues that emphasizing heuristics over other aspects of composing may encourage students to make the heuristic process an end in itself, a game which, when ostensibly completed, may leave the student still needing to find something to say (Kinney 143). An over-emphasis on the discovery process may draw time and energy away from simply getting things written down. Perhaps the strongest objection to the tagmemic system is that, in the words of another critic, tagmemics is built upon "a consistently empirical framework" which limits the student writer to the discovery of ideas "through physical features" alone, discouraging exploration of ideas and relationships not open to empirical verification (Wells 475). The preponderance of empirical terms seriously restricts the kind of writing intentions to which the tagmemic strategy might apply.

Another, more open and flexible discovery strategy is "dramatism," originally developed by Kenneth Burke as a method of analyzing "forms of thought," e.g., "poetry and fiction," "legal judgments," or "metaphysical structures" (*Grammar of Motives* xv). His system is based on a "pentad" of queries directed at "what people are doing and why they are doing it" (xv). The five components of the pentad are "Act, Scene, Agent, Agency, Purpose." Any "complete statement about motives," says Burke, "will offer some kind of answers to these five questions: what was done (act), when or where it was done (scene), who did it (agent), how he did it (agency), and why (purpose)" (xv). These terms do not function individually as elements of analysis; rather, the relationships between them—what Burke calls their "ratios"—are the key to their exploratory power. "These ratios," says Burke, "are principles of determination"; the "five terms would allow for ten [ratios](scene-act, scene-agent, scene-agency, scene-purpose, act-purpose, act-agent, act-agency, agent-purpose, agent-agency, and agency-purpose)" (15). By applying their analytic potential to a wide range of texts, ideas, and events, Burke demonstrates that the ratios can be extended to include relationships among three or more of the five terms. Noting the parallels between the pentad of queries and the journalists' traditional who? what? where? how? and why?, students of the pentad urge its relevance to the inventing of subject matter. For Burke, notes one advocate, "writing is a transcription of the process of composing ideas; it is not the product of thought but its actualization" (Comprone 336). This commentator suggests that writers use the pentad queries as a self-pacing guide, with the "agent" category addressed to the persona the writer is creating, for example, and the "agency" question directed to the kind of process the writer is using to produce the writing.

However, Burke himself—ever the flexible and wary interpreter of his own theories—has suggested that although his dramatistic terms may be put "to good use" in the classroom, writers should use them with caution. While their textbook use relies on their power to "generate a topic," they were really intended, says Burke, "to ask of the work the explicit questions to which its structure had already implicitly supplied the answers" ("Questions and Answers" 336). In other words, he intended them for use in analyzing a product, not a process; their application to the composing process itself clearly takes them far beyond their orignal purpose. Burke allows that this is not necessarily bad, for it may have practical usefulness, yet his warning illustrates the distortion liable to occur when theory is too hastily turned to pedagogical purposes.

Another discovery system that has received attention, and has exerted indirect classroom influence, is "prewriting." As we have seen earlier in this chapter, the term itself is often used simply to indicate the early part of the composing process, before the writing-down of text. But "prewriting" has also become the distinctive label of a discovery method developed by D. Gordon Rohman. Arguing that most students are taught to deal with the abstract "rhetoric of the finished word," Rohman suggests that students need to learn "the structure of thinking that leads to writing" (107). "Prewriting" is a series of activities which "imitate the principles" by which writing is generated: those activities are keeping a journal, practicing meditation, and making analogies. Keeping a journal is intended as a Thoreau-like exercise in the "discovery of myself for myself" (109), a way of articulating experience for oneself. Meditating is suggested as a way of imagining abstract ideas into concrete experience; analogy is urged as a method for seeing an experience in a variety of "as if" perspectives. Insofar as these activities require students to think through an idea, to give it body by developing it through analogies or other mind-play without the false comfort that a "solution" has been reached, they may aid student writers in developing what they want to say beyond the traditional orthodoxies of outlining and thesis-sentencing.

One survey of invention systems discusses a wide range of strategies from which teachers might choose (Harrington). Particularly for a complex set of terms like those in tagmemics, simply learning them well enough for practical use may draw energy away from actual composing. Thus, teachers who wish to use heuristics need to emphasize the commitment in study and practice needed for students to learn a heuristic system well. Teachers may find that this commitment absorbs energy that ought to be spent in other ways. However, explained carefully and clearly as a way of helping students shape their own composing, and taught with sufficient time to allow students to experiment and become familiar with their structures, heuristic strategies can help students learn ways to discover what might be said about a particular topic.

Revision, Pretext, and Protocols

As linear models of composing have been transformed into models emphasizing recursiveness, the importance of revision has become a major issue for writing teachers. The cognitive-process view of writing suggests that revising is logically the major point of intervention for teachers. If composing is viewed as a cognitive process with distinct—though recursive—stages, then, it can be argued, writing teachers should require students to "use" the composing process to its fullest potential by expanding their revising efforts. Influential research by Nancy Sommers and Sondra Perl has indicated that while experienced writers see revising primarily as a "global" process of reshaping a text fully and holistically, student writers tend to

see revision as a "local" process of "fixing" sentence structure, changing words and phrases, and correcting mechanical errors. Students
tend to interpret suggestions about revision as guidelines for "correcting" rather than as inducements to resee and reshape the whole
text. To emphasize the importance of holistic revision , many current
writing texts urge students to develop consistent, thorough revision
strategies, by learning how to resee and rework their writing.

Emphasis on revision as a natural element of "process teaching"
has, however, led to counterreaction and controversy in some interesting ways. For example, the habit of focusing revision on *written*
texts has been questioned; the appropriateness of revising for all
inexperienced writers has also been criticized. Textbook versions of
revision, for example, tend to emphasize multiple drafting; students
are urged to reread and rewrite texts not merely to "fix" errors but to
reshape organization, development, and style in ways that enhance
the writer's purpose. Recursive, nonlinear models of composing,
however, have emphasized the importance of "pretext," that which
is "written out" mentally. One researcher defines pretext as the
writer's "mental construction of 'text' prior to transcription"—"a
writer's tentative linguistic representation of meaning" which pre-
cedes and leads to "transcribing written text" (Witte 397). Some writers spend more time thinking out pretext than writing down actual
text. A crucial question thus arises: if much of a writer's thinking-in-
language, including the forming and reforming of sentences and even
tentative paragraphs, occurs *before* transcription, what role does that
leave the revising of written texts? If making pretext is indeed a major
aspect of composing, should the revising of written text be the focus
of teachers' influence? Or should teachers seek to shape students'
revising earlier, before it is written down?

These problems have been articulated by researchers who question whether systematic revision is equally appropriate to all student
writers or to all writing purposes. Those teachers who insist that students must make "a personal search for meaning through the course
of several drafts," says Maxine Hairston, are supporting an
"impractical, unrealistic, and, eventually, counterproductive" teaching strategy (451). Many routine writing purposes require no revision, she argues, while the more "reflective" purposes, fewer in
number, do require committed revising; our task as teachers is to
help students discern the level of revision appropriate to the purpose
at hand. Another researcher suggests that revisers and nonrevisers
differ essentially in mind and temperament, not just behaviorally out
of inexperience or indifference. Thus, the benefits of revising should
not be assumed; its gains and losses should be carefully taught. "One-
drafters are efficient writers," she argues, but they often miss out on

"options" deliberate revisers exploit (Harris 187). On the other hand, "multiple drafters" may waste time and energy revising pointlessly; they need to be taught not to "linger too long over making choices" (189). Teachers must be pluralists, patiently accepting the variety of student potential and the individualizing necessary to nurture it.

Though composing research will continue to look for evidence about writers' habits, it cannot provide models which satisfactorily account for this variety; the good judgment of writing teachers is the key here. Teachers need to consider what may be accomplished by trying to help students' composing at various stages. Often a finished text seems fixed and final to students, who may be reluctant to alter what was so arduously produced. At the least, teachers need to distinguish students for whom textual revision is meaningful from those for whom the making of pretext may be as important as written revision in producing effective texts.

Writer-Based Prose and Schema

Despite these controversies, the cognitive-process approach to writing has yielded some important insights for writing teachers. One of them is the influential concept of "writer-based" prose formulated by Linda Flower. She argues that the "ineffective writer" often turns to the "associative, narrative path of the writer's own confrontation with her subject" (19–20) in the course of composing, because she is enmeshed in the process of *making* meaning and cannot therefore *organize* meaning for readers. Writer-based prose shares the qualities of the "inner and egocentric speech described by Vygotsky and Piaget," including its elliptical quality, its connotative word-sense, and its nonlogical patterns (21). Such prose must be transformed into "reader-based" writing through the writer's imposition of reader-oriented structures upon her writing. In Piagetian terms, the growth of audience awareness is a function of decentering, during which writers gain the ability to perceive their work objectively. The concept of writer-centered prose has been fruitful in helping writing teachers see ineffective writing as a consequence of a particular kind of cognitive function; in this view, "errors" may be seen as strategic attempts to cope with unfamiliar writing situations and readers, rather than simply as violations of "rules" everyone should know.

Another important contribution of Piaget, Vygotsky, and other cognitivists to the psychology of learning—and thus to composition—is "schema theory," which attempts to account for the ways in which our understandings change as we develop. Following Piaget, early developmental psychologists proposed that learning occurred as a series of "assimilations" and "accommodations" during which the consciousness continuously encounters and is changed by new experiences. Current definitions of such theory tend to display positivist, even mechanistic terminology. "Cognitive schemata," says researcher Richard Beach, "are cognitive structures or scripts that help us organize information hierarchically" so that all new "information" may be "processed" into increasingly complex patterns (64–6). Though it is often cast in positivistic language, schema theory supports the view of writing as individual cognitive process: as teachers, says Janet Emig, we must account for "creative individual thought, for individuals writing. . . . [for] the constructs of the individual learner and writer" (*The Web of Meaning* 149). Protocol research—the study of the individual writer at work—flows naturally from this way of seeing writing. The pedagogical implications of schema theory suggest that teachers must be aware of different levels of understanding among students, in order to provide students with "experiences that will begin to move [them] toward the next level" (Petersen 42).

As we will see in Chapter Two, schema theory, along with other elements of the cognitive-process view of writing, has strongly influenced compositionists' understanding of writing and its teaching. However, schema theory may lead its adherents into advice laden with positivistic metaphors, represented, for example, by the phrase describing writing as "constructing texts." Cognitive theory's real aspiration—its striving to envision the complex and interactive process of composing—is thwarted when its practitioners apply the reductive language of the home remodeler to writing. Teachers of writing need to read the often jargon-laden descriptions of cognitive process warily, reminding themselves that schemas or "cognitive maps" are metaphors of mind rather than empirically verifiable descriptions.

Modal Systems

The changing concept of mode in discourse is another important sign of psychology's current influence on composition. The idea of modes, or "forms of discourse," first gained importance in the nineteenth century as composition theorists attempted to conceptualize the relationship between writers' psychological processes and textual form. They multiplied various "forms of discourse" in response to changing concepts of faculty and associationist psychology. Associationist psychology, for example, is the primary basis for the most influential nineteenth century modal system, that of Alexander Bain. There are "three ultimate modes of mind—Feeling, Volition, and

Intellect," he suggested, and the "forms of Discourse" correspond to each faculty:

> Those that have for their object to inform the Understanding [Intellect], fall under three heads—Description, Narration, and Exposition. The means of influencing the Will [Volition] are given under one head, Persuasion. The employing of language to excite pleasurable Feelings, is one of the chief characteristics of Poetry. (23) Furthermore, the Will can be moved only through the Understanding or through the Feelings (19).

Thus, three of Bain's five "kinds of composition" embody an association between actions of the intelligence and the moving of the will—i.e., between what the writer wants the reader to understand and what he wants the reader to believe or do, Bain might say. This linkage among psychic components reflects the mechanistic tendencies of associationist psychology, and to the modern eye appears reductive and outmoded. The very same terms are used, with very different premises, by another nineteenth century rhetorician, A. D. Hepburn, who classes the "forms of Discourse" according to the "objects of thought" each one addresses:

> 1. Description [is] the exhibition in language of the parts of a simultaneous whole. 2. Narration [is] the exhibition of the parts of a successive whole. 3. Exposition [consists] in the explication of general notions and propositions formed from them. 4. Argumentation [treats] the truth or falsehood of a proposition (in Kitzhaber 203).

Hepburn bases his definitions on the subject matter of the discourse types, rather than upon their psychological function. John Franklin Genung, an American rhetorician of the nineteenth century, echoes Hepburn by asserting that description, narration, exposition, and persuasion are "the particular forms that invention adopts, as it has to deal with material of various kinds" (Kitzhaber 203). Bain, Hepburn, and Genung use nearly identical terms to distinguish categories of prose composition, yet define those categories in radically different ways. The conflicts within these traditional modal categories have seldom been fully addressed, yet they still appear today in some rhetorics and readers, usually without any acknowledgement (or perhaps recognition) of their archaic psychological basis.

Recent psychological and linguistic theory have generated new perspectives on modal theory, of which the system of "discourse forms" developed by James Britton and his research team from the British Schools Council Project has become one of the best known. Britton has suggested three "function categories" of writing in schools, described in terms of the audience for the writing ("who is it

for?") and the purpose the writing serves ("what is it for?)"
("Functions of Writing" 15). Britton acknowledges the convergent
influences of cognitive psychology and linguistics, with Piaget and
Vygotsky as generative sources. Britton's interest in audience and
purpose would appear to derive from classical rhetoric's interest in
the speaker-audience relationship. However, his definition of the
writer's audience-sense utilizes a contemporary frame of reference.
He does not analyze the writer-audience relationship as always purposeful, i.e. involving a writer seeking to inform, persuade, or move
an audience. Instead, drawing on recent analyses of "language roles"
in human interaction, he suggests that the writer, purpose, and audience of a piece of writing are all related in one or two basic ways.
If writing reveals an intention to "get things done," whether by
instructing, persuading, "speculating," or "theorizing," then it serves
"some end outside itself" (18). This is "writing in the role of participant" (18), and Britton suggests the term "transactional" to describe
it. If writing renders "experiences real or imagined" in order that the
audience (which may be only the writer) may "contemplate narrated
experiences" (19) as a means of understanding them more clearly or
judging their value, then that writing becomes an end in itself, and its
form and style important in themselves. This use of language Britton
calls "writing in the role of spectator" (19), and he suggests the term
"poetic" to describe it.

Britton's scheme is represented by the following diagram:

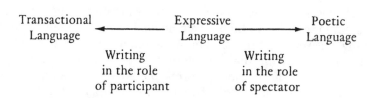

At the center of the spectrum is expressive language, which may
include both spectator and participant roles, but which assumes
shared interests and "close relations" between writer and audience.
This is the most common use of language in speech or writing, especially in children, because it does not require adaptation to an outside audience, but permits the writer or speaker to explore the world
within the security of "shared contexts" (32). As the child matures, or
as the adult defines his writing or speaking purpose, expressive language differentiates "into specific forms to meet specific demands
over a wide range of transactional and poetic tasks" ("Language and
the Nature of Learning" 33). Britton argues that "expressive language

signals the self, reflects not only the ebb and flow of a speaker's thought and feeling, but also his assumptions of shared contexts of meaning, and of a relationship of trust with his listener"; "[expressive language is] the mode in which young children chiefly write" (*The Development of Writing Abilities* 10–1). Thus, when younger writers are asked to write for an audience beyond their immediate world, they will succeed only to the extent they can visualize and address an audience outside their familiar experience.

What Britton perceives as the ubiquity of expressive speech and writing in schoolchildren leads him to propose a "major hypothesis" for school writing: "what children write in the early stages should be a form of written-down expressive speech. . . . As their writing and reading progress side by side, they will move from this starting point into . . . broadly differentiated kinds of writing" (*The Development of Writing Abilities* 10). Some rhetoric texts follow this pattern in their major sections, moving from "personal" writing (diaries, journals) through "descriptive" and "informative" to "persuasive" writing. Though there are differing forms and changing intentions involved in this sequence, there are also different audiences implied for the various types. Personal writing suggests a "relationship of trust" between writer and reader, while persuasive writing, at the other end of the spectrum, suggests abstract topics and a more distanced, generalized audience. Such a polarity may be seen, for example, in the assignments of the writing-test portion of the National Assessment of Educational Progress (NAEP), a nationwide program for measuring the educational gains of schoolchildren at different grade levels in the United States. The test program has been broadened in order to discover whether children were learning the flexibility needed to perform a variety of writing tasks for a variety of audiences.

One important example of Britton's influence on current thinking about modes appears in a well-known empirical study of students' composing processes. Describing her pioneering use of protocol studies in composing research, Janet Emig scrutinizes the physical and psychological minutiae of some high school seniors' writing habits, and induces composing patterns associated with the writing types she finds. In devising her categories, Emig notes the diagram of writing types constructed by Britton and his colleagues, which posits "expressive" writing as the primary mode of writing, especially for students. Agreeing with Britton's insight, she suggests that "all student writings emanate from an expressive impulse" (37). But then she argues that the other two terms in Britton's tripartite scheme "are at once too familiar and too ultimate" (37). Instead, she suggests two terms which describe the "relations between the writing self and the field of discourse": reflexive and extensive (37). Her diagram closely resembles Britton's:

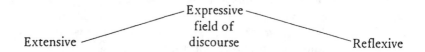

By "field of discourse" Emig says she means "areas of experience" (33). But her definitions make it clear that "field of discourse" is more than the relation of the "writing self" to the experience being handled in the writing. "Field of discourse" in Emig's system also includes the audience for the writing, and actually—like Britton's "function categories"—defines the complex interaction of the writer's intent, the nature of the subject matter, and the audience to which that matter is addressed.

For example, although Emig rejects Britton's term "poetic" in favor of her term "reflexive," both terms delineate a writer-subject-audience relationship. Writing reflexively, the "writing self" ponders and evaluates experience, attempts to answer the question "what does this experience mean?" (37), and is aimed at the self as the "chief audience" (91). Emig's term "extensive" identifies writing in "a basically active role"; such writing answers the question "how, because of this experience, do I interact with my environment?" (37), and is aimed at "adult others, notably teachers," as the "chief audience" (91). In other words, the extensive mode parallels Britton's transactional category, in which the writing self is in a "participant" role and intends to "get something done" with the writing. Emig's categories are limited to the school writing her students were engaged in, and lack the larger range of examples upon which Britton builds his categories.

Another instance of Britton's influence can be found in John Dixon's *Growth Thorough English*, his interpretation of the gist of the 1966 Anglo-American "Dartmouth Conference" on writing. This worldwide collaboration among composition teachers emphasized the roles of play and personal meditation in learning to write. Dixon suggests that the Conference participants were so fascinated by this theme that they ignored language in "the role of informing and explaining." This function—Britton's "transactional" category—requires the student to "imagine an audience other than himself and his classmates," and to organize language "on behalf of, in the interests of, and for [its] effect on, another person or other people" (124).

The Conference's omission of transactional writing from its program encourages a distorted view of what writing in schools ought to include, says Dixon. Students should be required to display a "social competence" in language, he suggests, embodied in such intentions as "explanations, requests, directions, invitations, reports, [and] instructions" (125).

What Dixon is arguing is what writing teachers already know: it is crucial for inexperienced writers to be able to write about what they know and relate it to others. It's false to talk about student writing as though it could be either entirely self-oriented or wholly social and other-directed. Any writing task that is to mean something to inexperienced writers must fall within the range of their lives and be directed at an audience meaningful to them (see Britton's audience categories in Chapter Three for a fuller development of this point). A journal, for example, can reflect the writer's own feelings about events and people while being formulated as a private-letter-to-the-teacher. Behind Dixon's advocacy of other-directed writing for students lies the idea of decentering. Audience awareness is precisely the writer's recognition of other points of view than his own, and of the ways in which his words strike others.

Despite Dixon's second thoughts, however, the Dartmouth Conference was the catalyst for the increasing interest in group and collaborative writing in the teaching of writing today. In the decades since the conference, group activities such as panel discussions, role-playing, and simulation games, and small-group work that encourages independent, self-motivated activity have all become important elements in teaching writing. Peter Elbow's influential texts, for example, emphasize writing groups as ways for students to take collective responsibility for themselves and each other as learners, in order to "claim more control over their own lives" (*Writing Without Teachers* vii) In the 1970's an NCTE Commission on Composition emphasized language as a mode of self creation: "through language we understand, interpret, enjoy, and in part create our worlds. . . . [language] can help students . . . live more fully" ("Teaching Composition" 219). It argued that "the teacher should encourage writing from personal experience" because "all writers . . . are trying to define their experiences, and, through those experiences, define themselves" (219).

Indeed, one of cognitive psychology's bedrock principles is that learning—including writing development—will occur most readily when what students learn and write about relates directly to their own experience. This principle was not invented by modern psychology. As Robert Connors points out, personal writing actually came into pedagogical fashion in the early nineteenth century, partly as a result of romantic theories of knowledge, and has remained a popular element of composition pedagogy ever since. Indeed, by emphasizing "narration" and "description" as major "modes of discourse," nineteenth century compositionists invited personal experience into the composition curriculum, where it remains today (Connors 177–8). Topics available to students' experience—confirming, expanding, or challenging it—support their authority in composing, bringing their attitudes and expectations into play. Setting the context for a writing topic is the teacher's responsibility; it can be done by establishing the rhetorical situation, to include the writing purpose and the audience. Today, most writing teachers tend to value assignments which combine a personal dimension with an emphasis on the relationship between writer, readers, and situational context. The best rhetoric texts emphasize contextual relationships, so that students' writing purposes will have the psychological fullness which invests writing with significance for students. As we will see in Chapter Two, the contextual view has gained influence in recent years, focusing teachers' attention on the importance of both reading and writing as reciprocal processes in composition.

Attitudes Toward the Student Writer

The lore of the Dartmouth Conference appeared frequently in the composition discipline in the years after 1966. Affirming the power of language to nurture self-discovery and interaction, the Darmouth conferees were, like a presidium, ratifying doctrines about language already articulated in the work of cognitive psychology and the writings of "progressive" educators like John Dewey. Piaget's concept of decentering, for example, has been a major source of theorizing about the developmental power of language. "One can learn the meaning of perspective," says one interpreter of Piaget, "only by pitting one's thoughts against those of others and noting similarities and differences" (Flavell 369). Collaborative activity among student writers in and out of the classroom reflects the Piagetian/Vygotskian faith in cognitive development through communication and collaboration. Another source of contemporary faith in communicative interaction—embodied in the progressive tradition and seldom acknowledged today—is John Dewey's insistence that "interaction" is a "chief principle for interpreting an experience in its educational function and force" (38). Dewey argues that any truly educative experience must derive from "personal needs, desires, purposes, and capacities" (42), too often ignored by teachers, says Dewey, because public education tends to emphasize the control of "external conditions" in the educational process, at the expense of "internal factors which also decide what kind of experience is had" (39).

The concept of stages in language growth has strongly influenced the way writing teachers view basic or remedial writers. The field of error-analysis has helped writing teachers view writing errors as signs of inexperienced writers' attempts to cope with unfamiliar standard usages. The roots of this view of error lie in Piaget's assertion that as she learns, the child will commit "systematic errors" in accommodating new cognitive structures to existing ones. In this view errors are seen not as deviations but as signals of the learner's ways of coping with new challenges. "Such systematic errors," says Piaget, "are found at all levels of the hierarchy of behavior" ("Comments" 4). This view of error has also influenced the composition discipline through ESL (the study of English as a Second Language), where error-analysis rather than rote memorization is used to help the language learner. Error-analysis has aided composition research by offering a constructive view of what grammar and coherence difficulties may reveal about writers' processes. It has aided composition pedagogy by helping teachers match teaching strategies to the errors students commit.

It has been particularly useful in helping inexperienced writers. In her seminal and influential study of problem writers—which will be explored further in Chapter Four—Mina Shaughnessy relies on her version of this approach to the writing difficulties of unskilled writers. Rather than using traditional grammar categories to define "error," she develops a new "language" of incomplete and unachieved grammatical intentions to describe the misused phrases and broken syntax of basic writers. Such formulations require teachers to regard "errors" as students' systematic attempts to manipulate what they do not yet fully understand, rather than as oversights which students could "correct" with more care. In order to respond to errors as attempts at mastery, teachers must try to understand the systems or patterns by means of which errors are produced, which may differ with each student. Teachers, says David Bartholomae, must study the "repeated instances of errors, in order to imagine what about the composition of the essays or sentences in them has resulted in error patterns" (Facts 210). Such a strategy does not make the teacher's job any less arduous, for it is nominally easier to mark errors with the symbols on the inside covers of grammar handbooks than to scrutinize sentences in hopes of finding patterns. But if the developmental view of error is to be enacted, teachers must individualize their perceptions of students' writing problems to help them towards a fuller literacy.

Another major influence on attitudes toward inexperienced or unskilled writers has come from the work of Carl Rogers, whose analysis of the feelings involved in the interaction between teacher and learner is particularly relevant to hesitant or fearful writers. In *Freedom to Learn*, Rogers rejects teaching defined as "imparting knowledge or skill." Instead, he argues, teaching must be defined as the "facilitation of change and learning"; it's the teacher's responsibility to encourage the process of learning, not to pass on "knowledge" that may soon be obsolete (104). We have seen this distinction implicit in the emphasis upon cognition as process. It appears, for example, in Bruner's distinction between the "expository mode" of teaching, in which the teacher employs "extrinsic" motivation, and the "hypothetical mode," in which the student "plays the principal role" in his learning and is "rewarded by discovery itself" (*On Knowing* 83). But Rogers' unique contribution to the composition discipline lies in his influential model of the ideal learning process. A "facilitating" relationship, says Rogers, involves "realness" (the facilitator's acknowledgment of his own feelings), "prizing" (the facilitator's nonpossessive caring for the learner), and "empathic understanding" (a nonjudgmental understanding of the learner's feelings) (106–12). These elements of the teacher-learner relationship will help produce a learner who is a "fully functioning person," says Rogers, adaptable to change and confident of herself as the agent of her own learning. Such qualities in the learner receive major emphasis, for example, in the NCTE's "Position Statement" on teaching composition: in learning to write students "learn about themselves and their world," and gain "the power to grow personally and to effect change in the world."

Classroom strategies have been influenced by Rogerian doctrine. His "methods for building freedom" for learners have been applied to the writing situation. Small-group work, simulation exercises, contract learning systems, and student self-evaluations all have been urged upon the writing class (see Chapter Six for a discussion of these methods). Two settings are particularly designed to nurture the feelings Rogers emphasizes: the writing lab and the small group. The writing lab or workshop has become an important part of many writing programs because it offers the individualized relationship usually seen as necessary to encourage poorer writers. The freedom of the workshop setting, coupled with the personal attention of the workshop instructor (who normally plays the role of "facilitator" in the Rogerian sense), offers the nurturing situation Rogers advocates. Small-group writing activity like that urged by Kenneth Bruffee and Peter Elbow (see Chapter Six) is also designed to create supporting relationships among students themselves. The present popularity of the writing lab and the small group is a response by writing teachers not only to increasingly unpredictable writing preparation among students, but also to the humane influence of Rogerian psychology.

Works Cited

Applebee, Arthur N. *Tradition and Reform in the Teaching of English: A History*. Urbana, IL: National Council of Teachers of English, 1974.

Bain, Alexander. *English Composition and Rhetoric: A Manual*. American Edition, Revised. New York: D. Appleton, 1866.

Beach, Richard and JoAnne Liebman-Kleine. "The Writing/Reading Relationship: Becoming One's Own Best Reader." *Conversations: Transactions in Reading and Writing*. Ed. Bruce Petersen. Urbana, IL: NCTE, 1986. 64–81.

Berthoff, Ann E. "Response to Janice Lauer, 'Counterstatement'." *Contemporary Rhetoric*. Ed. Ross Winterowd. New York: Harcourt Brace Jovanovich, 1975.

Bizzell, Patricia. "Composing Processes: An Overview." *The Teaching of Writing: Eighty-Fifth Yearbook of the National Society for the Study of Education*. Ed. Anthony R. Petrosky and David Bartholomae. Chicago: NSSE, 1986.

Bitzer, Lloyd. "The Rhetorical Situation." *Philosophy and Rhetoric* 1 (1968): 1–14.

Britton, James. *The Development of Writing Abilities, 11–18*. London: Macmillan, 1975.

———. "The Functions of Writing." *Research on Composing*. Ed. Charles R. Cooper and Lee Odell. Urbana, IL: NCTE, 1978.

Bruner, Jerome, et al. *Studies in Cognitive Growth*. New York: Wiley and Sons, 1966.

———. *Toward a Theory of Instruction*. Cambridge, MA: Harvard University Press, 1966.

Burke, Kenneth. *A Grammar of Motives*. New York: Prentice-Hall, 1945.

———. "Questions and Answers About the Pentad." *College Composition and Communication* 29 (1978): 330–5.

Connors, Robert J. "Personal Writing Assignments." *CCC* 38 (1987): 166–183.

Dewey, John. *Education and Experience*. New York: Macmillan, 1938.

Dixon, John. *Growth Through English Set in the Perspective of the Seventies*. 3rd ed. London: Oxford University Press, 1975.

Elbow, Peter. *Writing Without Teachers*. New York: Oxford University Press, 1973.

Emig, Janet. *The Composing Processes of Twelfth Graders.* Urbana, IL: NCTE, 1971.

———. *The Web of Meaning: Essays on Writing, Teaching, Learning, and Thinking.* Ed. Dixie Goswami and Maureen Butler. Portsmouth, NH: Boynton/Cook, 1983.

Faigley, Lester. "Competing Theories of Process: A Critique and a Proposal." *College English* 48 (1986): 527–42.

Flavell, John. *The Developmental Psychology of Jean Piaget.* Princeton, NJ: D. Van Nostrand, 1963.

Flower, Linda. "Writer-Based Prose: A Cognitive Basis for Problems in Writing." *CE* 41 (1979): 19–37.

Flower, Linda and John Hayes. "A Cognitive Process Theory of Writing." *College Composition and Communication* 32 (1981): 365–87.

Hairston, Maxine. "Different Products, Different Processes: A Theory About Writing." *CCC* 37 (1986): 442–56.

Harrington, David. "A Critical Survey of Resources for Teaching Rhetorical Invention." *CE* 40 (1979): 64–71.

Harris, Muriel. "Composing Behaviors of One- and Multi-Draft Writers." *CE* 51 (1989): 174–91.

Hartwell, Patrick. "Grammar, Grammars, and the Teaching of Grammar." *CE* 47 (1985): 105–27.

Hirsch, E. D. Jr. *The Philosophy of Composition.* Chicago: The University of Chicago Press, 1977.

Kinney, James. "Tagmemic Rhetoric: A Reconsideration." *CCC* 29 (1978):141–45.

Kitzhaber, Albert. "Rhetoric in American Colleges, 1850–1900." diss., University of Washington, 1953.

Kohlberg, Lawrence. *Child Psychology and Childhood Education: A Cognitive-Developmental View.* New York: Longman, 1987.

Lauer, Janice. "Toward a Metatheory of Heuristic Procedures." *CCC* 30 (1979): 268–9.

O'Hare, Frank. *Sentence-Combining: Improving Student Writing without Formal Grammar Instruction.* Urbana, IL: NCTE, 1973.

Passmore, John. *The Philosophy of Teaching.* Cambridge, MA: Harvard University Press, 1980.

Piaget, Jean. *Six Psychological Studies.* Trans. Anita Tenzer and David Elkind. New York: Random House, 1967.

———. "Comments on Vygotsky's Critical Remarks Concerning *The Language and Thought of the Child, and Judgment and Reasoning of the Child.*" "Addendum" to Vygotsky's *Thought and Language,* cited below.

Piaget, Jean and B. Inhelder. *The Psychology of the Child.* Trans. Helen Weaver. New York: Basic Books, 1969.

Perelman, Chaim. *The Realm of Rhetoric*. Trans. William Kluback. Notre Dame, IN: University of Notre Dame Press, 1982.

Polanyi, Michael. *Personal Knowledge: Towards a Post-Critical Philosophy*. Chicago: University of Chicago Press, 1962.

———. *The Tacit Dimension*. New York: Doubleday & Co., 1966.

Rogers, Carl. *Freedom to Learn*. Columbus, OH: Merrill Publishing Company, 1969.

Rohman, D. Gordon. "Pre-Writing: The Stage of Discovery in the Writing Process." CCC 16 (1965): 106–12.

Sledd, James. "Opinion. Product in Process: From Ambiguities of Standard English to Issues That Divide Us." CE 50 (1988): 168–76.

Vygotsky, L. S. *Thought and Language*. Trans. Eugenia Hanfmann and Gertrude Vakar. Cambridge, MA: MIT Press, 1962.

Wadsworth, Barry J. *Piaget's Theory of Cognitive Development*. New York: David McKay, 1971.

Wells, Susan. "Classroom Heuristics and Empiricism." CE 39 (1977): 467–76.

Wertsch, James V. *Vygotsky and the Social Formation of Mind*. Cambridge, MA: Harvard University Press, 1985.

Wright, Evelyn. "School English and Public Policy." CE 42 (1980).

Young, Richard, Alton Becker, Kenneth Pike. *Rhetoric: Discovery and Change*. New York: Harcourt, Brace and World, 1970.

Chapter Two

Writing and Reading,
Writers and Readers

I. The Individualist Tradition

Writing has traditionally been represented as a supremely isolated pursuit, at best requiring writers to keep apart from company, and at worst traducing them into alienation and despair. The image of lonely writers starving in their garrets for the sake of their art suggests the nobility of renunciation. That of oppressed writers seeking (in Virginia Woolf's terms) rooms of their own suggests the heroism of resistance to the tyranny of convention. Both figures embody the profound individualism which the act of writing has traditionally signified in our culture. It is one of Romanticism's particular legacies to portray the writer either as a god-like creator who transcends mere humanity, or as a noble outlaw heroically rejecting the prosaic consistencies of ordinary life. We tend to think of the writer's work as inherently solitary, requiring private time and circumstances for success, often at the cost of relationships and recognition.

This individualist perspective still claims a powerful hold on our imagination, and applies as well to readers as to writers. To write and to read are, in this view, affirmations of the sovereignty of the individual mind. Composing a text and composing a reading of that text become enactments of our unique personal identities. We see writing and reading in the same way we see political action in our pluralistic democracy: in atomistic terms, as the activity of selves whose separateness is not broached even in collective settings. The views we will explore in the first part of this chapter reinforce the notion that writing and reading are unique acts carried out by individuals in

44

distinct states of being. Even if we view writing and reading as inter-actions of writer, text and reader, we tend to see writer and text, or reader and text, as engaged autonomously in separate acts of composing.

Some perspectives on writing and reading have emerged in recent years which can help us clarify the issues involved in the individualist way of seeing. *Cognitive-process psychology* (whose major thinkers we examined in Chapter One) suggests that just as writing composes a text, so reading is also a form of composing: readers compose their versions of the text composed by the writer. Such processes are, in this view, individual cognitive functions; we can understand these processes, say the proponents of cognitive-process inquiry, by studying both actual writing and reading behav-ior. We then describe and model the processes we infer from such study, assuming that though such processes are manifested in differ-ent ways by individual writers and readers, they may be taken to represent writing and reading processes generally. Though the goals and methods of such research have been questioned, they continue to infuse both research studies and classroom textbooks.

While cognitive-process models focus on the composing behav-ior of individual writers and readers, *rhetorical analyses* tend to emphasize the contextual relationships between writers and read-ers. The field of rhetoric has traditionally studied the relationship among writers, texts, and readers, emphasizing the power of writers and texts to shape the roles readers play. *Literary theories* have also shaped our understanding of reader-writer relationships. Some liter-ary theorists, influenced by rhetorical perspectives, view writers and texts as determinative, shaping readers' roles and interpretations of meaning. Others see readers and reading communities as the real sources of meaning-making in discourse, arguing that texts have no real life until they are constituted in the act of reading.

Taken together, these perspectives offer a wide range of ways to interpret the relationship between writer and reader. Some empha-size the power of the text to shape readers' responses, others the constructive power of reading to shape the text. We will explore these influences in this chapter, focusing first on individualist ways of describing the writing-reading relationship, and then on the social and collaborative dimensions of writing.

Writing and Reading: The Cognitive Perspective

Let's consider what those who explore the cognitive aspects of writ-ing and reading say about their field. Here's the way two psycholin-guists articulate their goals: "In order to learn about the internal psychological processes involved in the act of writing," they approach writing "as language behavior unfolding in time, open to direct observation and therefore to systematic empirical investigation" (Kowal and O'Connell 110). In other words, from what writers are *doing*, these researchers hope to infer what and how they're *thinking* as they compose. Researchers construct models of what they believe is "going on" in the mind, as evidenced by observed behavior; such models are then tested and altered by further empirical studies.

Out of such study, process researchers hope (in Robert deBeaugrande's words) to bring to light "a small, powerful, and unified set of processing strategies" (241)—"schemas"—which represent the ways people use language. Schemas or "schemata" may loosely be defined as organizing structures or plans which enable writers and readers to integrate new information and ideas into existing ones. Unfortunately, it is difficult to find more precise definitions that are not tangled in scientistic patois: "schemata are cognitive structures or scripts that help us organize information hierarchically," one researcher pair suggests (Beach and Liebman-Kleine 64); "abstract, conceptual structures that organize prototypical knowledge of the world so we can bring it to bear in perception, comprehension, thought and bodily action," writes another (Phelps 165).

Based on their interpretations of schema theory, cognitive researchers draw up models of reading and writing behavior. This urge to build research findings into theoretical generalizations reflects the aspirations of a scientific approach: knowledge emerges cumulatively out of the constant retesting of hypotheses grounded in the cognitive paradigm. While hypotheses are constantly subject to testing and revising, research and teaching are governed by the most widely accepted hypotheses of a discipline. Thus, in composition pedagogy (according to the cognitive-process viewpoint) if we observe our students' writing behavior carefully enough, we can construct models of that behavior by accurately gauging the cognitive processes that generate it. And from such models, in turn, pedagogical strategies can be devised to shape students' writing behavior in desirable ways.

Writers and Readers Making Texts

Behind these aspirations to a scientific understanding of composing lies a distinct understanding of "mind": namely, the *constructionist* paradigm introduced in Chapter One—that mind is dynamic rather than static, active rather than passive, integrative rather than merely cumulative. Mind is not simply a recorder of information or a compiler of associations; it is a set of powers which transforms diverse experiences into wholes. This view of mind carries over into a similar view of discourse as dynamic and transforming, rather than merely mechanistic and transmissive. This dynamic understanding of discourse expresses itself both in psychology's cognitive-process view and in rhetorical models of discourse.

The cognitive-process view suggests that reading and writing are reciprocating elements, functioning only in response to each other. The phrase "writing process" has often been interpreted to mean the kind of thinking writers do while composing—a private and self-enclosed activity. But, says Louise Wetherbee Phelps, a fuller understanding of a reading-and-writing process sees it as a "cooperative enterprise whereby writers and readers construct meanings together, through the dialectic tension beween their interactive and interdependent processes"(162). Some writers suggest that this tension characterizes the individual composing consciousness. "The writer writing" and "the writer reading," meditates Donald Murray, are inseparable: "the writer hearing from the page what the writer does not expect to hear. The writer hearing (reading through the ear?) the line passing through the mouth before it is thought . . . the line changing as it is read"—these processes blur and intermingle (Murray 241). This interaction has provided another writer with a new starting-point as a teacher: "I don't know anymore how to teach students about writing without teaching them about reading" (Troyka 188).

Cognitive-process researchers tend to identify three important features which writing and reading share:

1. Writing and reading are both "intentional"—that is, active and purposeful. As Frank Smith suggests, neither are "passive and mechanical"; both are "purposeful and rational, dependent on prior knowledge and expectations" (2). Writing is not merely transmitting signals, nor is reading merely a receiving of them; the "wireless" or "channel" metaphor of communication, traditional to communication studies, simplifies and distorts the cognitive-process view of both writing and reading. In this view, writers do not encode their ideas into language framed in a text, so that the reader can decode the language and recover the writer's ideas intact "out of" the medium of language. The cognitive-process viewpoint insists that the writer's and reader's work include both invention and discovery. "Text" becomes a problematic entity, a reenactment of cognitive dynamics rather than a fixed record of settled meanings. A text is not a completed transaction until it is re-composed by readers who build their own representations of it. To teach writing and reading is, therefore, to

make writers and readers understand the deep kinship between the composing of a writer and that of a reader.

2. Writing and reading are both pulled by predictive, goal-driven activity, the writer/reader's need to foresee what comes next. Linda Flower and John Hayes maintain that "writing is a goal-directed process" in which "a hierarchical network of goals" directs the writing process, even as the goals themselves evolve through the process of revision (377). We do the same things as readers, as Lynn Q. Troyka points out: we "predict everything from words ('Once upon a _____") to concepts ('The arguments for giving up cigarettes are many. For example, _____). Without a preconscious anticipating and estimating of what to expect next . . . the brain would be unable to make connections and would not, therefore, comprehend" (191).

   Purposefulness has always been an issue in writing: traditional wisdom has it that one must begin with a purpose in mind. But the cognitive-process perspective suggests that composing is as much a process of discovering goals as it is enacting them. The writer's initial intentions energize composing, even as the act of composition revises and redirects those goals. And just as writers discover goals as they compose, readers become aware of their expectations as they read. Intentionality is as crucial to reading as to writing: without knowing where the text is going, readers cannot follow it. Reading is not simply a matter of "decoding" words and fitting them into sentences and paragraphs; it is a continuous process of shaping the groups of words in the text into patterns which fulfill readers' expectations.

3. Writing and reading are both context-dependent. Lacking the physical immediacy of speaking and listening, writing and reading must establish their own "situation"—context. Frank Smith describes the power of context in writing: "the writer is not free to produce words arbitrarily . . . [writers are bound by] two things, the subject matter . . . and the language the writer is employing" (41). Writers invoke context through the resources of language—diction, syntax, organization and format. Readers infer from these cues the "world" out of which the writer's subject matter and language emerge. The more complex are both writers' and readers' existing cognitive structures—schemata— the more fully will context emerge in the transactions of writers and readers.

   Writing and reading are twinned because comprehending is composing, says another researcher: "the comprehension of text . . . is the same kind of putting-together" as the composing of texts (Petrosky 20). Cognitive researchers suggest the same perspective in more technical language. Proficient readers and writers know how to "extract more information from [their] experiences and to further elaborate their schemata for . . . discourse," says one, because "young readers and writers gradually [learn to] read with a 'writer's eye' and to write with a 'reader's eye' " (Birnbaum 32). Inherent in this view is the intriguing assumption that writers "construct" readers as they write, while readers in turn "construct" texts as they read. Such a formulation involves both paradox and complementarity: writers invent the readers toward whom they direct the text, while—it may be said—readers invent the text in the process of reading it. Teachers of writing must understand the oppositional nature of this debate: while some theorists argue for the dominance of the writer and the text in the writing-reading transaction, others maintain readers' independence in the process of representing or constructing texts. As we will discover, this polarity manifests itself in both individual and social perspectives on writing, and has important implications for all writing teachers.

The Pedagogy of Cognitive Process

How fruitful the cognitive-process view has been for composition teachers in the last decade may be seen in the monographs and journals of writing pedagogy, in conference presentations, and, most of all, in the titles and contents of writing texts, where the term "process" has become ubiquitous. As "process" terminology has flourished, the code words of earlier generations have lost currency in the language of composition pedagogy. No longer are composition teachers seen primarily as enforcers of "grammar" rules whose task is to teach students "clear and correct expression." Instead, if they accept the cognitive-process view of composing, teachers see their mission as helping students master their own composing processes.

Process-oriented textbooks are strikingly different from the rule-bound traditional textbooks which they increasingly supplant. Rather than urging students to focus on planning ahead, writing outlines and observing editing rules, process texts emphasize the ostensible stages through which students should shepherd their writing, on the assumption that all students will be able to identify with the phases and processes identified in the text. Process texts emphasize the recursiveness of composing—the ways in which writers create new writing goals which in turn reshape the direction of the text. Process texts have revalued the current-traditional texts' emphasis on editing by identifying it as a final-stage operation, important only when the writer is ready to bring the text into conformity with socially-sanctioned codes.

As the most conservative and arguably the most potent of the forces that shape writing pedagogy, writing texts have institutionalized this shift toward process. Through their chapter headings writing texts often identify composing as having certain phases, thus giving these phases a presumed actuality for all students: "Discovering Your Subject"; "Developing What You Want to Say"; "Writing a First Draft"; "Revising Your Writing"; "Editing Your Work"; and so forth. As with widely available texts in any discipline, those in composition have the power to influence teachers more readily than students: "textbooks are instructional material more important for the writing teacher than for the writing student," suggests one researcher (Welch 271).

The process shift in the definition of the teacher's role has been regarded by many teachers and researchers as powerfully liberating. It is seen as a way of encouraging teachers to see themselves not as lawgivers and authority-figures obligated to pour their knowledge into their passively receptive students and enforce universal "standards" of editing, but as active participants in their students' learning, ready to empower them with an awareness of their own responsibilities as writers. It has generated some fruitful teaching strategies based on the conviction that if composing is a network of dynamic processes, teachers must discover fruitful ways to nurture these processes.

It is traditional wisdom to believe that writers need to know their actual readers as fully as possible. Student writers are still frequently urged to think of their readers and picture them as intimately as possible. Most writing texts give at least perfunctory advice to that effect, and some go into detail about how writers ought to envision their readers as they write: "writing must be directed to real people to be successful"; "you must always think of your actual readers as you write for them"; "poor writing is usually aimed at nobody in particular." This habit of urging writers to address real readers persists in the "handbook tradition" described in Chapter One, a tradition grounded partly in the legacies of oral rhetoric. If we don't know who we're writing (speaking) to, how can we judge what we want to say?

Yet there are many writing occasions in which writers may not know who their particular readers will be: letters to editors, businesses, and government agencies; proposals and reports in business, government, and foundations; and writings sent out for publication, among others. And, of course, students in academic settings often write for instructors whose expectations, rooted in specific disciplinary traditions, are neither understood nor anticipated by student writers. So writing teachers seem actually to be faced with two tasks: helping student writers learn to write effectively for familiar readers, and helping them compose for readers whose expectations and reactions aren't known. If writing and reading "selves" are both active as a writer writes, then writers must necessarily be readers not before or after they write, but while they write. How can writing teachers develop this simultaneity?

Donald Murray is one of the first writers to personalize the dry abstractions of schema research by picturing composing as a psychic dialogue. He argues that writers should awaken the readers in themselves, so that as they compose they read and respond to their own composing. He envisions writing as an interchange between a "writing self" and a "reading self," the self that reads monitoring the self that writes "during the writing process" (143). Viewing writing as cognitive dialogue "makes it possible for the teacher not only to teach the other self but recruit the other self to assist in the teaching of writing. The teacher brings the other self into existence, and then works with that other [reading] self" (143). When the "reading self" speaks and the teacher listens, "the teacher knows what needs to be taught or reinforced . . . in the next draft" (143). The reading self reflects and recreates the intentions of the writing self as the writer composes. Murray's interpretation of composing as a personal dialogue suggests his conviction that writing and reading are interdependent processes.

The effect of insisting that both writing and reading are composing processes is to draw attention away from the text itself. And if we give primary attention to the processes of writing and reading, then we tend to lose interest in the idea of a fixed text carrying the writer's meanings reliably to readers. Writing may be seen as a working-out of intentions which will never be communicated to readers quite as they are formulated. Indeed, if we see reading as part of composing it is pointless to speak of writing as "communicating" or reading as "receiving." Instead, "writing" and "reading" must be thought of as reciprocal acts of composing and constructing meaning. The important question about texts will not be "what does it mean?" It will be, quite literally, "what does the reader make of it?"

This constructionist perspective informs many recent pedagogical descriptions of the writer-reader relationship. One such study, offered by Christina Haas and Linda Flower, combines cognitive and rhetorical perspectives. Their vocabulary suggests their indebtedness to schema research as well as the constructionist perspective: "readers construct meaning by building multifaceted, interwoven representations of knowledge. The current text, prior texts, and the reading context can exert varying degrees of influence . . . but it is the reader who must integrate information into meaning" (168). Using the observational strategy common to most cognitive research, Haas and Flower attempt to identify "strategies" by means of which inexperienced and experienced readers "construct" meaning. Experienced readers, they find, use "rhetorical strategies" to "recreate or infer the rhetorical situation of the text," accounting for the "author's purpose, context, and effect on the audience" (176). Inexperienced readers, struggling to make sense of the subject matter of the text, do not "build a rich representation of text" because they are unable to envision the writer-reader relationship and the context within which it appears. As readers they find it difficult to predict and envision intentions and goals as they read; they are concerned almost entirely with reacting to the "information" of the text.

Inexperienced readers unable to build full "rhetorical representations" of texts miss those complex and implicit meanings developed by more experienced readers. Haas and Flower suggest that just as composition teachers teach writers, not texts, so they should "move from merely *teaching texts to teaching readers*" (169). These researchers also suggest pedagogical implications related to both cognitive and rhetorical approaches to composing. Students should be helped to identify the writer's goals and intentions even as they account for their own expectations in their reading. They should also be encouraged to do more than assimilate information; they should be urged to reconstruct the writer-reader relationship in order to develop their roles in that relationship.

Writing teachers increasingly see one of their tasks as helping inexperienced writers develop the reading self in them, until that reading self can identify with shifting viewpoints reflecting a variety of readerly roles. Teachers can help writers nurture their capacity to imagine readers, and project for those imagined readers the kinds of roles the writer wishes them to play. Writing teachers with this intention in mind strive to develop their students' abilities to be both writer and reader simultaneously, as a creative inner dialectic.

Yet, as we saw in Chapter One, the process approach to composing can be criticized on at least two major grounds: that it is too optimistic about what can be known about the mind's workings, and that it encourages pedagogical overgeneralization by suggesting the application of experimental findings and models to all student writers and readers. Both objections are as pertinent to reading as to writing, when these processes are seen as the cognitivists see them— i.e., as versions of composing. Kenneth Bruffee has articulated the first objection most visibly, in his advocacy of social-construction theory: when we talk about the mind's processes, he says, we are positing as real "our unconfirmed and unconfirmable inferences about what happens in the 'black box' of the mind" (777). We cannot really know mental processes with the thoroughness we claim, he argues, because, since our study of mind necessarily focuses on observable behavior, what we think of as knowledge about cognition is nothing more than inferences from such behavior—which we then "reify" into that which we think of as "objective" and "true."

Another difficulty with cognitive-process theory comes in the almost irresistible temptation it offers us to generalize its claims readily and uncritically to all our students. When we apply the "knowledge" we believe we have gained from cognitive research, we run the danger of distorting the uniqueness of individual cognition by imposing a general model upon it. To speak of "the writing process" as though it were compounded of universally demonstrable truths is to misrepresent our ways of knowing readers and writers. Especially when we encounter the work of those Stephen North calls the "Formalists," we must (in North's words) guard against mistaking "the elements of a Formal model for the 'real' things to which they correspond in some way" (242). Models of cognitive process are metaphors, not blueprints of mental activity; we are often tempted, say cognitive-process critics, to think that a diagram showing the "stages" of writing is a road map of a real landscape, when in fact it is actually a representation or rendering of that which can only be guessed at.

Writers and Texts Making Readers: Rhetorical and Literary Views

The cognitive-process viewpoint is not the only one that has extended our understanding of the writing-reading relationship. *Rhetorical theory* sees this relationship rather differently from the way cognitive-process theory views it. The cognitive-process view emphasizes the purposefulness of both writer and reader in constructing their versions of the text; it portrays both writers and readers as proactive and goal-driven. The rhetorical tradition, on the other hand, has generally focused on speakers and writers acting within a communication setting or situation, and defined listeners and readers as reactive rather than proactive or purposeful. This view of audience manifests itself, for example, in Edwin Black's suggestion that every speech situation features an "implied auditor" who becomes "a model of what the rhetor would have his real auditor become ... the image of a [listener]" (112–3). Such a model is created by the speaker's intention to have certain effects upon

listeners, who will take on the role embodied in the "implied auditor" by responding to the cues embedded in the discourse by the
speaker.

Such speaker-directed thinking has characterized the rhetoric of
writing as well, as exemplified by James Britton's discussion of writers in *The Development of Writing Abilities* (discussed more fully in
Chapter Three). In written discourse, says Britton, the writer must
"represent to himself . . . his readers . . . [by carrying out] a procedure
of self-editing, of arresting, reorganizing and adjusting his message
for his absent audience. He will be unable to do this unless he can
internalize his audience" (61–2). Britton argues that all writers, inexperienced or mature, can create images of intended readers by means
of this internalizing activity. The kind of writing Britton finds inexperienced writers most fluent in—"expressive" writing—is directed
at intimate or familiar readers. On the other hand, attempting to
envision unknown audiences causes inexperienced writers much
difficulty, Britton finds. It's important to note that Britton does not
say writers invent their audiences, only that they recall characteristics of actual readers they know in a way that helps them anticipate
the responses of those readers.

Others take Britton's proposal a step further by suggesting that
experienced writers do more than foresee the expectations of actual
readers. Various rhetorical and literary theorists argue that writers
hypothesize readers, projecting these hypothetical or "implied"
readers as role models for actual readers. Walker Gibson defines his
"mock reader" as the embodiment of the writer's intentions within a
text; if the actual reader cannot identify with this mock reader, then
"reading" cannot take place because the actual reader will be unable
to carry out the writer's intentions as inscribed in the text. Using
different terms, rhetorician Walter Ong identifies this hypothetical
reader as a "fiction" or "role" set by the writer; reading is the actual
reader's discovery of "the role the reader has to play" (12). That is, in
composing a text the writer composes a hypothetical reader who in
turn directs and guides actual readers into the roles the text asks
them to play. The readers "in" the text—hypothetical entities existing through textual cues—embody the attitudes and judgments
demanded of the text's actual readers.

Lisa Ede and Andrea Lunsford argue that writers invent hypothetical readers as embodiments of their composing intentions. The
writer's "*invoked* audience," they argue, is "called up or imagined by
the writer" (156) as the writer's "created fiction" (160). Writers may
also be clearly aware of their actual or "*addressed* audience"—
the "actual . . . readers of a discourse" who exist "outside of the text"
(167). However, since writers often do not know the addressed

audience, they "must rely in large part upon their own vision of the reader" (158). Through the image of readers which a writer invokes, "she invite[s] her audience to see themselves as she [sees] them" (163). It is through the writer's power of imaginative projection that audiences are invoked; they use "the semantic and syntactic resources of language to provide cues for the reader—cues which help to define the role or roles the writer wishes the reader to adopt in responding to the text" (160).

Some rhetorical theorists have cautioned against overestimating the writer's rhetorical control over the reader—that is, they suggest that the writer's imaginative projection of the reader is only one variable in the writer-reader relationship. For example, Douglas Park points out that the textbook tradition of urging writers to identify specific readers ignores the reality of composing, which "involves many different contexts dispersed through a text" (252). When writers asks themselves who their readers are, suggests Park, they will not be consistent in envisioning answers to this question, since only "at particular times [do] writers focus on audience as a discrete entity" (254). He argues that except when they are writing to specific, familiar readers, writers tend to be more conscious of the occasion of the writing itself, the conventions within which it is undertaken, and the settings in which it will be received, than of particular readers. Only sometimes, and inconsistently, do they envision readers not already familiar to them. But Park's analysis suggests that while writers' choices result from various pressures, their ability to imagine or project readers shapes their composing in purposeful ways.

From a different perspective Peter Elbow also warns against an overemphasis on reader-awareness. In the later stages of composing, he suggests, writers may be aware of readers; but for lengthy periods, and particularly in formulative stages of writing, writers are focused not on communicating but on thinking: "it is characteristic of much truly good writing to be, as it were, on fire with its meaning. Consciousness of readers is burned away; involvement in subject matter is all" ("An Argument" 54). Elbow invokes differences between Piaget's and Vygotsky's models of cognitive growth to support his suggestion that writers blend inner-directed and outer-directed impulses in their composing. When writers fail to compose in ways that engage readers, it is tempting, he maintains, to identify them as insufficiently decentered (following Piaget's model) and in need of moving (in Linda Flower's terms) "outward" from writer- to reader-based writing. On the other hand, he suggests, inexperienced writers constantly urged to consider their readers may become hyperconscious of readers, distracting them as they shape language to their own thinking. Students should be encouraged to set aside the tyranny of the reader-consciousness—and the communicative model of language from which it derives—in favor of giving language free play in the fields of discourse: "Instead of always using language in an audience-directed fashion," he urges, writing teachers should urge students to "unleash language for its own sake and let it function a bit on its own, without much intention and without much need for *communication*" (64).

Recent literary theory offers other perspectives on the interactions of writers, texts, and readers. Under the "New Criticism" which dominated literary interpretation through the middle decades of the twentieth century, the text itself was hailed as autonomous and independent of both writers' intentions and readers' responses. Only close readings could "find out" textual meanings, which though often ambiguous and multivalent were embodied in the text's unique linguistic structure. However, New Criticism's habit of seeing texts as embodiments of intrinsic meanings came to seem indefensible to readers sceptical that texts could be read independently of their intentions and contexts. In the 1970's and 80's many literary and textual theorists argued that meanings are not bound within texts, but shaped by the relationships among writers, readers, and their contexts.

One such literary theorist is Louise Rosenblatt, who sees the writing-reading relationship as a "transaction" based upon but not coexistent with the written text. Texts are "activated by the reader," so that a "live circuit" develops between "a specific reader and a specific text at a specific time and place" (14). The writer's intentions are not a strong element in her analysis of the writing-reading relationship; most of the "transaction" she envisions is that between an active reader and the "cues" which stimulate that reader's responses. Though "what the reader brings to the text will affect what he makes of it," nevertheless the reader must "respect limitations set by the [text's] verbal cues . . . [drawing] on his own resources to fill the gaps, to realize the blueprint provided by the text" (88). The kinds of responses readers bring to texts will constitute two major types of readings: "efferent" and "aesthetic." Efferent readings are those emphasizing what the reader "will carry away from the reading, where the reader's attention is "directed outward . . . toward concepts to be retained, ideas to be tested, actions to be performed" (24–5). Aesthetic readings center on "what happens during the actual reading event," with its "associations, feelings, attitudes and ideas" (25). Readings by different readers at different times may fall anywhere on a continuum between these two major modes of response.

For Rosenblatt the text's possibilities energize the writing-reading relationship. Wolfgang Iser, a phenomenologist who analyzes the

intuitive aspects of the writing-reading relationship, also emphasizes
the text by arguing its power to control readers. Sometimes he seems
to define reading purely as a subjective interchange between writer
and reader: in reading, "the thoughts of the author take place subjectively in the reader" so that "the reader will be 'occupied' by the[se]
thoughts" (*The Implied Reader* 293). However, his argument actually
foregrounds the text as the arena within which this subjective interchange occurs. Iser argues that readers will encounter an "implied
reader" in a text, an hypothesized figure, or paradigm, which can
help readers discover the text's potential meanings. Iser's implied
reader resembles the "mock" or "invoked" readers described by
rhetorical theorists; but while the rhetoricians identify their hypothetical readers as "fictions" or inventions of the *writer*, Iser characterizes the implied reader as a function of the *text*. The implied
reader comes to life as a "textual structure," in Iser's words; actual
readers identify with the implied reader in the process of responding
to the text's demands.

Iser does credit the actual reader's responses with some power:
"generally," he says, "the role prescribed by the text will be the
stronger, but the reader's own disposition will never disappear; . . .
[it will] form . . . a frame of reference for the act of grasping and
comprehending" (*The Act of Reading* 37). Iser sees the text as incomplete, awaiting the reader's acceptance of the invitation to respond
issued, as it were, by the implied reader. However, though Iser allows
the individuality of the actual reader some power in reading, like
Rosenblatt he gives preeminence to the text itself as the medi-
ator between the writer and reader. Iser does not maintain—as do
cognitive-process theorists—that readers may "compose" their versions of texts in response to the texts presented by writers. Rather,
the reader will discover meanings only by playing those readerly
roles, or "performances," directed by the writer through the implied
reader in the text.

Thus for Iser, writing-reading relationships are based on readers'
responses to texts. As with Rosenblatt, Iser talks little about the text
as the embodiment of the writer's intentions; his focus is on the ways
texts stimulate and control readers' roles. Reading may fulfill or fall
short of the text's potentialities; some readers will respond more
fully than others, depending on their sensitivity to the implied
reader. It's true that Iser posits "gaps" in many texts—tacit meanings
and unspoken possibilities—which must be filled during reading,
but these openings are themselves structured to elicit certain
responses from readers. Because Iser defines reading as responding
to intentional cues in the text, readers' efforts to clarify ambiguity or
difficulty in reading must inevitably take them back into the text.

Neither the actual readers' expectations nor the occasions of reading play decisive roles in readers' determination of textual meaning, as Iser construes that process.

Rhetoric and Texts

We should now consider some implications of the argument that by inventing or hypothesizing readers in the text, writers can manipulate actual readers' responses. Only through the language of the text—its "cues"—can the writer characterize the implied reader. Thus to envision a transmission of rhetorical power from writer through implied reader to actual reader, we must believe in the stability of texts. That is, we must accept that written language can carry writers' cues to readers without serious misunderstanding. And when we view the text as the reliable embodiment of the writer's intentions, we "privilege" the text by according it special status as a finished or completed thing, an artifact.

From here it is an easy step to the next major implication of the invented-reader perspective. Because the text is a finished product, and because it carries the writer's intentions, readers cannot be said to *construct* the text; they can only *construe* it and respond to it. As readers read the roles they must play, they are subject to the "script"—the text—which defines those roles. They "read themselves" from the text, discovering their roles and ways of responding from it. Readers are defined in terms of their enactment of the intentions embodied in the text; they draw life in relation to, and as functions of, the discourse itself. Writers compose the text's words, and so compose their readers.

To see a text rhetorically, then, is to be attuned to the ways in which it shapes and directs readers' responses. But readers can only respond to the writer's intentions insofar as they are embodied in the text and its signs. Thus, teachers who want to help their students become aware of their potential influence over readers must make them conscious of the reader-oriented cues they introduce into their writing. Writing teachers attending to rhetorical issues will want to help student writers foreground those textual structures that best accomplish their intentions with respect to their readers.

Rhetorician George Dillon articulates this sense of the writer's preeminence in the composing relationship: in most nonliterary writing, he says, "the writer has a scope to create roles and relations that is almost as large as that in literature," for "[w]riting (and reading) . . . is an act of social imagination: projection or construction of a self, an other, and a footing between them"(15). Readers are defined by writers' imaginative projections of them. Texts can be trusted to be reliable bearers of authorial intentions, and readers to willingly enact those intentions. As the manifestation of writers' intentions, texts make readers.

At first glance such a conclusion suggests a renewal of the traditional "product" focus of writing handbooks. But to the extent that such texts remain focused on formatting and editing—and more and more of them are now breaking away from these ancient habits—they will miss the real thrust of writers' textual power. For if texts are seen as embodiments of writers' intentions and sources of direction and control for readers, then writing teachers must help writers manipulate their texts in order to best achieve the desired effects. Student writers must be encouraged to envision their own intentions as they write, then with equal vividness imagine readers' reactions and responses to what they write. Writing teachers, that is, must teach writers to imagine readers as they compose, and to direct their writing to these imagined readers in a living, active dialogue, helping them envision readers' expectations and goals. In the next section we will see the idea of dialogue proposed as a primary descriptor of the writing-reading relationship.

II. The Social Perspective

The cognitive and rhetorical and interpretive approaches we have examined tend to frame the writer-reader relationship as an *individual interaction* between the writer and the reader. The cognitive perspective assumes a writer composing and a reader (re)composing, each striving to envision the intentions and expectations of the other. Some rhetorical descriptions of the writing-reading interaction (like those of Ede and Lunsford or Park and Dillon) focus the relationship between reader and writer within a given discourse situation. Some interpretive models, like those of Iser and Rosenblatt, focus on the interaction between text and reader and view the text as a reliable represention of intentions and cues.

But discussions of these approaches often sidestep a major difficulty in the individualist portrayal of writing and reading. If the writer envisions roles which readers must reconstruct from textual cues, by what means does a reasonable approximation between the writer's construction and the reader's reconstruction emerge? If writers project certain intentions in their texts which will be activated only by their readers' various representations of them, what is the nature of such a transaction? This question has spurred many theorists to argue that the writing-reading relationship cannot adequately be described in individualistic terms; it must, they argue, be portrayed as a profoundly *social experience*. The writing-reading relationship, they suggest, is defined and controlled by social, cultural, and institutional conventions.

Most people (including most English teachers) read texts day in and day out, in one form or another—newspapers, TV schedules, cookbooks, newsletters, church bulletins, shop manuals, students' assignments, sales letters, tax forms, tabloids, advertising brochures, sales reports, football stories, essays in monthly magazines, policy directives, the backs of cereal boxes. We read these texts because we want to, or have to, or need to; one way or another, they are integral to our lives. Some are associated with our work, some with our recreation, some with our family relationships and social obligations. All are opportunities emerging from daily contexts, part of the network of relations of which our lives consist. These relations are familiar in different ways: family discourse customs define some of our most intimate communications, while business and institutional conventions frame the discourse we enter at work, school and church.

Social perspectives thus require us to reconsider our teacherly habit of seeing writing and reading as private acts carried on by dutiful students in libraries and dorm rooms. Social perspectives on writing emerge from several different sources; we will examine three of the most important here. All three reject those cognitive-process and rhetorical approaches which focus on writing and reading as acts of individual composing. One source is the cross-disciplinary movement called *social construction*, whose proponents have studied the social processes of language and knowledge-making and stimulated new ways of thinking in the social sciences and humanities. Social construction suggests that what we see as "reality" is a "construct" built out of ways of seeing; what we accept as real is our way of organizing our world. Other sources of social perspectives in writing are easier to identify with specific fields of study. One is the *post-structuralist study of language and texts*, oriented toward literature, linguistics and discourse theory, and sharing social construction's tendency to see language-making as a collective human activity. Another is *ethnological research* on language and culture, a hybrid discipline with roots in anthropology, sociology, and linguistics. Each has important implications for our understanding of the writing-reading relationship and how we might teach it.

Social Construction and the Writing-Reading Relationship

The phrase "social construction" describes the combined views of a variety of modern thinkers who emphasized the social origins of human thought and behavior. One influential source of social

constructionist ideas can be found in "anti-foundationalism," especially as it is articulated in the work of Richard Rorty. It is our
ingrained habit, maintains Rorty, to think of "truth" and "the real"
as the foundation upon which our knowledge builds. But suppose language, through which our perceptions of truth are expressed,
is not "the mirror of nature" that we think it to be, with words referring directly to things and ideas that are objective and "beyond"
language. Suppose knowledge does not have an "objective" basis,
a "foundation." Suppose knowledge "will be a matter of conversation between persons, rather than a matter of interaction with non-
human reality" (157). If we grant this, then "the foundations of
knowledge" will be "propositions rather than objects" (160); that is,
since we share experience through language, what we know—
what we confidently call "knowledge"— will be "built" out of our
shared language.

Social constructionists thus hold knowledge-making to be a collective human activity. That is, what and how we say we "know"
does not come from the discovery of fundamental truths inhering in
some given order. We cannot know "reality" except as a function of
the interaction between individuals and their communities and
material contexts; there is no "foundation" or underlying "presence"
that language refers to. Instead, "reality" is "socially constructed."
"The real," says James Berlin, "is located in a relationship that
involves the dialectical interaction of the observer, the discourse
community (social group) . . . and the material conditions of existence" (488). What we see, think, and feel has no order or life for us
except as we experience it through this dialectic, which can occur
only in and through language. Kenneth Bruffee puts it this way: all of
what we know—"reality, knowledge, thought, facts, texts, selves"—
are "community-generated and community-maintained linguistic
entities" (774). In this view, knowledge is made possible by shared
language and is thus socially constructed, since language is the
power that enables us to articulate and shape our world. Thus, while
language does not determine experience, it is the only means by
which we can articulate—and thus know—our experiences. Knowledge is what is developed through shared perspectives, and is thus
always open to negotiation.

This view places language squarely at the center of our efforts to
declare what we know and value. For if we accept knowledge as
linguistically shaped, then traditional notions of what and how we
know become untenable. Our customary ways of talking about both
"physical reality" and moral "basic truths" become functions of what
discourse theorist M. M. Bakhtin calls the "polyphonic" variability
of language itself. The comfortable word "reality" must be seen as a

metaphor for how we construct our views of the world—reality is what we "make" out of language. The discourse by means of which we search for truth will be not analytical but dialogical; in Rorty's terms; "a matter of conversation between persons" (157). Our studies of texts and ideas will merge with a continuing "conversation of mankind" in which, concludes Rorty, "the hope of agreement is never lost so long as the conversation lasts" (318).

Influential versions of social construction have also emerged from the social sciences. Anthropologist Clifford Geertz has written extensively about the intimate connections between individuals and their sustaining cultures: "to see social institutions, social customs, social changes as in some sense 'readable' is to alter our whole sense of what such interpretation is," he remarks in characterizing cultures and ideas as "texts" within which individuals' ways of seeing are "written" (31). We should not seek intrinsic, universal principles of thought and belief to explain our individual experiences, he claims, because such principles do not exist—especially, for example, that "fundamental identity of mental functioning in *homo sapiens*, the so-called 'psychic unity of mankind' " proclaimed by many psychologists (150). Consider "common sense," he says, something we usually take to be an inherent part of our individual character. It is not a universal principle or a unique personal insight; instead, it is a culturally-developed norm: "common sense is as much an interpretation of the immediacies of experience . . . as are myth, painting, epistemology . . . [and is], like them, historically constructed"; it is no inherent human universal, but "can vary dramatically from one people to the next" (76). Thus, he concludes, to understand the relationship between individuals and their culture we must turn to the "constructive, or interpretive power . . . rooted in the collective resources of culture rather than in the separate capacities of individuals" (215). To make knowledge is to articulate the cultural attitudes and insights which frame our individual ways of seeing the world.

Social theorist Peter Berger extends this principle to the socially constructed self. Our self-knowledge emerges from social concepts internalized through language play: "society, identity, *and* reality are subjectively crystallized in the same process of internalization. . . . [and] language constitutes both the most important content and the most important instrument of socialization" (133). Language is both the means by which we articulate—or "construct"—our experience of what we call "the world," and the means by which that construct shapes us. "Language," says rhetorician C. H. Knoblauch, "is a function of its users, yet the users are themselves constituted by the processes of language. . . . and even as they practice language use, [they learn] the values, world assumptions, images of self and other— all the social realities that particular languages convey" (134).

Language also plays a crucial role in the social dialectics of Bakhtin and psychologist Lev Vygotsky. Their work in the Soviet Union during the 1930's, shaped by the dialectical thought of their era and nationality, has strongly influenced later social construction-ists. Vygotsky (who is both a cognitive and a social theorist and whose cognitive theory we considered in Chapter One) argues that children do not learn merely by having the cognitive ability to do so; learning is awakened, he maintains, only when "internal develop-ment processes" are stimulated through social interaction and "cooperation with . . . peers" (*Mind In Society* 90). That is, children learn dialectically as a function of the synergy awakened by social interaction. Though much of Vygotsky's work focuses on individual cognitive processes (in a kind of theoretical conversation with Piaget), his later work evidences his belief in the essential stimulus to learning provided by the individual's social relationships.

The dialectical view also informs the work of M. M. Bakhtin, who coined the term "dialogical" to describe his sense of the recipro-cal flow of discourse among the "voices" of a society. His vocabulary is abstract and sometimes superheated, but his sense of a world energized by language relationships into a "polyphony" of discourse has been greatly influential in composition circles. He argues from a literary perspective, suggesting that the diversity of voices found within the novel represents the vitality and diversity of language in its active human context. The novel, he suggests, draws into a tenu-ous whole "social dialects . . . professional jargons, generic langues, languages of generations and age groups . . . [and] languages that serve the specific sociopolitical purpose of the day, even of the hour" (263). The pull of diversity in human language always works against the centripetal power of integration and unity, continues Bakhtin, as "heteroglossia"—"the social diversity of speech types" (263)— contends against the formal unity that a common language embodies within a culture.

Composition theorists have been eager to apply Bakhtin's gener-alizations to the interactions of specific writers and readers, and some of his terms appear to invite such application. Each "living utterance," says Bakhtin, "having taken meaning . . . at a particular historical moment in a socially specific environment . . . become[s] an active participant in social dialogue" (276). The specificity of each utterance arises from the unique relationship between the speaker and the listener, whose "relationship . . . enters into the very inter-nal construction of rhetorical discourse" (280). Each "language moment" represents a specific interaction between speaker and listener, writer and reader. It is in its emphasis on context that the social perspective differs most crucially from the individualist view. While cognitive-process theory focuses on the dynamics of individual composing, social construction theory—Bakhtin's is a good example—emphasizes the power of cultural relationships to shape composing.

The power of Bakhtin's argument has stimulated current composition teachers and writers to explore ways of developing dialogical writing-reading relationships in their classrooms. Speaking of a student's efforts to deal with conflicting inner voices in addressing a socially controversial issue, John Trimbur suggests that the difficulty results from "the polyphony of voices that resonate in the writer's mind" as she attempts to resolve conflicting ways of speaking about the topic (Trimbur 219). "What this writer did," he concludes, was to "negotiate and resolve the conflicting claims of . . . different systems of authority" (218) as she constructed her own voice out of the chorus of attitudes she had internalized from her social development. Some writing teachers direct their efforts toward building a polyphonic classroom environment. One teacher records how she asks students to write responses to a series of stories which present conflicting attitudes, so that they are consistently required to revise their earlier "voices": students gradually "expand their means of conceptualizing their own experiences, interanimating the language they bring from their prior schooling, their homes, and communities with the new language of the text" (Goleman 138).

Various political implications can be discerned in the arguments of social constructionists. Bakhtin sees all language "as ideologically saturated . . . insuring a *maximum* of mutual understanding in all spheres of ideological life" (271). The values of a liberal pluralism may be inferred from the social constructionists' emphasis on different voices and cultures; in this view, diversity should be nurtured in writing classes. Writing and reading are seen as liberalizing forces, sensitizing individuals to otherness in their worlds. On the other hand, socialist and Marxist inferences may be drawn from social construction's emphasis on the power of the collective to shape discourse. Knoblauch suggests that in the ideologically-aware classroom students are situated "self-consciously within the objective social realities that impinge upon them," so that they gain "sociopolitical intelligence . . . sufficient for empowerment" (135). In this view, reading and writing are means toward political action. Similarly, James Berlin maintains that all discourse is inherently ideological because it's always a product of the "material, the social, and the individual" (488). Thus, he asserts, writing teachers have an inescapable ideological responsibility: they must help students challenge the discourse of dominant groups and disciplines, questioning their power in order to expose how "rhetorics can privilege some at the expense of others, according the chosen few an inequal share of power, perquisites, and material benefits" (490). In this view, it's important to scrutinize the ways in which those who hold power use language to deceive and exploit others.

An influential ideological voice from the political left is that of Paulo Freire, whose *Pedagogy of the Oppressed* sees literacy as the first step toward revolution and the rebuilding of a just state by collective action. Freire, a Brazilian educator with a Marxist viewpoint, argues that all teaching should be committed to "liberation" through the abolition of the "banking concept of education." "The pedagogy of the oppressed," he says, first "unveils the world of oppression" through a committed "praxis," then transforms the world by serving "all men [sic] in the process of permanent liberation" (40). The present dominance of the "banking concept of education," he says, means that most teachers see knowledge as "a gift bestowed by those who consider themselves knowledgeable upon those who they consider to know nothing." In this view students' actions include "receiving, filing and storing the deposits" of knowledge passed on by teachers (58). But inquiry should not seek simply to pass on a given order of ideas; real knowledge "emerges only through . . . the restless, impatient, continuing, hopeful inquiry men pursue in the world . . . and with each other" (58). Like other constructionists Freire argues that teaching must focus on "the transformational character of reality," which can be found out only through dynamic, continuous processes of human meaning-making. "Banking" education tends toward fixity; "problem-posing education" leads us to see our present experiences in terms of their "historical reality susceptible of transformation" (72–3). Only through dialogue can knowledge be made: "dialogue is the encounter between men, mediated by the world, in order to name the world"; by "speaking their word" men "transform their world," but only when they name it together (76–7). Thus education must be "dialogical par excellence" so that the "students' view of the world" constantly emerges in dialogue with the teacher, who must "be with" students in a collective enterprise of knowledge-making (101).

This emphasis upon the political power of language raises an obvious but nonetheless crucial question: namely, is language to be seen as an instrument of human effort, or as its master? When we speak of "self," do we mean an autonomous entity who uses language to define and express that which he or she is, prior to language? Or do we mean by "self" a voice expressing the socially constituted attitudes and conventions which comprise it? The rhetorical and cognitive-process approaches we have explored earlier take the instrumental view of language. They locate the constructionist argument within the individual, seeing writing and reading as means by

which we enact our unique capacities through language, and affirm
our individual powers of meaning-making. Social construction,
on the other hand, proposes that since we develop or "construct" our
sense of self from communal ideas and attitudes, language is
the means by which we discover and articulate our individuality
within the cultural contexts that frame us. Language provides the
means for discovering selfhood, not by affirming our separate
uniqueness, but by giving voice to all the culturally-based understandings which constitute our experience. Thus the "I" which we
take to be the "subject" of our own experience is a composite entity
articulated in language out of communal experiences. Because our
ways of defining experience are relational and contextual, terms like
"subject-object" and "self-society" are deprived of any intrinsic or
"foundational" meaning separate from their contexts.

These efforts to define human experience in social terms have
created considerable opposition. Attempts to establish communality
and consensus as a way of knowing, for example, have been strongly
criticized by opponents of social construction. If knowledge is that
which has been arrived at by some agreement within a community or
a culture, yet if the process of knowing is itself a continuous, unceas-
ing conversation among the voices of a community or culture, then
where and when does this conversation become stabilized enough to
warrant agreement? This difficulty has direct application to writing
teachers. We may work with our students in small groups, or with the
whole class as a group, acting as facilitators, mediators, and editors,
but at some point we must individualize our relationships with
them. "We do not teach bodies of consensus-builders; we can only
teach their members," says one writing teacher in a critique of the
pedagogical applications of social construction (Petraglia 45). Nor
does social construction theory adequately explain where change
comes from in the conversational model. If knowledge is that which
is constructed through collaboration and agreement, from what
source do challenges and revisions arise? If all the voices in a community operate from within consensus, must revisions not begin
outside? But if they do, how do they join the conversation in order to
negotiate new understandings? Oppositional voices clearly must be
allowed into the constructionist process of knowledge-making; yet
the collaborative model, based on consensus, often seems to reject
the initiative and force of individual thought.

Thus, social construction cannot avoid the discourse of oppositions; it flirts with a kind of determinism—one that, as we will see,
poststructuralism openly embraces—by reversing the terms of individual construction and defining individuals as the instruments of the
language which defines them. In effect, discourse theorists have

revised the self-vs-society antinomy into a language-vs.-self opposition: do we control language, or does it control us? While committed theorists like Rorty assert language's dominance without worrying unduly about the specific consequences for individual writers and readers, some composition scholars have not found it so easy to gloss over this vexed issue. One such scholar finds terms like "self" and "mind" qualifying equally as "fictions" in the individualist or the collective perspective: "to tell a writer that he invents by letting the collective speak through him. . . . is no less extreme than current views suggesting that a writer invents by releasing a mysterious, hidden entity" (Lefevre 83).

Other social constructionists view the tension between language's individualizing potential and its determinative socializing force as fruitful and generative; such a tension, they argue, impels us to better understand the ambivalent power of language. One theorist metaphorizes the nature of language in biological terms: she proposes "an ecological model of writing, whose fundamental tenet is that writing is an activity through which a person is continually engaged with a variety of socially constituted systems" (Cooper 367). The "ecological model," she continues, "postulates dynamic interlocking systems which structure the social activity of writing" (368). Both statements appear to subdue the powers of individual writers to those of social "systems." But she balances this emphasis on social determinism with a countering recognition of writers' powers to frame social systems through language: "writers interact to form systems," she adds, because "systems are not given . . . instead they are made and remade by writers"(368). Sometimes systems structure writers, sometimes writers structure systems; the antithetical quality of traditional foundational inquiry—with its subject-object, self-world oppositions—still lurks in the arguments of social constructionists.

Social constructionists in composition see this persistently antithetical tendency as healthy and necessary. Indeed, they maintain that a primary task of writing teachers is to disconcert students by encouraging them to recognize the oppressive power of discourse conventions. In the constructionist view, dominant conventions of mode, form, and style enable individuals to use language, but at the same time impose conformity upon individual expression. Because discourse is essential to our representations of experience, we need to teach our students to recognize and manipulate those prevailing discourse conventions which affect our ways of knowing, in order to resist and change what is oppressive about them. Thus, the constructionist view of language carries with it an implicit paradox: discourse can only empower those who recognize its determinative force. If we view the interaction between the individualizing power of the human mind and the collective social authority of language as reciprocal rather than oppositional, then that interaction may be seen as the essential dynamic of the "conversation" by which we make meaning. In this view, teachers should confront students with this antinomy—the reciprocity between convention and individuality—to make them fully aware of the socially constituted nature of the forms and codes within which they are asked to write.

Poststructuralist Discourse Theory

The term "poststructuralism" is an indeterminate and often confusing label; it does not describe a particular theoretical school or a specific cluster of theorists, but rather, a wide range of recent thinkers and their systems. Unfortunately, it is often used interchangeably with its parent term "structuralism," which does describe a school of largely European linguists and discourse theorists that includes Ferdinand de Saussure, Claude Lévi-Strauss and Roland Barthes. The writings of these structuralists have provided the foundations upon which later theorists—poststructuralists—have built their unique and original insights into the nature of language and thought. One of poststructuralism's most prominent and controversial manifestations, "deconstruction"—the effort to critique all language as unstable and indeterminate in its meanings—is both an extension and a critique of structuralism's tenets. This and other "isms" spawned by poststructuralist thought have strongly affected not only literary theory but linguistics, rhetoric, and social and political theory.

Because poststructuralism has had a powerful influence on recent theories of writing and reading, writing teachers need to understand some of its basic tenets—not because they can be translated into particular teaching strategies, but because they challenge our traditional ways of understanding reading and writing. Reading poststructuralist theory is difficult because it relies on an abstruse vocabulary to establish its interpretations of discourse; many readers find its terminology nearly impenetrable. Indeed, Jane Tompkins asserts that "you can't 'apply poststructuralism' " in the classroom at all, because, as poststructuralists view it, language is always already exercising its power over us beyond any self-conscious theorizing about it (747). Recognizing that poststructuralism is far too loose and baggy a monster to attempt any systematic taming here, we must be content with briefly examining some of its more accessible pronouncements.

Poststructuralist theory insists upon the determinative power of discourse in formulating human experience, and expresses a strongly anti-foundational view of language. Like social constructionist thought, poststructuralist theory holds that language makes knowledge possible. But poststructuralist thinkers go further by asserting that words are not names for things or experiences in themselves, but arbitrary signs conferred by the collective authority of culture upon elements of our experience. Language is a system of relationships among words, a "web of meaning," to use a common poststructuralist figure of speech. There is no "underlying truth" to which language refers, or upon which it builds. "We" and the "world" are simply words, constructs existing only in the relationships among the words themselves. What we perceive as differences or oppositions between the terms "self" and "world," for example, are linguistic relationships only, not entities; they do not exist for us until we encounter them through language. There is no connection between "signifier"—sign, word—and the "signified"—what we are accustomed to call "content" or "object." If we try to say, for example, that language names what "is," poststructuralists would argue that there is no correspondence between a something that is named, and the signifier that is taken to be its name.

"You and I, the reader or subject and the 'text,' or any object 'out there,'" says Tompkins, "are not freestanding autonomous entities, but beings that are culturally constituted by interpretive frameworks . . . that our culture makes available to us, and these strategies are the only way that we have of conceiving who we are" (734). Each writer and text is "situated" within a system of conventions and codes which frames the production and the representation of the text. Thus, a favorite locution of postructuralist argument is to say that writers and readers are both "written" by language: "A situated self," says theorist Stanley Fish, "is a self whose every operation is a function of the conventional possibilities built into this or that text" (346). The intentions and expectations of writers and readers interplay with the conventions of textual genre and occasions of publication to define each act of writing and reading. No writer or reader, adds Fish, composes texts or performs readings within their "own set of isolated beliefs without systematic constraints" (346). Thus, for poststructuralists the term "discourse community" is important, denoting, in the words of another theorist, a "group of individuals bound by a common interest" and a "social framework regulating textual production" (Porter 38). All discourse within a community is shaped by its conventions. However, writers and readers usually participate in several such communities simultaneously (for example, each class for which a student writes may invoke a different discourse community), with varying textual conventions operating in different situations.

Two French discourse theorists, Roland Barthes and Jacques Derrida, have had the greatest influence upon current poststructuralist theory. Both speak of language as determinative in human meaning-making. Barthes posits the existence of something called "Text," which differs from (lowercase) texts. The latter are specific pieces of discourse written in a particular time and place; the former is the network of all texts deriving from and participating in the universal flow of discourse. While texts are read, "Text is experienced only as an activity, a production" which "cuts across a work, several works" because all texts are simply a set of relations with other texts, all participating in and contributing to that flow of discourse which is Text (76). "The Text's metaphor is that of *network*," says Barthes, from which all texts—and thus all writing and reading—emerge and to which they return (78). No text is a new or original creation, but another version of similar earlier texts; he calls this textual stream "intertext": "every text, being itself the intertext of another text, belongs to the intertextual" (77) The logic of poststructuralism reverses the traditional terms of composition: because the web of linguistic relations is the only source of human meaning, the Text writes the writer; writers and readers are "written" by Text. That is, they formulate those linguistic conventions and codes embodied in Text, the generative source of all discourse.

Derrida pushes his obtuse word-play beyond the limits of many readers' tolerance, but he does so intentionally, in order to disturb their accustomed ways of talking about writing and texts. He shares Barthes' emphasis upon the power of language to determine meanings, and like Barthes proposes that language has no connection to any idea or thing, and contains no intrinsic meanings. Words have no foundational reference or significance: "the elements of signification function due not to the compact force of their nuclei, but rather to the network of oppositions that distinguishes them, and then relates them to one another" (10). Influenced by Ferdinand de Saussure's doctrine of "the arbitrary nature of the sign," Derrida coins the term "différance," then frees it from conventional syntax to represent his view of the way language works: "différance ✖" (6). "Différance" cannot be predicated because it does not exist as part of a syntactical system; it is not a proposition, but the "silence" of comparison and contrast between two arbitrary signs. Tompkins reads Derrida as saying, "not that language or a word is taking the place of something, [but] that anything that is perceptible is dependent for its being there upon its position within a system" (744). That is, the only way we have of making meaning is by reading the play of differences among the "signs" amid which we live. How we see ourselves and our world is constituted by and through the network of language, which acts as a screen through which we experience the world.

Derrida's use of "deconstruction" as a way of analyzing language rests upon this sense of the variability and shiftiness of all discourse. His view is made clear in an interview with Gary Olson, who points out that Derrida encourages "our self-reflexive examination of the notion of 'composition,' the field, and our institutional relationships" (3). When discourse threatens to become hegemonic—when it dominates communal and institutional ways of seeing and knowing—it is ripe for deconstruction, because in Derrida's words deconstruction "questions the thesis, the theme, the positionality of everything, including, among other things, composition" (8). It is crucial to analyze the models of discourse which underlie our own writing and teaching of writing, says Derrida: "once you have analyzed and questioned and destablilized the authority of the old models, you have to invent each time new forms according to the situation . . . the audience, your own purpose, your own motivation to invent new forms" (9). An important element in teaching composition, he maintains, is to require students to examine the "authority" and "finality" of the models, "what interests they serve—personal, political, ideological. . . . [and] to change the models and invent new ways of writing" (9).

For some poststructuralists the political dimensions of discourse are paramount, particularly with respect to discussions of discourse communities. Poststructuralists argue that the political power of discourse must be recognized and understood through careful analysis. In this perspective, no writing and no writing pedagogy is "ideologically innocent," in the words of one poststructuralist writer: "discourse communities are organized around the production and legitimation of particular forms of knowledge and social practices at the expense of others" (Chase 13). It is our responsibility, he continues, to teach our students to recognize and criticize "the inclusion *and/or* absence of particular cultural values, processes and dynamics in any discourse on composition," and to judge whether this "and/or" serves "emancipatory interests" (14). Our efforts to understand the discourse systems through which we shape our meanings are the first steps in the process of deconstruction. As the poststructuralists see it, the deconstructive enterprise is not intended to destroy discourse but to gain awareness of its enormous power over our lives. Only if we can understand this, they suggest, will we be in a position to attempt to reconstruct our ways of knowing as we might wish.

Language, Sociology, and Ethnography

Another influential social perspective on writing and reading comes from empirical social research conducted through direct observations of speakers, writers, and readers. One intriguing form of this is "code research," the study—pioneered by British sociolinguist Basil Bernstein—of how class differences acting through family and school affect individual language mastery. Code research began with Bernstein's questioning of conventional responses to some childrens' language shortcomings. Why, he asked, do some children fall short of others in using language for learning and directing their lives? He formulated his response within the perspective of social construction: "the structure of social relationships determines the principles of communication and so the shaping forms of consciousness" (*Towards a Theory of Educational Transmissions* 24). It is, he concludes, because language is a fundamentally social, not individual, capacity. Class differences determine how children learn and use language: "class acts crucially on ... *both* the family and the school" (*Towards a Theory of Educational Transmissions* 27). Individual language difficulties are almost always a function of the agents of social control—families, schools, work. Thus, to understand relative levels of mastery we must look not at individual histories but at the entire social structure within which children learn to speak, read, and write.

The concept of code contains two pairs of definitions: two types of family structure—"personal" and "positional"—are said to evoke two types of language code—"elaborated" and "restricted." The middle class embodies a family structure Bernstein terms "personal," based on a "weak classification and framing" of roles encouraging flexibility, initiative, and cooperation. In families with flexible authority relationships, "differences between persons," rather than age or sex differences, govern individual identity, resulting in "person-centered families" in which verbalization itself helps formulate individual differences (*Towards a Sociology of Language* 185). Children in such families gain "a strong sense of autonomy" which allows them to exploit an elaborated code of language use (185). Attributes of an elaborated code include grammar and usage carefully edited to conform to standard English, wide vocabulary, and most importantly, "universalistic meanings" which are context-free and flexible because the speaker has the individual freedom to use language as a means of exploration and growth (79). One of the empirical evidences adduced by Bernstein for code differences is "hesitation phenomena"; middle-class children were observed to hesitate more often and for longer durations than working-class children in closely observed discussions (87). Bernstein takes this phenomenon to mean that because middle-class children value language as an expression of individual uniqueness and authenticity, they tend to select and edit their language more carefully than working-class children, whose restricted code does not encourage such language play.

The typical working-class speaker, says Bernstein, gains identity in a family governed by strong "boundary maintenance" based on "strong classification and framing" of individual roles clearly delineated by age and sex. The parents of such families generally work in jobs which offer little freedom, openness, or inventiveness; working-class jobs entail clearly and narrowly defined duties under the scrutiny of a supervisor who makes sure things are done by the rules. Thus it follows, argues Bernstein, that in working-class families "the authority structure is based upon clear-cut, unambiguous definitions of the status" of each family member (*Towards a Sociology of Language* 184). This family structure produces a "restricted" code of language use, featuring reduced syntactic alternatives, reduced vocabulary range, and "communalized" language contexts which depend upon shared acceptance of speech roles among speakers and listeners. Users of a restricted code also rely on what Bernstein calls "particularistic meanings," which depend upon localized relationships and shared assumptions about society and work. In Bernstein's view, the class system has produced the restricted code for the working class by limiting the "distribution of knowledge" and the opportunity to explore concepts outside a rigidly defined social position (175).

This analysis suggests that because the teaching of writing tends to emphasize individual processes, the personal voice, and audience-awareness, it implicitly favors middle-class students and puts working-class students at a disadvantage. Nor will curriculum reform itself necessarily improve working-class students' opportunities, argues one scholar of Bernstein's work, since "to the extent that the tasks specifically involve writing in the necessarily decontextualized, competitive environment of the school, it is just as likely that any new, more proficient writing curriculum . . . will be most readily mastered by those students whose pattern of socialization makes them best positioned to profit from schooling in general" (Tuman 47). Bernstein's analysis also calls into question the good intentions of many writing teachers in developing basic writing strategies, since these strategies generally rely on individual remediation to address students' language problems. For—in Bernstein's view—what schools identify as language deficiencies are actually functions of socialization, not individual cognitive difficulties: "power and control are made substantive in the classification and framing which

then generate distinctive forms of social relationships and thus communication," thereby shaping "mental structures" (11). Much as
Vygostsky does, Bernstein identifies language as an individual
capacity powerfully controlled by social contexts.

Like poststructuralist discourse theory, ethnography, the anthropological study of the elements of a culture, sees language as a cultural determinant shaping the attitudes and behavior of individuals.
Ethnological research investigates the ways language works in con-
sort with other forces—religious, social, economic—that shape the
daily lives of a people. Anthropology no longer claims to make
"objective," bias-free assessments of a culture; rather, "ethnographers are first of all concerned with the contextual fields that
contain the phenomena being observed . . . [and with] multiple
perspectives–their own, the subjects', other outsiders . . . [and with]
the meaning-making processes of their subjects" (Kleine 117).

The ethnographic work which has most influenced composition
studies is Shirley Brice Heath's *Ways with Words*, a study of the
language differences between two rural North Carolina communities
as revealed in schoolchildrens' language attitudes and behavior.
Heath takes an instrumental rather than a determinative view of
language; she sees her ethnography as a means of teaching those
whom she studied "how to recognize and use language as power"
(266). She shares with social constructionists a belief in the power of
socially generated attitudes and behaviors to shape individual learning, and a commitment to social collaboration and dialogue as ways
of teaching language. Language is an expression of social cohesion,
in her view, its powers tied closely to the individual's communal
relationships.

She worked closely with the schoolteachers of the communities,
helping them "in observing patterns of behavior in groups of children" (273). She asked the teachers to study their own ingrained
attitudes about teaching language, the better to understand why their
students did not behave linguistically as they wanted. The teachers
discovered that as a part of mastering reading, speaking and writing
skills effective for school, students had to "learn school" itself—the
"basic rules of cooperation and participation" required by the classroom (281). Because teachers did not understand the kinds of homes
and family relationships their students came from, "teachers found
they drew more and more on what the students could bring to class
to teach the teachers about their reading and writing needs" (314).
Finally, "with imagination, [and] initiative . . . teachers were able to
create interest and motivation in the students and to involve them in
. . . reading and writing tasks" (314).

Heath defends the essential role of social collaboration in an individual's efforts to master the languages of different communities. She sees community integration as the goal of language mastery: "students [brought] community knowledge into the classroom and classroom knowledge into the community" (356). As they learned to work within the language environment of the classroom, some students were able to succeed at higher grade levels than their parents. Heath does not conclude, however, by celebrating the collaborative methodology as a bold new pedagogy. She ends by noting regretfully the "linguistic and cultural capital" of the rural childrens' communal ways which prevent them from mastering the school culture, which remains the province of townspeople "who control and limit the potential progress of other communities" (368–9). Language empowerment is rooted in social change; without pervasive shifts in present patterns of cultural dominance, suggests Heath, no pedagogical strategy can by itself bring change.

The Pedagogy of the Social Perspective

However, despite the problematic issues of self-vs.-language raised by poststructuralist arguments, and Heath's reservations about the difficulties of teaching social empowerment, group collaboration and communal interaction have been hailed by many composition teachers as welcome correctives to individualist patterns in writing pedagogy. Two major developments in the teaching of writing have resulted directly from social perspectives on discourse: the emphasis on community in writing and the development of collaborative strategies in writing classrooms.

One outcome of social perspectives is an emphasis on community in writing. This emphasis arises in some form from all the major influences examined above. To the social constructionists "community" suggests the collectivity of thought and discourse in whose "conversation" all individuals must participate in order to make meaning for themselves. This definition suggests conservatively that individuals can only use language in terms sanctioned by the community; at the extreme, it suggests that individuals are merely the voices of the collective speaking through them. That is, poststructuralist tend to see community in textual terms, as that web of "intertext" which controls all discourse in a given field. To the ethnographers, on the other hand, community suggests the complex of forces, including language, that shape but do not wholly determine the attitudes and behavior of its individual members. Various adjectives have been applied to particularize these notions of community:

interpretive community, language community, discourse community, among others.

Composition scholars have tended to prefer "discourse community" as a generic term whose definition goes something like this: a group whose interests, attitudes, and values are rooted in common ways of knowing, and who communicate through common ways of speaking and writing. Left unspoken in this general definition is whether such a community is to be thought of as comprised of actual people speaking and writing in particularized settings—as the social constructionists and ethnographers would have it—or of texts and intertext which "write" writers and readers—as poststructuralists are likely to insist. Both ways of glossing "discourse community" have their usefulness, depending on how strongly we view language controlling its users through its collective rules and conventions.

Teachers of writing and reading have been concerned with students' empowerment within and across discourse communities. If a discourse community does indeed control discourse within its field, then anyone not familiar enough with its conventions to use them in writing or reading will be unable to participate in the community itself. But, composition scholars have argued, asking students to join in unfamiliar discourse communities is just what we teachers do. "Every time a student sits down to write for us," says David Bartholomae, "he has to invent the university for the occasion" by learning the language of "History or Anthropology or Economics or English" and their "peculiar ways of knowing, selecting, evaluating, reporting, concluding, and arguing that define the discourse of [their] community" (134). We require them, in other words, to join new and different discourse communities and thereby to struggle with language they cannot understand, framing ways of knowing they do not grasp. To enroll students in any college course is to plunge them into potentially new discourse communities; such confrontations cannot be avoided. Not all compositionists, however, take the position that entering academic discourse entails students' abandonment of their customary discourse communities. Just as many educators argue that minority students should not abandon their own dialects as they learn standard English, so Joseph Harris proposes that students should not necessarily forego their own language contexts in learning academic discourse, but should be taught instead to "*reposition* themselves in relation to several continuous and conflicting discourses" and to "reflect critically on those discourses . . . to which they already belong" (Harris 19). It is the instructor's responsibility, says another, to help her students see the "hidden curriculum" behind a given writing assignment through "discourse analysis—that is, to help students analyze the conventions and expectations of the kind of discourse they are being asked to produce" (Bizzell 238).

Other writers, taking that position further, argue that because writing *is* so deeply context-specific, students cannot learn to write except within specific discourse groups. Such a position is supported by the poststructuralist emphasis upon the "situatedness" of all discourse—its rootedness in those discourse conventions within which both writer and reader act. In this perspective, writing teachers ought to avoid teaching writing *per se*, and instead teach writing *situations*, emphasizing the uniqueness of every writing event. Thomas Kent makes this argument strongly: "no formal pedagogy can be constructed to teach the act of writing or critical reading," he maintains (36). Straight writing courses (as they exist in most schools and universities) are of no use to students, because they cannot help them come to grips with the particularities of each separate situation. All writing emerges from writers' and readers' "specific dialogic . . . interactions with others' interpretive strategies"; and if English-department writing courses can "only supply background knowledge" of writing goals and responses, then the teaching of writing and reading must be the "province of the academy itself" (39). A course in technical writing, for example, will be of far less use than writing required of students in a specific engineering class whose discourse is embedded in the terms and ideas of that discipline.

Social perspectives have also generated an emphasis upon collaboration in the writing classroom. Kenneth Bruffee, the most influential advocate of collaborative learning, maintains (following Vygotsky's theory) that because thought is internalized social dialogue, we must help students "learn to think well collectively" by understanding how their discourse is embedded in "social context" and "community life" ("Collaborative Learning" 640). The task of writing teachers, he continues, "should be to . . . [engage] students in conversation among themselves at as many points in both the writing and the reading process as possible" ("Collaborative Learning" 642). Because language is the means by which we construct our world, teachers should make students conscious of their rootedness in language and devise settings which enforce knowledge-making through social discourse.

If we see our students' opportunities as writers and readers in these terms, how can we help them join the conversation of a given community? It is crucial to help inexperienced writers and readers understand the conventions which underlie texts in a particular discourse community. The goal need not be to draw students out of familiar discourse—that of family, peer groups, work—but to help them become fluent in different kinds of discourse and able to move among them. Careful classroom discussions of unfamiliar texts and their generative concepts, vocabulary, logic, figures of speech, and voices can help inexperienced readers explore new forms of discourse. Students can be encouraged to articulate their own levels of awareness individually and in groups, gradually becoming familiar with the language characteristic of different disciplines and communities.

Such collaborative discussion is a major feature of David Bleich's pedagogy of reading and writing. He shares with the cognitive-process approach both its constructionist perspective and its view that reading is a purposeful activity driven by the reader's own goals and expectations. Bleich describes the early stages of reading in strongly individualist terms, as a series of responses and "resymbolizations" emerging solely from each reader's own personal identity. He maintains that meaning is always "motivated" or "deliberately sought," a construction of each knower's experience (*Subjective Criticism* 99). Because readers "resymbolize" texts for themselves when they read, each reader's "text" is an individually constructed entity or representation. But precisely because each reader develops separate representations of a text in early stages of reading, Bleich argues that a further stage is crucial: the collaborative process of negotiating shared meanings. Without finding any contradiction in his position, Bleich argues that though reading is the accumulation of individual responses, each reader's responses and resymbolizations will take on full significance only when they are brought together and tested against one another in a communal setting. The most effective reading community is the reading and writing classroom, Bleich believes, because its participants will articulate their motivations and "negotiate" their individual responses into collective understandings that will become "new knowledge" (293). Thus "reading communities" will engage in "communal negotiation" to discover meaning about their own and others' writings.

Most writing teachers who like Bleich emphasize collaborative learning tend to rely on group interaction in their classes, with the traditional instructor-student relationship broadened into a network of student-student relationships facilitated by the instructor. Reading and writing assignments are often done by two or more students working together, sharing the drafting and revising tasks. Collectively-written drafts are shared with other groups for responses and feedback. Evaluation may also be part of the collaborative effort: grades will reflect not only the instructor's judgments but those of the writer's peers as well. Collaborative learning relationships have become an important part of many writing courses; strategies for sharing writing and reading will be explored at length in Chapter Six.

Works Cited

Bakhtin, M. M. *The Dialogic Imagination: Four Essays.* Ed. Michael Holquist, trans. Caryl Emerson and Michael Holquist. Austin: University of Texas Press, 1981.

Barthes, Roland. "From Work to Text." *Revue d' Esthetique* 3 (1971). Rpt. in *Textual Strategies: Perspectives in Poststructuralist Criticism.* Ed. Josue V. Harari. Cornell, NY: Cornell University Press, 1979. 73–81.

Bartholomae, David. "Inventing the University." *Perspectives on Literacy.* Eds. Eugene R. Kintgen, Barry M. Kroll, Mike Rose. Carbondale, IL: Southern Illinois Press, 1988. 273–285.

Beach, Richard and JoAnne Liebman-Kleine. "The Writing/Reading Relationship: Becoming One's Own Best Reader." Petersen 64–81.

Berger, Peter. *The Social Construction of Reality: A Treatise in the Sociology of Knowledge.* Garden City, NY: Doubleday, 1967.

Berlin, James. "Rhetoric and Idealogy in the Writing Class." *College English* 50 (1988): 477–94.

Bernstein, Basil. *Class, Codes, and Control: Towards a Theory of Educational Transmissions.* Vol. 3. Boston: Routledge & Kegan Paul, 1975.

———. *Theoretical Studies Toward a Sociology of Language.* London: Routledge and Kegan Paul, 1971.

Birnbaum, June Cannell. "Reflective Thought: The Connection between Reading and Writing." Petersen 30–45.

Bizzell, Patricia. "Cognition, Convention, and Certainty: What We Need to Know about Writing." *PRE/TEXT* 3 (1982): 213–43.

Black, Edwin. "The Second Persona." *Quarterly Journal of Speech* LVI, 2 (1970), 109–19.

Bleich, David. *Subjective Criticism.* Baltimore: Johns Hopkins University Press, 1978.

Britton, James, et al. *The Development of Writing Abilities 11–18.* Schools Council Research Studies. London: Macmillan Education, 1975.

Bruffee, Kenneth. "Collaborative Learning and the 'Conversation of Mankind.' " *CE* 46 (1984): 635–52.

———. "Social Construction, Language, and the Authority of Knowledge: A Bibliographical Essay." *CE* 48 (1986): 773–790.

Chase, Geoffrey. "Accommodation, Resistance and the Politics of Student Writing." *College Composition and Communication* 39 (1988): 13–22.

Cooper, Marilyn M. "The Ecology of Writing." *CE* 48 (1986): 364–75.

de Beaugrande, Robert. "Writing and Meaning: Contexts of Research." Matsuhashi 1–33.

Derrida, Jacques. "Différance." *Margins of Philosophy.* Trans. Alan Bass. Chicago: University Chicago Press, 1982; 3–27.

Dillon, George. *Rhetoric as Social Imagination: Explorations in the Interpersonal Function of Language.* Bloomington, IN: Indiana University Press, 1967.

Ede, Lisa, and Andrea Lunsford. "Audience Addressed/Audience Invoked: The Role of Audience in Composition Theory and Pedagogy." *CCC* 35 (1984): 155–71.

Elbow, Peter. "Closing My Eyes as I Speak: An Argument for Ignoring Audience." *CE* 49 (1987): 50–69.

Fish, Stanley. *Doing What Comes Naturally: Change, Rhetoric, and the Practice of Theory in Literature and Legal Studies.* Durham, NC: Duke University Press, 1989.

Flower, Linda, and John Hayes. "A Cognitive Process Theory of Writing." *College Composition and Communication* 32 (1981): 365–87.

Freire, Paulo. *Pedagogy of the Oppressed.* Trans. Myra Bergman Ramos. New York: The Seabury Press, 1970.

Geertz, Clifford. *Local Knowledge: Further Essays in Interpretive Anthropology.* New York: Basic Books, 1983.

Gibson, Walker. "Authors, Speakers, Readers, and Mock Readers." *CE* 11 (1950): 265–69.

Goleman, Judith. "The Dialogic Imagination: Something More Than We've Been Taught." Newkirk 131–42.

Haas, Christina, and Linda Flower. "Rhetorical Reading Strategies and the Construction of Meaning." *CCC* 39 (1988): 167–83.

Harris, Joseph. "The Idea of Community in the Study of Writing." *CCC* 40 (1989): 11–22.

Iser, Wolfgang. *The Implied Reader.* Baltimore: The Johns Hopkins University Press, 1974.

———. *The Act of Reading.* Baltimore: The Johns Hopkins Press, 1978.

Kent, Thomas. "Paralogic Hermeneutics." *Rhetoric Review* 8 (1989): 24–42.

Kleine, Michael. "Beyond Triangulation: Ethnography, Writing, and Rhetoric." *Journal of Advanced Composition* 10.1 (1990): 117–25.

Knoblauch, C. H. "Rhetorical Constructions: Dialogue and Commitment." *CE* 50 (1988): 125–40.

Kowal, Sabine and Daniel C. O'Connell. "Writing as Language Behavior: Myths, Models, Methods." Matsuhashi 108–132.

Lefevre, Karen Burke. *Invention As A Social Act.* CCCC Studies in Writing and Rhetoric. Carbondale, IL: Southern Illinois University Press, 1987.

Matsuhashi, Ann, ed. *Writing in Real Time: Modeling Production Processes.* Norwood, NJ: Ablex Publishing Corp., 1987.

Murray, Donald. "Teaching the Other Self: The Writer's First Reader." *CCC* 33 (1982): 140–47.

Newkirk, Thomas, ed. *Only Connect: Uniting Reading and Writing.* Portsmouth, NH: Boynton/Cook Publishers, 1986

North, Stephen. *The Making of Knowledge in Composition: Portrait of an Emerging Field.* Portsmouth, NH: Boynton/Cook Publishers, 1987.

Olson, Gary. "Jacques Derrida On Rhetoric and Composition." *Journal of Advanced Composition* 10.1 (1990): 1–21.

Ong, Walter J., S.J. "The Writer's Audience Is Always a Fiction." PMLA 90 (January 1975): 9–21.

Park, Douglas. "The Meanings of Audience." CE 44 (1982): 247–57.

Petersen, Bruce T., ed. *Convergences: Transactions in Reading and Writing.* Urbana, IL: NCTE, 1986.

Petraglia, Joseph. "Interrupting the Conversation: The Constructionist Dialogue in Composition." JAC 11.1 (1991): 37–56.

Petrosky, Anthony R. "From Story to Essay: Reading and Writing." CCC 33 (1982): 19–36.

Phelps, Louise Wetherbee. *Composition as a Human Science: Contributions to the Self-Understanding of a Discipline.* New York: Oxford University Press, 1988.

Porter, James. "Intertextuality and the Discourse Community." *Rhetoric Review* 5.1 (1986): 34–47.

Reither, James and Douglas Vipond. "Writing as Collaboration." CE 51 (1989): 855–67.

Rorty, Richard. *Philosophy and the Mirror of Nature.* Princeton: Princeton University Press, 1979.

Rosenblatt, Louise M. *The Reader, the Text, the Poem: The Transactional Theory of the Literary Work.* Carbondale, IL: Southern Illinois University Press, 1978.

Smith, Frank. *Understanding Reading: A Psycholinguistic Analysis of Reading and Learning to Read.* Hillsdale, NJ: Lawrence Erlbaum Associates, 1988.

Tompkins, Jane. "A Short Course in Post-structuralism." CE 50 (1988): 733–47.

Trimbur, John. "Beyond Cognition: The Voices in Inner Speech." RR 5.2 (1987): 211–25.

Troyka, Lynn. "Closeness to Text: A Delineation of Reading Processes as They Affect Composing." Newkirk 187–97.

Tuman, Myron. "Class, Codes, and Composition: Basil Bernstein and the Critique of Pedagogy." CCC 39 (1988): 42–51.

Vygotsky, L. S. *Mind In Society: The Development of Higher Psychological Processes.* Ed. M. Cole, V. John-Steiner, S. Scribner, and E. Souberman. Cambridge, MA: Harvard University Press, 1978.

Welch, Kathleen. "Ideology and Freshman Textbook Production: The Place of Theory in Writing Pedagogy." CCC 38 (1987): 269–82.

Chapter Three

Discourse Systems
What They Offer Writing Teachers

In Chapter Two we examined writing and reading in their individual and social perspectives. In this chapter we will consider some general models of discourse which attempt to account systematically for the forms, purposes, and audiences of writing. We will also consider models of what I will call "micro-rhetorics," descriptions of structural patterns in sentences and paragraphs. Each model attempts to encompass elements of discourse into a systematic whole; each has its strengths and its flaws. All have implications for the teaching of writing, however. If we are to choose intelligently among these strategies, we need to understand their strengths and also their difficulties and ambiguities.

Although linguistics, psychology, and philosophy have all contributed to our understanding of composing, rhetoric is the discipline traditionally associated with the study of spoken and written discourse. Yet in the twentieth century, the study of rhetoric has shifted largely to speech departments, in the wake of the split between English departments (which took over literature and composition) and speech departments (which appropriated, partly by default, public speaking and the rhetorical tradition behind it; see Chapter One). Some scholars, of course, are still willing to label themselves rhetoricians and their work "studies in rhetoric"; Kenneth Burke views his studies of symbolic action as rhetorical in important ways. But those studying writing and reading in such fields as linguistics, psychology, sociology, and anthropology generally prefer the term "discourse" to reflect their sense of the scientific nature of their inquiries.

A theory of discourse is a systematic attempt to describe the variables in human communication and the way they interact. The discourse systems examined in this chapter emphasize writing and fall into two major categories: those "relational" systems that focus on *the dynamic relations among writer, text, and reader;* and those I will call "categorizing" systems that emphasize *the static character-istics of texts.*

We will consider three relational systems: Kenneth Burke's, James Moffett's and James Britton's. Kenneth Burke's analyses of man's symbolic activity, including writing, have proved enormously suggestive for discourse theory in general. Though neither James Moffett nor James Britton acknowledges Burke as a direct influence, their models of writer-text-reader interaction reflect a Burkean interest in intention and response in discourse. We will also consider two categorizing systems: those of James Kinneavy and Frank D'Angelo. Their work proposes textual categories based on the writer's intentions and the structures of mind said to be implicit in textual structures.

Relational Systems: Burke, Moffett, Britton

These contemporary discourse systems combine traditional rhetorical elements with elements of the constructionist theories we examined in Chapters One and Two. At the heart of the matter are differing views on the relationship between language and thought. As we saw in Chapter One, cognitive-process theories have in recent decades asserted the inseparability of thought and language. But in classical rhetoric there is a tradition of "ornateness"—a tendency to distinguish what is said from how it is said—that remains influential today. Invention is discussed separately from elements of structure and style in some influential classical treatises and in many current handbooks as well. In these texts, invention is presented as the process of developing ideas and issues by means of topics (*topoi*) that speakers and writers may use to gain the adherence of the audience. Style, on the other hand, is presented as argument's dress, clothing the speaker's claims in pleasing and telling fashion. Rhetorician Louis Milic terms this the doctrine of "ornate form"; thoughts can be "dressed in a variety of outfits," and the speaker's role is to find the dress appropriate to the occasion (Milic 67). Students learn style by imitating a lush variety of diction, sentence patterns, and figures of speech.

The doctrine of ornateness—that form and content are at least implicitly separable, as distinct "stages" of composing—remains an underlying constant in discourse theory. It is an element of the "instrumental" view of language discussed in Chapter One—the view that language "expresses" thoughts and attitudes formulated prior to and independently of it. It may be found in writing handbooks, where exercises in sentence combining and paragraph patterns imply that, for teaching purposes at least, the stylistic elements of discourse are separable from "content" or "meaning." This separability exemplifies the notion, as C. H. Knoblauch and Lil Brannon put it, "that rhetoric defines nothing more than a system of optional communicative vehicles for ideas that have been independently ascertained . . . a catalogue of all-purpose, ready-made structures" for discourse (46). The view of composing as a series of linear stages from idea through language to writing even appears, for example, in an NCTE-sanctioned definition of "writing competence" as "the ability to discover what one wishes to say and to convey one's message through language, syntax, and content that are appropriate for one's audience and purpose" (Odell 103). The tradition of ornateness carries a price: it seems to justify a patronizing view of rhetoric as decoration ("oh, that's just rhetoric") or persiflage. Knoblauch and Brannon suggest that writing teachers who "still tend to accept these beliefs about discourse" will find no support among today's theories of discourse (46). While this is largely true, the instrumental view of language remains a strong undercurrent in our ways of talking about rhetoric and discourse.

In contemporary discussions of the nature of discourse, these traditional rhetorical attitudes contrast with a unitary view of the relationship between thought and language. That body of theory we have called "constructionist" in Chapters One and Two maintains that language is at the heart of our efforts to build knowledge. And if language is the primary means by which we articulate and define our experiences, then words are much more than the dress of thought; words and thoughts are coeval, one and the same. In this view, style and form generate meaning, not merely reflect some prior mental order or understanding. In the discourse systems that follow, elements of both views can be found; attention to textual patterns and forms is balanced by analyses of the cognitive and situational elements of discourse.

Kenneth Burke and Dramatism

Though the dynamic interrelations of speaker, speech, and hearer have received attention in systems of rhetoric throughout the ages, no theory more convincingly describes the interactive nature of all discourse than Kenneth Burke's. Because of its ambitious generalizing and its intended application to all human symbolic activity, Burke's readings of language as symbolic action are as relevant to written discourse as to other communicative modes. Burke's pentad of "motives" for symbolic communication has been widely used (and somewhat misunderstood) by those attempting to devise heuristic systems for composition (see Chapter One for a discussion of some heuristic systems).

The work of Kenneth Burke has furthered the contemporary view of discourse as unitary and dynamic. In *The Philosophy of Literary Form* Burke defines the "verbal act" as "symbolic action," emphasizing that all human utterances are "stylized answers" to situations which occasion them (8). His terminology suggests how thoroughly unitary is his view of all communication, particularly discourse: "the symbolic act is *the dancing of an attitude*" [his italics] (9). For Burke, a "symbolic act" is any purposive human action that communicates meaning. In *A Grammar Of Motives* Burke devises a system for analyzing any purposive act, from political gestures and the making of war to the dramatized actions of tragedy. To provide a framework for his analyses of symbolic action, Burke propounds a "dramatistic" method of analysis featuring a "pentad" of "five key terms" to analyze "what people are doing and why they are doing it" (xv). These terms are Act, Scene, Agent, Agency, and Purpose. But each term lacks meaning as a separate item; only the relationship, or "ratio," between them confers significance upon them, and gives them analytical force. Any symbolic action, linguistic or otherwise, contains an act, a scene wherein it occurs, an agent, an agency by which it is committed, and a purpose which generates it. But because any symbolic act is by nature dynamic and relational—the structure of the pentad rests on this assumption—merely applying the individual, static terms in an attempt to define a dynamic process is meaningless. Meaningful analysis of the symbolic act can come only from a description of the relationships among the terms, relationships Burke calls "ratios" or "principles of determination." Thus, to borrow an analogy from linguistics, the pentad comprises what Burke argues is a grammar of meaning which, like language grammars, can describe any of the potentially infinite number of symbolic actions.

Although Burke alludes to a wide range of symbolic activity, he is primarily interested in language. Rhetoric, for Burke, is the art of achieving identification between speaker and listener, writer and reader, to the point of "consubstantiality," or identity of understanding. Rhetoric is "the use of language as a symbolic means of inducing cooperation in beings that by nature respond to symbols" (*A Rhetoric of Motives* 43). Cooperation emerges from consubstantiality, which in turn is achieved by a speaker or writer only by a "strategy of 'naming' in such a way ... as to achieve identification" with the intended audience (Holland 68). Burke understands rhetoric, then, as the purposive use of language. The pentad provides an analytic tool for evaluating the rhetorical effectiveness of a statement, or its success in achieving identification between speaker or writer and audience. Applied to discourse, the "key terms of dramatism" can analyze the statement itself (the Act), the speaker or writer (the Agent), the medium in which the statement occurs (the Agency, or the form of the statement), the occasion in which it occurs (the Scene), and the intention which generates it (the Purpose)—but each only in the context of all the other key terms.

Within this framework are two crucial assumptions which underlie the rhetorical tradition from its classical beginnings, and to which Burke gives renewed emphasis: first, that human beings are capable of reason in their discourse, and second, that they articulate their reasoning in language. In Burke's view, any discourse may be viewed as an actor-agent's seizing of an occasion to communicate something. For "the agent is an author of his acts, which are descended from him," and the ratio between agent and act always implies a "temporal or sequential relationship" (*Rhetoric* 16). Thus, the most important ratios for Burke are those between Act and Agent, Scene and Purpose, and Agency and Purpose. The dynamic interactions among these elements of discourse control the meaningfulness of all symbolic acts.

Burke's vision of the dynamic interaction of discourse elements has been influential for many teachers of writing. Unfortunately, the pentad's practical value for analyzing particular pieces of discourse isn't given much demonstration by Burke. After propounding the elements of the pentad in *A Grammar of Motives,* for example, Burke devotes the rest of the volume to analyzing philosophic schools and general patterns of thought in pentadic terms; he does not bring the pentad to bear upon specific pieces of discourse except in passing. His major interest in *A Grammar of Motives* is to locate underlying principles for the pentadic terms within major philosophic schools of Western culture. His primary interest in *A Rhetoric of Motives* is to establish kinds of behavior in thought or action which would achieve "identification." The *Rhetoric* is tradition-oriented, that is, and does not utilize the pentadic elements developed in the *Grammar*. In the *Rhetoric* Burke prescribes strategies for persuasive discourse that generally fall within Aristotle's three means of persuasion: logos or reason, ethos or character, and pathos or emotion. Thus, for many readers today the central locus of Burke's influence remains in the potently heuristic early chapters of *The*

Grammar of Motives in which the pentadic terms are given the most concentrated presentation.

James Moffett's Universe of Discourse

Burke's emphasis upon the relationships among discourse elements has furthered the contemporary view of discourse as dynamic interaction. The recent work of James Moffett is an example of a relational discourse theory specifically applied to written discourse. In *Teaching the Universe of Discourse*, Moffett argues that the elements of discourse—"speaker, listener, subject"—exist meaningfully only in relation to one another: all discourse is "somebody talking to somebody about something" (10). Moffett relies on the terms of Piaget's developmental psychology to ground his categories of discourse. Assuming that the deepest impulse to communicate is the egocentric need to express something, Moffett places discourse along a spectrum ranging from "egocentric" expression to "decentered" statement. The process of decentering in discourse occurs, says Moffett, in different ways: it can move "from implicit embodied idea to explicitly formulated idea," "from . . . small known audience . . . to a distant unknown and different audience," or from emotion in the "there-then" to emotion in the "here-now" (57).

Moffett posits two basic relations, or (to borrow Burke's term) ratios, within which discourse may be defined:

A. The rhetorical distance between writer and listener (I-you).
       and
B. The abstractive distance between writer and subject (I-it).

The "I-you" or rhetorical scale features the writer "abstracting for" an audience at varying removes from the writer. The "I-it" scale features the writer "abstracting from" "raw experience" into varying levels of generality.

Rhetorical distance between speaker and listener increases as the distance between the "I" and the "you" grows. The closest relation occurs in reflection and meditation, while the widest distance comes in addressing an unknown, general audience:

A. Reflection—intrapersonal (writing for oneself).
B. Conversation—interpersonal (speaking with intimate listener).
C. Correspondence—interpersonal (writing for intimate audience).
D. Publication—impersonal (writing for general audience).

Likewise, the abstraction between speaker and subject (the "I-it" relation) occurs as the inventing mind arranges its materials "in hierarchies of classes and subclasses" (19) increasingly distant from immediate experience. Thus, discourse ranges from immediate personal experience to conceptual abstraction:

A. What is happening—drama—recording.
B. What happened—narrative—reporting.
C. What happens—exposition—generalizing.
D. What may happen—logical argument—theorizing.

This schematization allows Moffett to categorize all major forms of written discourse in a hierarchy which encapsules both psychological and rhetorical variables (see Figure 1).

Moffett does point out that his one-dimensional figure flattens the diversity of the variables he is representing. Despite this admission, he does not hesitate to apply his ambitious scheme to a wide spectrum of discourse. He organizes his diagram along two axes of abstraction or distance: the "I-you" axis of rhetorical distance, and

Figure 1

Interior Dialogue (egocentric speech)			P
Vocal Dialogue (socialized speech)	Recording, the drama of what is happening.	PLAYS	O
Correspondence Personal Journal Autobiography			E
Memoir	Reporting, the narrative of what happened.	FICTION	T
Biography Chronicle			
History	Generalizing, the exposition of what happens.	ESSAY	R
Science			
Metaphysics	Theorizing, the argumentation of what will, may happen.		Y

the "I-it" axis of referential abstraction. The writer-audience, "I-you" relationship ranges from the child's speech for himself only, through close audiences on to the most generalized readership, rhetorically distanced from the writer. The writer-reality, "I-it" connection ranges from what Moffett takes to be the most immediate form of experiential rendering in language—drama, "what is happening"— to the generalized theorizing of metaphysics, the most abstract kind of cognitive activity. Such a scheme appears to offer teachers conceptual support in devising a coherent sequence of writing tasks.

And indeed, though he warns that his theory must not "be translated directly into syllabi" (54), Moffett's system has gained considerable pedagogical influence. The "I-you" relationship seems to obey a rhetorical progression, from communicating with a familiar, undifferentiated audience to publication for a general, diversified audience of unknown expectations. Such a progression implies that teachers should require personal writing before setting writing tasks for more distanced or diversified audiences. Again, the "I-it" relationship relies on Moffett's interpretation of Piaget's concept of decentering, which, argues Moffett, involves progression "from talking about present objects and actions to talking about things past and potential," "from projecting emotion into the there-then to focusing it in the here-now," and demands the ability to see "alternatives . . . and [stand] in others' shoes" (57).

This progression implies a sequence of writing tasks moving from familiar, personal-experience topics to abstract, impersonal issues. Recent textbooks at the secondary and college level often reflect just such a progression, from diaries and personal experience essays to research papers. Moffett's system can help teachers find value in assignments outside academic writing; it emphasizes the importance of asking students to write at various levels of abstraction and complexity, and for a variety of audiences. Finally, it obliges students to see that no single form of discourse is a thing unto itself, but is part of a continuum of rhetorical possibilities to be explored in preparation for future writing tasks.

However, Moffett's system is strained by ambiguous and confusing premises. Some ambiguity is inevitable, of course, in any discourse system posited on a specific model of mind. It is tempting but often difficult to devise practical rules and strategies from a complex theory. For example, British rhetoricians of the later eighteenth and nineteenth centuries based their rhetorical analyses upon a mental geography whose poles were the "faculties" of "will" and "understanding." To make rhetoric out of this psychology required rhetoricians to define modes of writing which appealed separately to the various faculties—exposition relying on the faculty of understanding, and persuasion requiring the involvement of the will. This categorizing created narrow, rigid definitions of the "forms of discourse," while it also wrenched definitions of mental function. The same kind of dislocation undermines the integrity of Moffett's categories, which are based on several different psychological premises held together uneasily by Moffett's skillful prose.

The ambiguity in Moffett's concept of "abstraction" weakens the "I-it" portion of his system. Moffett begins by basing the "I-it" relationship upon what he calls the mind's process of "abstracting *from raw phenomena*" (18) in building concepts about experience. What Moffett is outlining here is a theory of "concept formation," which psychologists today view as an essential part of any theory of cognitive process. In places Moffett appears to articulate a "structural" view of concept formation, based on Piaget's ideas of assimilation and accommodation: the features of day-to-day experience, says Moffett, "are not only selected but reorganized, and increasingly as we go up the scale of the nervous system, integrated with previously abstracted information"(22). But more often, he uses language suggestive of an "empirical" view: concepts emerge, he says, as the mind constructs "an object out of the indivisible phenomenal world by singling out some environmental features and ignoring others" (20). In a teaching textbook written as a companion volume to *Teaching the Universe of Discourse*, Moffett presents what appears to be a simplistic Lockean sequence: "reason . . . operates on what the senses represent to it of external reality, most of which has been filed away in the memory" (*Student-Centered Language Arts, K–12*, 8). It would perhaps be unfair to judge Moffett's discourse theory on the basis of shifting premises, were those premises only incidental to the theory; but Moffett makes them central to his argument by basing the "I-it" relationship upon them. "I-it" experience is given blurred and shifting definition in Moffett's work, here as a function of cognitive structures interacting with sense experience, there as the direct impact of sense stimuli upon "memory" and "reason."

Moffett uses the illustration of a person sitting in a cafeteria: he can record what is happening, he can talk later about what happened, he can generalize about what usually happens in such situations, or he can speculate about what may happen (36 ff). Locating the beginning of abstraction in empirical experience immediately narrows the scope of the concept-forming process, implying that all concepts begin with sense experience. This naive empiricism conflicts with the Piagetian concept of cognitive structure which Moffett invokes elsewhere. Piaget argues that cognitive growth is controlled by universal structures of mind called up by, not originating with, external experience. Thus Moffett's assertion that recording experience as narrative is psychologically prior to other modes of discourse (because it reflects the immediacy of empirical experience) is puzzling. What if there are modes of experience quite independent of empirical stimuli, which form the basis of certain kinds of discourse? What if, as some psychologists argue, the mind often generalizes or theorizes independently from any empirical stimulus, immediate or original? What if, in terms of Moffett's system, the "it" of the "I-it" relationship does not always begin as a bit of sense experience recordable in the present tense, but originates as a form of deeper cognition? The mind appears to be far more complex than Moffett's associationist bias would allow; the "I-it" progression of discourse is not necessarily related in the fashion Moffett indicates.

Perhaps, then, the record of "what is happening"—whether couched in "vocal dialogue" or in journal entries—is not always less abstract, with less "I-it" distance, than theorizing about "what may happen." Consider the genre of meditative writing, for example. The *Pensées* of Pascal take the form of a series of fragments connected by certain thematic links, reflecting the drama of Pascal's probing intellect in immediate and continuous conflict with received opinion. Deeply personal in tone and address, they bear the surface marks of the self-oriented writings at the top of Moffett's hierachy. Yet the *Pensées* are profoundly abstract, theoretical, and appear aimed at a general audience of inquiring intellects.

Students, too, are capable of writing personal forms containing generalizations and theorizing. Such writing may be considerably more complex than the progressions suggested by Moffett's spectrum. Another example of writing that simultaneously embodies the whole range of Moffett's spectrum is Loren Eiseley's *The Immense Journey*. These essays begin as reports of biological and anthropological lore, then generalize about the physical universe, then theorize about man's place in that universe. Extraordinarily concrete and deeply felt in tone, these essays make a drama out of Eiseley's perceptions even as they argue for a certain attitude toward the world. The experience rendered by Eiseley's presentations is as complex as it is whole; it recognizes few of the gradations outlined in the "Spectrum of Discourse"—or rather, it comprehends nearly all of them in a very unhierarchical way.

Another difficulty in Moffett's argument is his deliberate conflation of "abstraction" and "generalization." He argues that "the ranging of the mind's materials in hierarchies of classes and subclasses" (19)—thinking from the general to the specific—is the same activity as extending a "referent in time and space"(19), Moffett's phrase for thinking from abstract to concrete. As an example he cites "pop fly" as both more specific and more concrete than "parabolic trajectory" (20). Yet this illustration does not justify Moffett's over-extension of the term "abstraction." When we speak of something being "concrete," we mean that it exists in a form available to the senses; if it is not available to the senses, we speak of it as "abstract." But something "specific" is not necessarily concrete; it is only more particular within its class. It is true that "pop fly" is more specific and more concrete that "parabolic trajectory," because the former is a kind of parabola we can see, but, for example, the love of a parent for a child is more specific than the general concept of love, yet not necessarily more concrete; it may be enacted concretely in a hug, yet it also exists as a specific love when not enacted concretely. It's important that students understand the difference between the logic of class hierarchy and the envisioning process that renders experience concretely. To implement the useful strategies borne of Moffett's system, teachers must insure that they do not blur the meanings of both processes and the language appropriate to each.

James Britton and Language Roles

Britton acknowledges his debt to Moffett's scale of abstraction in formulating part of his system. But by resting his classifications of writing on the intentions implicit in them, rather than like Moffett upon their ostensible reality-reference, Britton avoids some—but not all—of the ambiguities plaguing Moffett's system. In formulating his "language functions" and "audience roles," however, Britton uses the relational or contextual approach inconsistently, making the entirety of his system somewhat disjointed in its presentation. Despite its flaws, however, Britton's discourse system has wielded enormous influence among teachers of writing since its publication in the mid-1970s.

In Chapter One we briefly examined Britton's version of writing modes or as he terms them, "functions"—transactional, expressive, and poetic. To better understand his entire system of discourse we must now look closely at the way Britton relates writing "functions" to what he terms "language roles." He asserts that with respect to any experience, we may either be participating in it or evaluating it out of a desire to understand it better. When the linguistic representation of the world enables the user to participate in the world, then language is being used "in the role of participant" (80). The user employs language in the world "in order to operate in it," to "seek an outcome" in the actual world by communicating information or commands (transactional writing or by using persuasion (80). The function term for this purpose is "transactional." However, if the user wishes to represent the world, not in order to participate in it, but in order to evaluate it "without seeking outcomes in the actual world," then he is using language "*in the role of spectator*" (80). When language is used in the role of spectator, it strives only to present experience in a certain way. The function term for this purpose is "poetic."

Britton models his transactional functions on Moffett's scale of abstraction, ranging from the specific to the general, with recording and reporting viewed as renderings of specific experience, followed by patterns of generalization and ultimately by hypotheses about generalizations. But Britton tries to avoid suggesting a hierarchy among these functions; instead he argues that each of these functions is a "stance" adopted by the writer to achieve a specific purpose for a specific audience. Generalizations and speculations are products of different language stances or approaches to experience through language, rather than purported attributes of experience itself. Britton denies Moffett's implication that "higher" levels of abstraction are likely to appear in, for example, scientific writing but not in the younger writer's work. Britton, noting one eleven-year-old's generalization that "people get mad very easy" (97), frequently reminds the reader that abstraction is not a hierarchically distributed characteristic of certain kinds of experience, but a perspective on experience through language.

Britton's spectator role presumes a detachment from the immediacy of experience, superficially resembling the abstractive "distance" at the far end of Moffett's "I-it" scale. But Moffett's "distance" purports to measure a movement away from the sense world to an abstract representation of that world, a movement that implies a scale of empirical associationism. Britton's scale implies an intentional framing or representation of experience through language itself; spectator-role writing is primarily imaginative writing— stories, poems, plays. The spectator role presumes a detachment from the immediacy of experience, superficially resembling the abstractive "distance" at the far end of Moffett's "I-it" scale. Poetic writing, in the role of spectator, is language used "to recount or recreate real or imagined experience for no other reason than to enjoy it" (91) or evaluate it. Poetic writing becomes "an immediate end in itself, and not a means: it is a verbal artifact, a construct" (93). Thus, maintains Britton, poetic writing, unlike transactional writing, cannot be independently "contextualized"—i.e., understood in separate bits—but must be read in terms of its own intrinsic unity.

Transactional and poetic writing are not characterized by a relationship with any particular audience. Transactional writing, in the role of participant, is "language to get things done: to inform

... to advise or persuade or instruct people" (88). Such writing "is an immediate means to an end outside itself" (93) and can be "contextualized" piecemeal by the reader—that is, the reader can isolate portions of transactional writing and still find them meaningful. The audience for the poetic function may be the writer herself or others playing a spectator role. But Britton defines expressive discourse in terms of a specific kind of audience—that of a close group of readers familiar to the writer, and sharing the writer's attitudes and expectations. Thus, expressive writing will be "utterance at its most relaxed and intimate, as free as possible from outside demands, whether those of a task or of an audience" (82). Indeed, it's "free to move easily from participant role into spectator role and vice versa" (82). Here Britton shifts the premise of his function categories from role definition to audience awareness, an alteration he does not clearly acknowledge in his scheme of functions (see Figure 2).

Though he does not link his writing "functions" with audience relationships except in the expressive mode, Britton does construct a separate system of writer-audience relationships to which he gives the general name "context of situation" (60). For the writer, says Britton, "context of situation" involves "writing this kind of thing in this sort of society for this sort of person" (61). But context involves more than just the nature of the writer and the reader. It also involves all the relevant assumptions within the culture they share: in order "for language to function effectively there must be 'tacit acceptance' by both speaker and hearer of all the relevant conventions, beliefs and presuppositions" (61).

In written discourse, moreover, the writer does not have immediately available clues for construing the audience, as does a speaker. Rather, the writer must "represent to himself a context of situation, and this includes his readers" (61). What Moffett calls the "I-you" relationship is, in Britton's view, the reader's invention, a mind's eye representation of audience invoked continuously by the writer as he composes. As we saw in Chapter Two, this way of describing discourse represents that relational viewpoint characteristic of contemporary analyses of the writer-reader relationship. Unfortunately, Britton doesn't fully extend his description of the "invented"

Figure 2

Participant Role	———————————————	Spectator Role
TRANSACTIONAL	EXPRESSIVE	POETIC

The Development of Writing Abilities (11–18), p. 81

audience to each function or audience category, nor does his system incorporate any insights from other treatments of the writer-reader relationship.

The audience categories as formulated by Britton appear in Figure 3.

Because their writing samples and the audiences for them were limited to school situations, Britton and his researchers were obliged to include the teacher as an audience component. In the range of readers from "self" to "unknown audience," however, a general similarity to Moffett's "I-you" scale can be seen arising from their common debt to the concept of cognitive egocentricism. Writing for the self, says Britton, is "a written form of 'speech for oneself'" (66)—a phrase borrowed from Piaget's concept of egocentric speech, which both Britton and Moffett posit as the beginning of the child's language use. Primary audiences for school children are teachers, who can serve as "trusted adults," teachers engaged in a "teacher-learner"

Figure 3

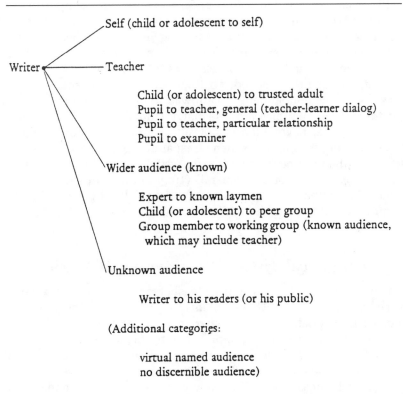

Self (child or adolescent to self)

Writer

Teacher

Child (or adolescent) to trusted adult
Pupil to teacher, general (teacher-learner dialog)
Pupil to teacher, particular relationship
Pupil to examiner

Wider audience (known)

Expert to known laymen
Child (or adolescent) to peer group
Group member to working group (known audience,
which may include teacher)

Unknown audience

Writer to his readers (or his public)

(Additional categories:

virtual named audience
no discernible audience)

—adapted from Britton, p. 66

dialogue with the child, or teachers acting as "examiners" to whom the child reports (68–70). Within the school situation, argues Britton, children may also begin to write for a "wider audience" that includes peers and known laymen, and for an "unknown audience" which is the common target for poetic writing tasks. This range of possible audiences is presented by Britton in the same way Moffett characterizes his "I-you" scale: as a hierarchy of readers requiring an increasingly sophisticated objectivity on the part of the writer.

The developmental implications of Britton's audience categories are brought out by the survey of school writings done by Britton and his colleagues. Transactional writing is the most frequent type of school writing. Expressive and poetic functions appear much less often among school writing, though the poetic function is present until the later secondary years. "The overall pattern," says Britton, "is marked by the substantial increase of writing for the teacher as examiner, together with some move towards writing for a more public audience in the fifth and seventh years" (182). Associations between audience and function appear markedly, for example, in the consistent relation between expressive writing and the "trusted adult," and between transactional writing and the "teacher as examiner." The latter audience increasingly dominates school writing in the later educational years. The teacher's traditional role as students' only audience for all school writing impels Britton and his colleagues to urge that students be allowed to do more expressive and poetic writing. They also propose that, if students are to be prepared for writing tasks beyond the school setting, "work in school ought to equip a writer to choose his own target audience and, eventually, to be able, when the occasion arises, to write as someone with something to say to the world in general" (192). Training in writing skills ought, in Britton's view, to allow children fuller opportunities to confront a full range of functions and audiences.

Categorical Systems: Kinneavy and D'Angelo

There is much of value for writing teachers in the relational systems we have just reviewed. These systems help us see the variety of roles and writing situations that inexperienced writers need to explore, and suggest some teaching approaches to encourage such exploration. The two categorical systems we will consider next are more interesting as ambitious but flawed theories than they are as pedagogical influences. James Kinneavy by means of "aim" and Frank D'Angelo by means of "conceptual pattern" attempt to construct typologies of discourse based on textual patterns. Both systems are text-centered, foregrounding discussions of structural and semantic elements of texts and avoiding discussions of audience and situation. Both theorists claim cognitive grounds for all textual structures, Kinneavy referring to such grounds as "aims" and D'Angelo as "conceptual patterns." But neither clearly addresses problematic elements in the relationship between mind and language, nor cites cognitive or psycholinguistic arguments that might support his case. Thus, teachers of writing who insist on the situated and social nature of writing will find these systems of little use in understanding written discourse.

Yet there are at least two reasons why writing teachers (who have papers to read and department chairpersons to cope with) should nevertheless study categorical discourse systems like those of Kinneavy and D'Angelo. First, an understanding of the issues involved in identifying textual characteristics can help teachers gain a wider view of the often incomplete writing intentions embodied in student writing. Such an understanding can help teachers become aware of the textual patterns—often unrealized or incompatible—which inform a piece of student writing. Second, an awareness of these efforts to anatomize texts can help teachers devise ways to familiarize inexperienced writers with some of the possibilities of textuality itself, the look and feel of formal writing. That is, it can help students who have read and written little see how such writing—especially writing in the academy—differs from their customary discourse; they can experience the end result of carefully shaped composing for a variety of academic and professional purposes. For these reasons we need to look at these two efforts to create a typology of discourse.

James Kinneavy's Aims of Discourse

A Theory of Discourse is an ambitious effort to build a comprehensive discourse system. Kinneavy's purpose is not, like Moffett's and Britton's, to demonstrate the dynamic variables which generate a given text. Instead, he focuses on the text rather than on the processes which generate it. In the text, he maintains, the dynamic elements of discourse—intention and response—are embodied and are available through textual analysis. What Kinneavy attempts is an anatomy of human communication, with an emphasis on the characteristics of texts, which he arranges in terms of four "aims" represented by means of a "communications triangle."

This model, drawn from the field of information theory, represents communication as a sort of telephone network. "Basic to all uses of language," says Kinneavy, "are a person who encodes a message, the signal (language) which carries the message, the reality to which the message refers, and the decoder (receiver of the message)" (19). Kinneavy's triangle looks this way:

Figure 4

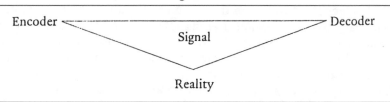

Before we explore the uses to which Kinneavy puts this schematization, we should note his own acknowledgment of its limitations. His reliance on the language of electronic information-processing requires him to organize his analysis within its terms, whose scientistic connotations many composition scholars see as reductive. Kinneavy acknowledges the disadvantages of this diagram—its oversimplification of communication's complexity and its inability to represent the interactive, reciprocal nature of oral and written communication. It implies that communication flows in straight lines and that there is a "reality" somewhere outside that flow, to which it "refers."

Moreover, Kinneavy's separation of "reality" from the communications flow implies that the "real" is prior to language. This premise stands in direct opposition to the constructionists' view that language itself is the basis of meaning and knowing—that "the real" is what we frame in language. When Kinneavy proposed his system in the early 1970s, constructionist views of language and anti-foundationalist philosophy had not yet been widely promulgated in discourse theory. It is clear now that the current constructionist perspective is fundamentally opposed to the foundationalist view that underlies Kinneavy's theory. Thus, in studying Kinneavy's theory we have an interesting opportunity to compare a traditional foundationalist argument with those anti-foundationalist views we studied in Chapter Two.

Kinneavy distinguishes two major categories of study based on the communications triangle. "Linguistics" comprehends the study of the signal (language) itself and the interaction between language and reality, both constituting the means of communication. "Discourse," of most concern to Kinneavy here, is "the study of the situational uses of the potentials of the language" (22), and is "characterized by individuals acting in a special time and place" (22). Though this definition of discourse seems to differ little from the situational definitions offered by Moffett and Britton, major differences quickly appear.

Kinneavy argues that the fundamental determinant—and thus the center of a discourse system—is "aim." But by "aim" Kinneavy does not mean the intent of the speaker or writer, or the purpose with respect to the hearer or reader. Instead, he defines "aim in discourse" as that "aim which is embodied in the text itself—given the qualifications of situation and culture" (49). For Kinneavy "aim" and "text" are coterminous entities, the one a part of the other. Text is a "totality of effect" which is "generated by the things talked about, the organization given the materials, the accompanying style" (49). Text includes the notion of "effect" as "a reaction of some kind of acceptance or rejection" generated by the interaction of textual elements. What happens in the writer's mind as he works, or in the reader's mind as he reads, is of interest to psychology, Kinneavy says, but not to discourse analysis.

It is here that Kinneavy's discourse theory is most at odds with constructionist and anti-foundationalist understandings of language. For the constructionists, the text is merely an index or sign of those generative processes of intention and response; it is the processes themselves that must be studied. The text itself is indeterminate, existing only as writer's or reader's construction; composing itself is the meaning-making element of discourse. Contrastingly, Kinneavy argues that the text itself contains or embodies purpose. The formulated text is the vital core of all discourse; intention and response are in some sense "in" the text and must therefore be read "from" it: "aim," he says, is that "which is embodied in the text itself" (49). Thus, aim can be recovered from a study of the text itself.

Aim determines discourse in four possible ways, he argues, referring to his communication model: by representing the sender, the receiver, the reality being presented, or the form of the text (signal) itself. Each aim defines its own discourse:

> In *literary discourse* the [textual] artifact is present; in *informative and scientific discourse* the reality is represented; in *expressive discourse* the reaction of the [sending] self is displayed . . . [and] in *persuasion*, the acceptance [by the receiver] is implicitly or explicitly requested in the text (60 [italics mine]).

The majority of texts, Kinneavy acknowledges, have more than one aim. But the possibility of multiple aims in one discourse does not, in Kinneavy's view, weaken his system, for he argues that, however singular or combined, it is still aim that is the basic determiner of discourse. Thus, Kinneavy's purpose is to create an anatomy of discourse (see Figure 5) which abstracts "the different norms" of each aim, "and consider[s] them in isolation" (63). These norms "are distinct from the various aims of discourse"; they are respectively "the distinctive nature, the distinctive logic, the characteristic organizational patterns, and the stylistic features" (63) of texts representing each aim.

A quick look at one of the four "aim" categories reveals how Kinneavy's anatomizing works, and suggests his reliance on the same kind of straightforward empiricism found in Moffett's thought. Reference discourse is that whose aim is "to designate or reproduce reality" (39). There are three kinds of reference discourse, each characterized by a different attitude toward reality. *Informative* discourse is one of these; it assumes that reality is understood and that "the facts about it are simply relayed to the decoder" (39), so that "factuality," content comprehensiveness and informative surprise value" (129) are the hallmarks of informative logic. Factuality must always be verified; if the facts are established inductively, then they must be verified empirically. If the facts rely on assumptions not empirically verifiable, then they must verify themselves according to deductive logical patterns. The organization of informative discourse, continues Kinneavy, may rely on the principle of "comprehensiveness," or "surprise value," or "importance," or "logical ordering principles of deduction and induction" (161). Kinneavy uses journalistic writing as his main source of examples in discussing informational discourse, so that the "inverted triangle" news presentation and the "5W's" of comprehensiveness appear as his salient points. As for style, informative discourse involves three issues most often: "readability, avoiding dullness, and pacing" (181). Informative diction tends to be jargon-free, denotative, and concrete; about informative syntax, Kinneavy has very little to say.

Kinneavy's analysis applies the same norms of logic, organization, and style to two other kinds of referential discourse, scientific and exploratory, and to persuasive, literary, and expressive discourse. He discusses the theoretical antecedents of his concepts, criticizes the weaknesses in previous theory and methodology, and indicates needed study. Indeed, the sections entitled "The Nature of . . . " under each of the four primary discourse types are valuable reviews of contributory theories and concepts, well worth studying as theoretical surveys. The essay on persuasive discourse, for example, contains a concise review of rhetorical theory from Aristotle to Burke.

Beyond the wide range of Kinneavy's eclecticism, however, another point of interest claims our attention: the striking similarity between Kinneavy's "aims" and Britton's "functions." Britton's "transactional" writing shares some of the features of Kinneavy's "referential" and "persuasive" writing, while his "poetic" function is very similar to Kinneavy's "literary" aim. Their joint use of the "expressive" category, on the other hand, implies a similarity which does not exist:

KINNEAVY	BRITTON

A. *Referential discourse*
 1. Informative
  a. presents facts
  b. strives for completeness
  c. relies on surprise value
 2. Scientific discourse
  a. impersonal
  b. demonstrates hypotheses
  c. strives for certainty
 3. Exploratory discourse
  a. creates hypotheses, does
   not prove them
  b. often personal

B. *Persuasive discourse*
 1. Focuses on decoder
 2. Induces to belief or action
 3. Deals with probable or
   plausible

C. *Literary discourse*
 1. Emphasis upon internal
   structure of text
 2. Organic unity in structure
 3. Logic of developing
   probability

D. *Expressive discourse*
 1. Focuses upon encoder, the
   "speaking self" (398)
 2. Self discovers its identity
   through expressive discourse
 3. Self formulates a "Being-for-
   the-World" (406) in expression
 4. Style is linguistic expression
   of these selves

A. *Transactional (informative)*
 1. Recording, reporting, narrating,
   describing events and places.
 2. Analogic, analogic-tautologic,
   tautologic writing
  a. objective
  b. increasingly speculative and
   generalized
 3. Analogic (low-level), analogic
   writing
  a. personal or impersonal
  b. informal generalization

B. *Transactional (conative) writing*
 1. Regulative writing
  a. instructs, demands, imposes
   authority
 2. Persuasive writing
  a. attempts to influence
   behavior or action
  b. attempts to change attitudes

C. *Poetic writing*
 1. Emphasis upon "phonic
   substance of language
   itself" (90)
 2. Pattern of arrangement crucial
 3. Writer's feelings as subject

D. *Expressive writing*
 1. Writing for the self
 2. Intimacy between writer,
   audience
 3. Meaning often assumed as
   shared contexts

The most obvious similarity lies in the poetic category. Britton's "poetic" writing is concerned with the shape and sound of language rather than its impact. The function of poetic writing, Britton continues, is to allow the evaluation of experience, or its re-creation for pleasure. Any poetic text exists as an object of contemplation, not as a means to achieve an effect upon the reader or a release for the writer, though these functions may contribute secondarily to the making of the work. Kinneavy's "literary" discourse has an identical feature: it emphasizes the structure and unity of the text, which must develop an aesthetic purpose. As is his habit, Britton goes beyond Kinneavy in articulating some pedagogical implications of poetic writing. He urges the importance of poetic writing tasks in the early years of the school curriculum, since such writing rapidly loses ground to transactional writing tasks at higher educational levels. Britton brings audience into his consideration of poetic writing—an element that does not interest Kinneavy in literary discourse—by pointing out a possible association between the fading of poetic writing and the replacement of the "teacher-learner dialogue" with the "pupil-to-examiner" audience type in later school years.

Britton and Kinneavy both use the term "expressive" to denote a certain kind of writing. But Kinneavy's concept of expressive writing has little in common with Britton's. Following his habit of locating the attributes of writing-reading processes in texts rather than in writers and readers, Kinneavy defines "expressive" as a purpose somehow inherent in the subject matter rather than in the mind of the writer. Kinneavy's definition catches the flavor of his eclectic influences: "expressive discourse is . . . psychologically prior to all other uses of language" because the "expressive component . . . involves a man with the world and his fellows to give him his unique brand of humanity" (396). Here Kinneavy turns sharply away from his familiar theoretical grounding, proposing that the "selfhood" which he says is developed in expressive writing be described in Heideggerian terms. Thus, he describes three categories of "self-identity" developed in expressive writing: "Being-for-oneself," "Being-for-others," and "Being-in-the-world." He then analyzes the Declaration of Independence to show the interplay among these elements of identity, as conceived in terms of national (rather than personal) selfhood. Kinneavy's analysis of expressive writing is considerably more abstract than Britton's, and, unlike Britton's, does not propose specific pedagogical applications.

Britton's analysis of expressive writing reflects a very different influence, the Piagetian concept of cognitive egocentricity which Britton draws upon in developing its teaching implications. Expressive writing is a written-down version of "speaking for oneself," the form of discourse typical of young children who have not learned to use language beyond shared contexts and personal meanings. Britton's discussion of expressive writing focuses on its crucial role in a child's growth. Britton is interested in the psychological context of expressive utterance, the shared meanings upon which it depends, and, in particular, its importance to a child's cognitive development. By means of student protocols, Britton demonstrates the importance of the expressive function in the efforts of young writers and concludes that such writing should be a major part of schoolchildren's language experience.

Kinneavy's work does not offer the range of insights and teaching applications afforded by Britton's system. It is flawed both by its ambiguous theoretical justification and by the inconsistent treatment it gives the different kinds of discourse it purports to discuss. For example, persuasive discourse gets a thorough introduction in his review of traditional and modern rhetorical systems, yet the subsequent analysis of Roosevelt's first inaugural address is framed almost exclusively in Aristotelian terms. It would appear that although Kinneavy analyzes the theoretical force of such twentieth-century analyses as Burke's, he is unable to synthesize Burke with other rhetorical approaches or suggest how useful Burke might be, along with Aristotle, in a genuinely fresh approach to persuasive discourse. Perhaps the least developed portion of A Theory of Discourse is its largest section, attempting to classify various kinds of referential discourse. From the elaborate framework of categories and norms adduced by Kinneavy in preparation for the chapters on major discourse types, the reader is led to expect a thorough analysis of each type of referential discourse and of each example. Such an analysis simply does not appear. And, because his analysis is incomplete, he fails to present a genuine synthesis or new understanding of informative discourse. It is inevitable that any system attempting to build a hierarchy of categories for all writing will overlook some types of writing. But the real disappointment in Kinneavy's study is that, for all the information it amasses, it does not offer the genuinely fresh "theory" of writing its title promises.

Frank D'Angelo's Conceptual Theory of Rhetoric

In A Conceptual Theory of Rhetoric Frank D'Angelo bases his discourse system on his claim that rhetorical forms derive from certain mental processes. His presentation does not support this ambitious claim, however, both because some elements of his theory are inadequately developed and because other elements rely on familiar categories of school-text rhetoric. Despite its theoretical weaknesses, however, D'Angelo's system is worth study because it offers ways of helping students perceive textual structures.

D'Angelo argues that all discourse forms and styles are embodiments of thought patterns: "conceptual patterns in discourse are symbolic manifestations of underlying thought processes," he argues (33). Such processes manifest themselves at the sentence, paragraph, and larger structural levels, as expressions of mind: "similar conceptual structures" are " 'topics' when they serve a heuristic function . . . 'patterns of arrangement' when they are used to organize discourse" and " 'stylistic' when they inform sentences" (35). Implicit here are two related premises: cognitive psychology's focus on mental processes, and transformational grammar's concept of underlying linguistic patterns that "generate" language use. "What are the innate organizing principles, the deeper underlying mental operations, the abstract mental structures that determine discourse?" he asks (26). D'Angelo argues deductively, from the principle of innate conceptual patterns, that "if the same innate structural patterns underlie all languages, then discourse patterns in different languages . . . must be basically alike" (26). And if "common structural features of discourse can be identified, he concludes, then "discourse universals" may be said to exist (26).

D'Angelo begins with the underlying "topics" he believe inhere in every writer's composing. A traditional view of the topics, he maintains, is that they are "content-laden," "pre-fabricated arguments" to be used wherever appropriate in the discourse (38). Actually, he continues, topics are mental processes embedded in cognition itself, possessing a "psychological reality" which allows them to "probe any subject whatever" (38). The scheme he proposes to illustrate his view appears in Figure 6, which contains many forms of discourse traditionally termed "modes," "expository methods," and the like. The hierarchical arrangement of the diagram reveals the generative assumptions of the scheme: each kind of category ("static," "progressive," "repetitive," and "nonlogical") controls a range of topics which embodies the major characteristic of its class. Few discourses are purely one type; most combine two or more of the conceptual patterns represented by the topics. D'Angelo's claim of generative power for his topics rests on his argument that they signify activities of mind. However, many of his categories—especially those in the group labeled "static logical topics"—have customarily described textual patterns rather than cognitive processes. There is a bit of sleight-of-hand in D'Angelo's relabelling textual patterns as mental operations, as though it were a given that completed textual structures could be considered identical with the composing processes that produced them.

However problematic this declared link between process and form may be, D'Angelo does maintain that conceptual strategy becomes the form of the written product—its arrangement. "The concept of arrangement is closely connected to that of invention," says D'Angelo, because "the writer begins with a mental image or plan of the discourse" which "corresponds roughly to the order of the discourse itself," in the same sense in which the Aristotelian efficient cause, "extrinsic to the discourse," corresponds to the formal "intrinsic" cause (56). The abstract topical categories become incarnate as observable patterns of organization; they undergo this reification only because they are identical in conceptual essence. They are "dynamic organizational processes" which manifest themselves as "conventional, static patterns" (57). These patterns appear in any discourse, in various combinations, and they may be clarified by two analytic methods: *syntagmatic analysis* and *paradigmatic analysis*. Each of these strategies represents a way of distilling out the organizational essence of a discourse.

Syntagmatic analysis is sentence-level scrutiny of the logical and grammatical progression of a text. It owes a major debt to the Christensen paragraph model (examined later in this chapter). Syntagmatic analysis, says D'Angelo, "follows the linear order of elements from one sentence to another and from one paragraph to another. Thus, if a discourse consists of five paragraphs, containing a total of 250 [sic] sentences, then the structure of the discourse is described in terms of this order" (60). Syntagmatic analysis depends upon two assumptions crucial to the Christensen method: that paragraphs have a lead or topic sentence, and that logical progression from sentence to sentence is primarily a matter of varying levels of generality. If all paragraphs could be shown to have a topic sentence, D'Angelo's premise would be convincing. But since topic sentences aren't universal in paragraphs, D'Angelo's first premise lacks credence. Variation in generality levels is also difficult to interpret in some types of paragraphs, but frequent enough to give it more credence. D'Angelo uses Christensen's method of numbering sentences according to their generality, with 1 signaling the most general level. Though D'Angelo does not clarify how this procedure may be "generative" for a writer, his illustration offers a useful method of analyzing sentence progression in a written text.

Syntagmatic analysis reveals logical movement in the sentence. Paradigmatic analysis focuses on the structural movement of a text beyond the sentence level: it is the "analysis of a text in which certain sentences or other linguistic elements are extracted from the sequential order and placed in a schematic pattern or paradigm" (60). The paradigms emerging from such analysis have no preconceived categories or labels in D'Angelo's system; each text will yield up its own unique pattern. To demonstrate, D'Angelo analyzes a sequence of paragraphs to illustrate a classification progression:

1. The motives which lead people to seek a college education divide the students into *three types.*
2. The *first type* are *the few* who love learning.

3. The *second type* are *the many* whose motive is preparation for a professional career.

4. The *third type* are *the majority* whose parents are "putting them through college because it is the expected thing to do" (97–98).

Stylistic paradigms constitute the last portion of D'Angelo's system, for "style in the theory of conceptual rhetoric is inseparable from form" (104). To illustrate at length the "relationship that exists between style and structure" (109), D'Angelo analyzes a five-paragraph sequence from Thomas Wolfe, emphasizing repetition, parallelism, and alternation of sentence structures. Wolfe's syntax, says D'Angelo, achieves a rhythm of "alternation and progression" (120) based primarily on the parallel repetitions of noun, prepositional and participial phrases, which amplify the polarities of life and death, permanence and change. After analyzing style within the sentence, D'Angelo focuses on "intersentence relationships." Repetitions of parallel structures link most of the passage's sentences and paragraphs together in a progression of assertions about life and death, permanence and change. "Progressions in sentence and paragraph length" are a "constant feature" of the passage, with the first paragraph the shortest and the last paragraph the longest (129).

D'Angelo then summarizes syntagmatic and paradigmatic schemas of the passage. Syntagmatic analysis emphasizes the repetition in the passages, all the sentences maintaining the same level of generality. On the other hand, paradigmatic analysis emphasizes the duality in the passage. Between the two a tautology develops: "some things will never change," "these things will always be the same." D'Angelo repeats his claim that the patterns discovered in the text are "formal principles of repetition and alternation" which are "deeply rooted in the nature of man and in the world around him. They are universal patterns of experience exemplified in particular works" (145).

D'Angelo's categories of analysis—syntagmatic and paradigmatic—offer a useful framework for analyzing the logical and rhetorical structures of prose. They deserve to be more widely known than they are, as tools both for research into the textual characteristics of rhetoric and logic, and for illustrating these characteristics in the classroom. One or two intensive classroom exercises using his analytic strategies could help students see the structural connectedness that marks good writing.

D'Angelo's categories do not add up to a convincing "conceptual theory." Repeatedly, D'Angelo affirms the universality of his conceptual patterns, yet he is offhand and cryptic in supporting his claims. Of the conceptual topics, for example, he remarks that they lend themselves "to easy memorization" in order that students may "internalize these topics (and the questions which they suggest) so that they can be used for subsequent invention" (47). But he gives no illustration of how this may work for a given purpose or audience. Again, when D'Angelo insists that paradigmatic analysis is designed "not only to reveal the underlying principles that inform discourse, but also to make them generative (in the sense of actually producing discourse)" (86), he does not clarify how paradigms might actually serve a heuristic purpose for student writers.

Indeed, D'Angelo ignores the fact that his "conceptual paradigms" have no life apart from a particular discourse, since they are not so much general patterns as they are generalized paraphrases of particular texts. Thus, students must first master the ability to penetrate prose structure, recognizing the internal patterns there, before they bring D'Angelo's categories into play. D'Angelo's analysis is valuable primarily as a method for helping students organize their own perceptions of prose structure. The "conceptual rhetoric" offers a useful method for classroom analysis of texts; as a theory of mental process it demands more reasoned support than D'Angelo's slim volume permits.

Micro-Rhetorics: The Sentence

The systems discussed above are concerned with the categories and processes of whole texts, and have blended discourse theory with rhetorical insights. Other systems focus on smaller units of written discourse—sentences and paragraphs. Like the categorical systems reviewed above, these micro-rhetorics are text-centered, foregrounding discussions of structural and semantic elements of texts and avoiding discussions of audience and situation. They tend to be psycholinguistic in orientation, justifying the study of syntactical and semantic elements of writing as clues to the mind's processes of making meaning through language.

Francis Christensen's Generative Rhetoric of the Sentence

In the mid-1960s Francis Christensen proposed two "generative rhetorics"— one for sentences and another for paragraphs—which have influenced the development of current micro-rhetorics. Confessing his weariness with the classical basis of sentence models in many texts, Christensen argues that traditional Latinate descriptions of sentence patterns is no longer relevant in English prose. Instead, he suggests, "the typical sentence of modern English, the kind we can best spend our efforts trying to teach, is what we may call the cumulative sentence" (2). Invoking a rather simplistic version of transformational grammar, Christensen posits that the essence of sentence formation is "a process of addition" (2) which adds to a "main clause" modifiers that, depending upon their position with respect to the main clause, may move forward or backward in direction of modification. His own sentence best illustrates this paradigm:

> The main clause, which may or may not have a sentence modifier before it, advances the discussion; but the additions move backward, as in this clause, to modify the statement of the main clause or more often to explicate or exemplify it, so that the sentence has a flowing and ebbing movement, advancing to a new position and then pausing to consolidate it, leaping and lingering as the popular ballad does (2).

He appears to be arguing that the major propositions in a sentence are always expressed in a "main clause," and are extended and particularized by additional clauses and phrases placed before or after the main clause. This proposition is intriguing but weakened by the ambiguity in the term "addition." It is unclear whether Christensen means "main clause" in the sense of noun phrase + verb phrase, the basic propositional form of a sentence in versions of transformational grammar. If by "main clause" he does mean such a "kernel sentence," Christensen does not clarify the relationship between transformational rules and his principles of addition and direction of movement.

Despite its ambiguous linguistic definition, Christensen's system offers a practical model for both sentence analysis and sentence-building. In its three major principles—addition, direction of modification, and level of generality—the Christensen paradigm illuminates the potential flexibility and complexity of the English sentence in a way that permits inexperienced writers to analyze sentences and to generate their own within the formula. It allows students to recognize the major propositions of a sentence, as contained in a definite unit of the sentence—the independent clause. It encourages their recognition of optional structures for modifying and particularizing these propositions. And it requires writers to be aware of different levels of generality and specificity among their sentences. The major objection to Christensen's model, which he anticipates, is that such a model best fits descriptive and narrative aims in writing. The examples he uses reflect this bias:

1 The flame sidled up the match,
2 driving a film of moisture and a thin strip of darker grey before it.
—Faulkner

1 He could sail for hours,
    2 searching the blanched grasses below him with
       his telescopic eyes,
    2 gaining height against the wind,
    2 descending in mile-long, gently declining
       swoops when he curved and rode back
    2 never beating a wing.
—Walter van Tilburg Clark

These sentences, and most of the others he uses as illustrations, exhibit a single independent clause followed or preceded by modifying structures—often participials—which add concreteness to an essentially visual event. The independent clauses are numbered 1, and the modifying phrases (participials, absolutes, prepositionals) are numbered in descending numerical order depending on whether they modify the main clause or one of the subordinate elements of the sentence. Christensen does not deny that the cumulative pattern is most appropriate to narrative-descriptive purposes. Indeed, he defends the pedagogical value of such writing as the best teaching vehicle for student writers who must ultimately write "utilitarian prose": "We can teach diction and sentence structure far more effectively through a few controlled exercises in description and narration than we can by starting right off with exposition" (6).

Sentence Combining

One reason Christensen's system gained influence was that it anticipated the methodology of sentence combining. Though its 1970s popularity has waned considerably, this strategy for manipulating sentence elements is still worth our attention because within limits it remains a useful pedagogical tool, and because its now declining popularity is another instructive instance of the continuing shift in composition's underlying paradigms.

Sentence combining originated as a pedagogical outcome of transformational grammar's early influence; it arose from a conception of the sentence which appeared directly appropriate to the classroom application of this new linguistic theory. The key was the idea of the "kernel sentence" and its transformations—the core of early transformational theory. According to this theory, all sentences begin as simple declarations or affirmations that are "kernels" comprising the "deep structure" of a sentence—its underlying structure. By means of various transformations creating negatives, questions, passives, and relatives, these simple kernels are bundled together to form more complex "surface structures" whose efficiency is measured by the information packed within the embedded structures.

This description of syntactic complexity attracted teachers looking for ways to improve on the conventional, static categories of traditional grammar. If it could be claimed that the most "mature" sentences were those containing the largest number of transformations, then a pedagogy could be devised based on exercises intended to improve the writer's "transformational" ability, as measured on a quantified basis.

Such a promise proved seductive to researchers interested in composition pedagogy. The concept of the kernel sentence offered an attractive foundation for a sequence of sentence-building tasks characterized by repetition and variation. From its beginnings, however, transformational grammar theory altered its theoretical premises frequently as descriptions of "deep" and "surface" structures changed. For example, new theories about "deep structure" operations gave rise to more complex versions of transformations generating surface structures. So-called "generalized transformations" (involving more than one clause or "sentence string") were postulated to explain "embedding"—the production of adjective, appositive, possessive, relative, and absolute sentence structures.

These generalized transformations became the basis of sentence combining at the height of its popularity. The concept of embedding gave rise to the idea of "syntactic maturity," a measure of sentence skill based on the observable increase in sentence length and number of embedded structures over time. A new pedagogy of style emerged, featuring the conversion of choppy, unmodified base clauses into complex, embedded structures, by means of exercises in generalized transformations.

Another important influence on teaching methods carried over from early transformational grammar is Kellogg Hunt's proposal for the "T-unit" (or terminable unit) as the best gauge of progressive age-level differences in writing. He has defined a T-unit as an independent clause plus all its subordinate structures; he argues that syntactic maturity is a condition best indicated by T-unit differentials. Influenced by Hunt's work and using his T-unit as the primary measure, John Mellon later proposed that "growth of syntactic fluency can result only from increased use of sentence-embedding transformations." Thus, "embedding transforms, together with measures of depth of embedding, cluster size, and unique nominal patterns, constitute the appropriate criteria for describing . . . syntactic fluency" (20) and comprise the basis for a pedagogy of sentence-making. His program of sentence combining, and those of other researchers extending his early proposals, targeted embedding transformations as the core of transformational pedagogy.

In the 1970s and early 1980s many texts relied on sentence combining as a method for helping students write more complex and fluent sentences. One text (Daiker et al.) featured a series of combining exercises that taught generalized transformations first by introducing the syntactic forms they take (relative clauses, participles, appositives, absolutes, prepositional phrases), then by introducing combining strategies ("rearrangement," "repetition," "emphasis"). The text's authors attempt to minimize the piece-work quality of sentence combining by developing a series of "kernels" which, when combined into individual sentences, may then be structured into a unified paragraph or multi-paragraph discourse. The "strategies" emphasized in this text focused on organizational and structural rather than merely grammatical skills. Students were urged to learn strategies of repetition, emphasis, and coherence that contribute to the rhetorical power of writing. Long, often multi-paragraph passages of kernel strings and of pre-combined sentences were featured, the former requiring lengthy combining activity at various discourse levels, the latter requiring analysis and recombination for additional effectiveness.

Another sentence-combining text embodied a different approach: it de-emphasized syntactic categories, taking students instead through programmed exercises in embedding modifiers and in adding coordinating and subordinating structures to kernel sentences (Strong). This text assumed that requiring students to learn units of syntax is counterproductive and unnecessary at the outset of sentence-combining work. Rather, students were asked to combine sentences in response to general coordinating and subordinating signals, so that they could gain confidence in their basic sentence competence. Only in the second portion of the text were syntactical units named as targets for combining activity; in the later portion also, longer kernel strings and multi-paragraph exercises were introduced, on the principle that students cannot build longer units of discourse until they develop skills and confidence at the single-sentence and single-paragraph level.

Sentence combining flourished because empirical studies showed that under its regimen students could indeed learn to write more complex sentences. Seldom has a specific kind of writing drill been so intensively measured by quantitative methods, most of which indicated that it does produce measurable gains in sentence complexity at all age levels. One group of researchers reported that students doing sentence combining in a one-semester course made greater gains than students not doing it, both in measures of syntactic maturity and in overall quality as evaluated holistically (Combs). Other research tended to show that while gains produced by sentence combining were real enough, improvement in sentence construction ceased as soon as students stopped combining drills (Jones). At its best, sentence combining offers a sentence-building activity requiring some creativity, rather than the sentence-repairing drills so ingrained in the handbook tradition discussed in Chapter One.

The premise that writers and readers can learn by starting with small units of text—for example, sentences or "kernels"—and from them build larger units is open to question, however, in view of the process theories of composing discussed in Chapter Two. Cognitive-process models define reading and writing as holistic and context-dependent, driven by writers' and readers' expectations and goals as they compose and represent texts. In this view neither writers nor readers form sentences by starting with small parts and building bigger parts out of them, like bricklayers building walls; instead, the processes of writing and reading are seen as large-scale cognitive operations that embed smaller or "local" units of meaning in larger or "global" meanings as the text is developed. Teaching strategies emphasizing small-unit exercises run counter to current cognitive-process theory, which paints a complex picture of composing strategies that move back and forth between the whole and the part. Teachers therefore need to be cautious about the potential for reductiveness when asking students to combine sentences as a way of improving writing skills.

Though some writing texts and teachers continue to use sentence combining as a remedial strategy, it is not a panacea for inexperienced writers. Making sentences from given parts does not require inventive thinking, does not help students learn focus and organization, does not help them control voice and tone, and does not sharpen editing for mechanics and usage. Sentence combining is like making model airplanes out of labeled parts; genuine inventiveness has no part in it. A sentence-combining problem may, for example, illustrate how relative clauses may be shortened to modifiers. But here, as in the most complex combinations, the sentence structures available to students will be limited to those allowed by the design of the task itself. Given the openness of composing itself, combining prefabricated sentence parts will be useful only for student writers who specifically need such exercise.

Micro-Rhetorics: The Paragraph

Studies of paragraph structure carry the same advantages and disadvantages as sentence-level analyses for writing teachers. They offer ways of discussing the patterns of written texts, presenting patterns and terminology that can help students talk about paragraphs and the ways their logical structures may be strengthened. The first three proposals which follow, all published in the 1960s, are as text-centered as the categorical systems considered earlier. These paragraph rhetorics also suffer from another serious weakness, in the perspective of more recent composition theory. That is, they tend to be "arhetorical," lacking full rhetorical context and focusing on the features of one paragraph at a time—when every paragraph is actually part of the larger structure of its text. That is, paragraphs have relationships to other paragraphs in the text, just as every sentence must be seen in its relationship to other sentences in the text. The danger of paragraph rhetorics is their tendency to encourage students to look at one piece of the text as though it had a life separate from that of the whole. Teachers should keep this persistent danger in mind as they consider ways of using these patterns in the classroom.

Francis Christensen's Generative Rhetoric of the Paragraph

Francis Christensen expresses a distaste for textbook models of the paragraph that parallels his distaste for text models of the sentence. Citing the bewildering variety of paragraph principles found in writing texts, Christensen proposes a model based on the same "generative" principles contained in his sentence rhetoric: addition, direction of movement, level of generality, and texture. The first sentence is "nearly always" the topic sentence, he argues; when it is, it begins the logical movement of the paragraph, as "the sentence whose assertion is supported or whose meaning is explicated or whose parts are detailed by the sentences added to it" (22). Though he doesn't say so directly, he appears to define the topic sentence as the most general sentence in the paragraph. Two types of sequences are related to the topic sentence, he says: coordinate and subordinate. In a coordinate sequence the topic sentence is developed by other sentences using repetition and parallel structures. In a subordinate sequence the topic sentence is developed by other sentences at various levels of generality, using a variety of structures.

Seldom, however, do coordinate or subordinate sequences occur in pure form in paragraphs; the mixed form, says Christensen, is the most common, with a blend of coordinate and subordinate sentences. As in his sentence rhetoric, Christensen here illustrates the working of his paradigms by breaking each paragraph into its constituent sentences, numbered and placed by means of their relation both to the topic sentence and to the immediately preceding sentence. Christensen offers the following examples of coordinate and subordinate sequences:

Coordinate Sequence

1 He [the native speaker] may, of course, speak a form of English that
  marks him as coming from a rural or an unread group.
  2 But if he doesn't mind being so marked, there's no reason why
    he should change.
    3 Samuel Johnson kept a Staffordshire burr in his speech all
      his life.
    3 In Burns's mouth the despised lowland Scots dialect served
      just as well as the "correct" English spoken by ten million of
      his southern contemporaries.
    3 Lincoln's vocabulary and his way of pronouncing certain
      words were sneered at by many better educated people at the
      time, but he seemed to be able to use the English language as
      effectively as his critics.
          (Bergen Evans, *Comfortable Words,* in Christensen, 24)

Subordinate Sequence

1 The process of learning is essential to our lives.
  2 All higher animals seek it deliberately.
    3 They are inquisitive and they experiment.
      4 An experiment is a sort of harmless trial run of some action
        which we shall have to make in the real world; and this,
        whether it is made in the laboratory by scientists or by
        fox-cubs outside their earth.
        5 The scientist experiments and the cub plays; both are
          learning to correct their errors of judgment in a setting in
          which errors are not fatal.
          6 Perhaps this is what gives them both their air of
            happiness and freedom in these activities.
    (J. Bronowski, *The Common Sense of Science,* In Christensen, 23)

The mixed sequence is by far the most common paragraph
arrangement, says Christensen, citing a wide range of examples with
varying coordinate and subordinate patterns indicated by progressive and regressive numbering. The analytical power of the mixed-
sequence model may be measured by applying it to an expository
paragraph—for example, to the first paragraph beneath the heading
above, "Francis Christensen's Generative Rhetoric of the Paragraph":

Mixed Sequence

1 Francis Christensen expressed a distaste for textbook models of
  the paragraph that parallels his distaste for text models of the
  sentence.

2 Citing the bewildering variety of paragraph principles found in
   writing texts, Christensen proposes a model based on the same
   "generative" principles contained in this sentence rhetoric:
   addition, direction of movement, level of generality, and
   texture.
   3 The first sentence is "nearly always" the topic sentence, he
      argues; when it is, it begins the logical movement of the
      paragraph, as "the sentence whose assertion is supported or
      whose meaning is explicated or whose parts are detailed by
      the sentences added to it."
      4 Though he doesn't say so directly, he appears to define the
         topic sentence as the most general sentence in the
         paragraph.
   3 Two types of sequences are related to the topic sentence, he
      says: coordinate and subordinate.
      4 In a coordinate sequence the topic sentence is developed
         by other sentences using repetition and parallel structures.
      4 In a subordinate sequence the topic sentence is developed
         by other sentences at various levels of generality, using a
         variety of structures.

The first sentence is certainly the leading sentence here, the most
general sentence of the paragraph and the indicator of its drift. But
it's not really the topic sentence; the second sentence actually
announces the topic of the paragraph (the Christensen paragraph
model) and is therefore more specific in its content than the first
sentence. The third sentence is more specific yet (thus is numbered
at the "3" level) because it begins a description of the principles
named in sentence two. And sentence four is even more specific
because it defines one of its terms ("topic sentence") more thoroughly. Sentence five returns to level 3 generality because it further
defines the principles named in sentence two. It is less general than
the fourth sentence, but more general than the last two sentences,
which return to the "4" level because each further defines one of the
terms in sentence five.

It appears that the structure of this paragraph fits generally into
the pattern identified in Christensen's paradigm. However, Christensen's system does not appear to offer a way of describing what the
lead sentence actually does in this paragraph. The problem lies in
Christensen's ambiguous handling of the concept of the topic sentence itself. In the introduction to his system he asserts that the "top
sentence" in the paragraph—i.e., the most general sentence—is
"nearly always the first sentence of the sequence" (22), a generalization that would appear to allow very few exceptions. Yet later he cites

several examples of paragraphs with no topic sentence, or with sentences as general as the topic sentence, but unrelated to what appears to be the paragraph's main focus. Though Christensen suggests that many such "false" topic sentences probably tie into the discourse at a level beyond the paragraph, his system functions best as a descriptor of structure at the single-paragraph level.

A. L. Becker's Tagmemic Paragraph Analysis

Another set of paragraph models has been proposed by A. L. Becker, one of the original proponents of the tagmemic grammar that generated the invention strategy discussed in Chapter One. To adduce the tagmemic model, Becker surveyed many student paragraphs, rather than quoting from professional writers as Christensen did. As a way of "partitioning discourse," says Becker, tagmemic analysis generates "grammatical markers of paragraph slots" that are "nearly identical for all types of paragraphs" (34). Becker agrees with Christensen that levels of generality are crucial in paragraph structure. But various "lexical" (word-related) elements are needed, he continues, to account for the ways in which levels of generality are made "explicit" in paragraphs (34). Thus, the tagmemic model of expository paragraph structure offers two kinds of "slot arrangements" which represent varying levels of generality, and two major categories of lexical (word and phrase) indicators of these levels of generality. One expository model relies on the TRI pattern "in the T [topic] slot the topic is stated, in the R [restriction] slot the topic is narrowed down or defined, and in the I [illustration] slot the topic, as restricted in R, is illustrated or described at lower level [sic] of generality" (34).

These slots can be filled in various ways. The T slot "can be filled by a simple proposition, or a proposition implying a contrast, comparison, partition, etc." (35), while the I slot can contain examples, analogies, or comparisons. The slot order may be reversed, so that an IRT pattern controls the paragraph in a specific-to-general sequence. Lexical markers of paragraph structure fall into two categories, what Becker calls "equivalence classes," and transitional markers. Equivalence markers are parallel words and phrases, linking pronoun references, synonymous words and phrases, and other lexical devices for echoing and repeating key terms. Transitional words are conjunctions, conjunctive adverbs, and phrases that imply logical movement (for example, in other words). Other elements of paragraph structure—indentation, verb sequences, and phonological (oral) markers—are mentioned by Becker, but given little emphasis.

Thus, the structure of a given paragraph may be delineated primarily in terms of grammatical slots and lexical markers, according to the tagmemic system. The usefulness of this model can be briefly illustrated by applying it to the same paragraph used to test the Christensen model, the first paragraph under the heading "Francis Christensen's Generative Rhetoric of the Paragraph" above:

(T) Francis Christensen expresses a distaste for textbook models of the paragraph that parallels his distaste for text models of the sentence. (R1) Citing the bewildering variety of paragraph principles found in writing texts, Christensen proposes a model based on the same "generative" principles contained in his sentence rhetoric addition, direction of movement, level of generality, and texture. (I) The first sentence is "nearly always" the topic sentence, he argues; when it is, it begins the logical movement of the paragraph, as "the sentence whose assertion is supported or whose meaning is explicated or whose parts are detailed by the sentences added to it." (I) Though he doesn't say so directly, he appears to define the topic sentence as the most general sentence in the paragraph (R2) Two types of sequence are related to the topic sentence, he says: coordinate and subordinate. (I) In a coordinate sequence the topic sentence is developed by other sentences using repetition and parallel structures. (I) In a subordinate sequence the topic sentence is developed by other sentences at various levels of generality, using a variety of structures.

The tagmemic interpretation of this paragraph may be read in the following way. The T sentence indicates Christensen's readiness to offer an alternative to textbook paragraph models. R1 narrows the disapproval into a specific proposal. The following two "I" sentences amplify elements of R1, including "direction of movement" and "level of generality." R2 is another restriction of the "T" sentence, at approximately the same level of generalization as R1, introducing the term "sequence" as a way of summarizing the four principles in R1 and giving a heading for specific structural types. The final "I" sentences illustrate types of sequence. Certain lexical markers also figure in the paragraph's structure. The terms "paragraph" and "principles" link the first two sentences, "topic sentence" the middle two, and "sequence" the last three. The initial parallelism in the last two sentences emphasizes the equivalent generality of each sequence named. Transitional devices include repetition of Christensen's point of view in rejecting outworn paragraph models and proposing his own in their place: "Christensen expresses a distaste," "Christensen proposes," "he argues," "he says."

Becker identifies the other expository paragraph arrangement as P-S or Problem-Solution: "the P slot, often in question form, is the statement of a problem or an effect which is to be explained, and the S slot states the solution or cause of P. If it is extended the S slot very often has an internal structure of TRI (an example of embedding at the paragraph level)" (35). Interestingly, a quick look at the Christensen paragraph above reveals what could be termed a Problem-Solution pattern. The utility of textbook paragraph models, called into question by Christensen, is the "problem," and the "solution" is the proposal of "generative principles" that govern all paragraph structure. The "solution" portion of the paragraph is further sub-divided in terms of a restriction-and-illustration pattern which amplifies the nature of the "solution." It seems clear from this exam-ple and from the single example of the P-S pattern offered by Becker that the P-S pattern repeats the basic format of the TRI pattern. The "problem" which heads a P-S pattern will inevitably be followed by a listing or an analysis of the items involved in a "solution", in the presentation of which varying levels of generality in the R-and-I pattern will normally occur. Without more examples from Becker, it is hard to know whether he wishes to present the P-S model as a true paradigmatic alternative to the TRI model, or as a kind of shadow of TRI. The present analysis indicates that the TRI pattern is more universal in its applicability, because it accounts for a more complex interrelation of generality and logic.

Paul Rodgers' Rhetoric of the Paragraph

A third paragraph model is termed by Paul Rodgers a "discourse-centered rhetoric of the paragraph." Citing Christensen's reluctance to claim descriptive universality for his model, Rodgers argues that "piecemeal inductive observations" have failed to generate a set of descriptors sufficiently broad and complex to account for all para-graphs. What's needed, says Rodgers, is "a concept of the para-graph that will comprehend all paragraphs," "a flexible, open-ended discourse-centered rhetoric of the paragraph" (41). Rodgers offers a set of paragraph descriptors that, he implies, suggests better than less complex systems the actual conditions governing paragraph choices. Christensen's model is rejected because in Rodgers' view it omits crucial elements in striving for generative simplicity. Rodgers argues, for example, that neither inductive nor deductive patterns actually account for most paragraph divisions. "Both types of movement exist at all levels of discourse, in units smaller than the sentence and larger than the paragraph," he points out, and while "indentation fre-quently does mark" breaks in levels of generality, "other consider-ations" often take precedence over logical movements (42). Indeed, he says, "logical, physical, rhythmical, tonal, formal, and other rhetorical criteria, set off from adjacent patterns by indentations," (43) all may govern what he calls "stadia" or various patterns that take paragraph form. "A tight deductive formula" can never account for these complex factors; only an "inductive study of the art of paragraphing" can begin to define the diversity of paragraph elements (43).

Rodgers does not wish to propose a universal model for the paragraph; he thinks paragraphs are too diverse to justify such a proposal. Instead he summarizes elements he has noticed in the paragraphing practice of some skilled writers. He chooses a sequence of paragraphs from Walter Pater's highly mannered essay "Style" to illustrate how a complex interplay of factors affect a skilled writer's paragraph choices. In Pater's essay Rodgers finds characteristics which would defy "a strict traditional paragraph analysis" (45). Some groups of separately indented paragraphs could be condensed into larger textual units, for they form "a single synthetic logical stadium broken into [separate] paragraphs . . . for physical or editorial reasons" (45), not for any reason related to internal structure.

Traditional paragraph analysis, Rodgers reiterates, would find Pater's strategy baffling. By means of this analysis, and through analyses of other unusual paragraph strategies elsewhere in Pater's essay, Rodgers demonstrates that often in Pater's writing "other legitimate criteria have overridden the tug of logic" (47). That is, Pater's paragraphs are not always—or even usually—informed by a specific rhetorical or logical pattern identifiable as a paradigm. Rather, his reasons for indenting to make paragraphs are unpredictable and responsive to local contexts. Rodgers does not defend all of Pater's choices for paragraphing, nor is he able to show convincing reasons why some of them are made. But Rodgers succeeds in demonstrating how diverse the bases of paragraph choice may be for a skillful writer. By implication, he suggests that attempts to formulate "generative" paragraph models must account for more than levels of generality, logical movement, and syntactical structure. Rodgers' analysis of Pater's style demonstrates how extraordinarily subtle and various is Pater's strategy, which takes into account not only logical development and coherence but also many other factors: reader expectation, paragraph size and readability, rhythm within and across the "stadia," parallelisms and juxtapositions within the stadia, and, Rodgers concludes, "tonal fluctuation" and "Pater's unusual penchant for underplaying important ideas grammatically while stressing them rhetorically" (48). The art of paragraphing emerges from Rodgers' analysis as an intuitive process of choice among a range of possibilities far too diverse for any single paradigam to explain.

Compared with Rodgers' proposals, those of Christensen and Becker have a seductive simplicity about them. Christensen, for example, never clearly explains why he chooses levels of generality as the crucial variable in his generative model. He says only that "the structural relations I have disclosed are real (they were discovered by induction)" (32), without explaining how they were induced and how the controversy concerning the topic sentence was confronted as he devised his model. His range of examples suggests that he perused the published work of contemporary professional writers for paragraphs to illustrate his paradigm, criticizing a few which deviate too far from his principles as illogical or erroneously punctuated (30). Rodgers, on the other hand, argues that the "inductive study of the art of paragraphing has an immense neglected potential" (43) which, he appears to suggest, may lead to "a concept of the paragraph that will comprehend all paragraphs" (41). Thus he usefully subverts the models of Christensen and Becker, to the extent that these models are based on simplifying assumptions about paragraph constituents. After reading Rodgers, it is difficult to believe that other models have sufficiently taken into account the complexities of paragraphing.

Wisely—and unlike Christensen—Becker and Rodgers claim only analytical value for their models; they draw few pedagogical conclusions from their analyses. Paragraphs are responses not only to cues within a certain group of sentences, but to signals from every-where in the discourse of which they are a part; the significance of a paragraph draws from the whole of which it is (or ought to be) an integral unit. Sentence form is governed by a grammar. But there is no "grammar" of the paragraph, for paragraphs emerge from a diverse and somewhat arbitrary set of customs perceived differently by different writers. Requiring students to generate paragraphs in response only to a given internal structure oversimplifies the number and diversity of clues writers actually take into account in forming paragraphs. Writing teachers should be wary of single-paragraph exercises, therefore, because such exercises suffer even more than sentence combining from the same disadvantage: a lack of rhetorical context. While lack of context does not necessarily strip sentence combining of its limited value, paragraph choices mean virtually nothing unless they emerge from a whole discourse context. Students may be asked to compose a single paragraph on some topic, but what emerges is not a paragraph but a mini-discourse.

Another, quite different discussion of paragraph theory reflects recent cognitive and constructive perspectives by presenting a "reader-oriented theory of the paragraph" with clear pedagogical applications (Eden and Mitchell 416). "Text-centered approaches," argue these researchers, "abbreviate the writing process; they treat the text rather than the reader as its endpoint" (420). Instead of thinking of paragraphs as ways of organizing sentences into formal patterns, they maintain, we should think of them as "signaling systems" which "depend for their effectiveness on the exploitation of ... the reader's conventional expectations and perceptual patterns" (416–7). These expectations cannot be packaged in formal patterns like Christensen's; though they can be stated generally, they can be enacted only in specific writing contexts which will not yield to textbook patterns of "coordination-subordination" or "topic-restriction." The authors argue that paragraphs are not merely visual patterns, however; they are also text-structures with implicit cognitive elements. Readers expect paragraphs to be logically coherent and unified because their visual presentation implies such qualities; readers also anticipate receiving cues about the paragraph's focus and its relationship to other units of the text.

That is, readers expect their experience of a text to be shaped in part by its paragraphing. And because paragraphs are part of reading behavior, say these researchers, teachers ought to help students learn to use paragraphing as they compose. Students should be encouraged to use paragraphs flexibly, shaping and reshaping them in response to the changing configurations of texts. Students should be encouraged to study and imitate the paragraphing of experienced, published writers. And they should "not be taught that the paragraph is a self-contained rhetorical form," but that it stands in relation to other units of writing (429).

Paragraphs have genuine life only as units within a discourse. And the integrity of a paragraph within a discourse is more likely to appear in revision than in other composing stages, for many of the clues that generate paragraphs are available to the writer only in a draft of the whole piece. Like sentence combining, paragraphing as an isolated exercise forces contextless composing upon students. Teachers should require single-paragraph exercises (such as can be found in many texts) only from inexperienced writers, and only as a means of introducing the nature of paragraphs themselves to students. Such exercises should never replace longer writing tasks and should be used only to make students aware of the basic fact that paragraphs are discourse units. Students can only learn to shape effective paragraphs by composing them within contexts that give them significance.

Works Cited

Becker, A. L. "A Tagmemic Approach to Paragraph Analysis." *College Composition and Communication* 16 (1965): 144–56.

Britton, James, et al. *The Development of Writing Abilities* (11–18). Schools Council Research Studies. London: Macmillan Education, 1975.

Burke, Kenneth. *The Philosophy of Literary Form*. 1941. New York: Vintage, 1957.

———. *A Grammar of Motives*. New York: Prentice-Hall, 1945.

Christensen, Francis. "A Generative Rhetoric of the Sentence." CCC 14 (1963): 155–61.

———. "A Generative Rhetoric of the Paragraph." CCC 16 (1965): 144–56.

Combs, Warren G. "Sentence-Combining Practice: Do Gains in Judgment of Writing 'Quality' Persist?". *Journal of Educational Research*, 70 (1977): 318–21.

Daiker, Donald, Andrew Kerek, Max Morenberg. *The Writer's Options*. New York: Harper and Row, 1979.

D'Angelo, Frank. *A Conceptual Theory of Rhetoric*. Cambridge, MA: Winthrop, 1975.

Eden, Rick and Ruth Mitchell. "Paragraphing for the Reader." CCC 37 1986): 416–30, 441.

Holland, Virginia. *Counterpoint*. New York: The Philosophical Library, 1959.

Hunt, Kellogg. "A Synopsis of Clause-to-Sentence Length Factors." *English Journal* 54 (1965): 300–09.

Jones, Mary Ann. "Sentence Combining in Freshman English: Measuring the Rate of Syntactic Growth." Conference on College Composition and Communication, Dallas, TX, 1981.

Kinneavy, James. *A Theory of Discourse: The Aims of Discourse*. Englewood Cliffs, NJ: Prentice-Hall, 1971.

Knoblauch, C. H. and Lil Brannon. *Rhetorical Traditions and the Teaching of Writing*. Portsmouth, NH: Boynton/Cook, 1984.

Mellon, John. *Transformational Sentence-Combining*. Urbana, IL: NCTE, 1969.

Milic, Louis T. "Theories of Style and Their Implication for the Teaching of Composition." CCC 16 (1965): 66–-9, 126.

Moffett, James. *Teaching the Universe of Discourse*. Boston: Houghton Mifflin, 1968.

———. *Student-Centered Language Arts, K-12*. 2nd ed. Boston: Houghton Mifflin, 1976.

Odell, Lee. "Defining and Assessing Competence in Writing." *The Nature and Measurement of Competency in English*. Ed. Charles R. Cooper. Urbana, IL: NCTE, 1981. 95–138.

Rodgers, Paul. "A Discourse-Centered Rhetoric of the Paragraph." CCC 17 (1966): 2–11.

Strong, William A. *Sentence Combining and Paragraph Building*. Teachers' Edition. New York: Random House, 1981.

Chapter Four

Pressure Points
Literacy, Writing Testing, Basic Writing

Scene: Early in the fall semester, two English instructors are sitting in the departmental lounge furnished with castoff chairs and sofas. Between bites of tuna salad and bologna sandwiches they drift into a discussion of their respective sections of freshman composition:

Bill: Good grief, my eleven o'clock section is really bad. I mean, you know, there's hardly one of them that can write a complete sentence. I gave them an impromptu on "My First Day at College" and one of them wrote, "That is really an interesting topic. I want to take it home and maul it over in my mind." The rest of them wrote things like "Once fully assembled, the orientation director introduced himself to us," or, "I was forwarded from his class to another freshman English class." I'm gonna get lots of laughs from this bunch, if nothing else.

Jane: Well, they probably got a laugh from that dumb topic you assigned them, too. I'll have to admit mine wasn't a lot better, though: you know, "Describe Something You Learned Recently." Isn't that terrific? One kid wrote a theme around the topic "What Goes Around Comes Around"; another one talked about "human sufferage" and political debates that are "seeping us back into dark ignorance." One said that TV was a lot of "fantastic grabble" and another said he was tired of reading so much "satirism" where people were "casting dispersions" on one another.

Bill: I'm telling you, students these days are really bad. Some of the kids in my class didn't write more than ten minutes before they just quit and left. When I was in college I would've been embarrassed not to do my best. The other kids in my classes at least tried too. We didn't dare not try, you know, we felt as though we were lucky to be in college and we knew the professors wouldn't take any garbage from us.

Jane: Yeah, right, I remember in my class the instructor was a TA who really had high standards. He would take up students' papers and then read the worst ones aloud, with all the misspellings and everything, so the kid who wrote it would just cringe with embarrassment. I mean nobody dared hand in a paper that wasn't absolutely perfect. You'd see some of the kids the night before really working on their papers, really sweating them, not just handing in some sloppy first draft like the kids today do. You know what would happen in my classes now if I read some of the bad papers aloud? The kids would just laugh, you know, just get a kick out of hearing other people's dumb mistakes and their own. They wouldn't care. I asked one girl why her first out-of-class paper was worse than her first impromptu, and she said she didn't really have time to work on it; she had to go through sorority rush and she was really busy. Can you believe that?

Bill: You'd think they'd do better work now that they do most of their writing on computers. That's what the computer company said would happen if we bought their computers and made students use them. They said students would get turned on to writing once they discovered they could interact directly with instructors on the computer—said students would feel "empowered" and would "get control of the writing process" once they learned how easy revision is on the screen.

Jane: Yeah, I remember. But all I hear students complaining about now are how they couldn't get the margins right or how the monitors closed the computer lab and they couldn't finish or how their files crashed and they lost everything. Students used to show me papers they said the dog chewed; now they hand in stuff that looks the same, except that they say the printer chewed it instead.

Bill: Don't they have any pride any more? It must be the way kids are raised these days, or the way they're just passed through school without having to do any work. When I was in high school I really had to work hard; my English teacher was a demon. He'd tell my parents if he thought I wasn't doing enough work. Schoolteachers these days really coddle the kids, and their parents don't care either. Just want the kid to come to school, get a degree, and get a good job. They think they pay good money, why shouldn't their kid do well?

Jane: Right. Something has happened to students these days. They just aren't like we were in school. Maybe I should go to work for the government; you know, a day's work, a day's pay, who notices?

Maybe Bill and Jane were tired of tuna and bologna, or had stayed up too late the night before, reading student papers. Or perhaps they were simply articulating an academic deteriorationism, the usual counterpoint to a more optimistic faith in individual potential and human progress. Should our instructors' plaints be viewed in the long perspective of cultural change, or even in the short view of a day's dyspepsia?

Are there any visible evidences to justify the unhappiness of our brownbag philosophers? This much, certainly, can be said: *something* has changed in American education; things are not as they were in school when our teachers were there, and the students they confront in college classes now are not the same kinds of students *their* teachers confronted in earlier generations. The evidence for this may be found, for example, in statistical comparisons between the number and kind of college students in earlier decades and in recent years. These comparisons reveal important differences in enrollment sizes and the socioeconomic and racial makeup of student populations.

Literacy, Social Change and Testing

The most visible change in postsecondary education in recent decades is the vast increase in numbers of students finishing high school and going on to college. Since the early 1960s many academic communities have grown into cities, with dormitories rising on every available acre of ground. The construction boom in academic housing during the 1960s and 1970s resembled the frantic building of barracks during the mobilization years of World War II. The numbers show why such haste was necessary: for example, of every one thousand students who entered fifth grade in 1942, only half graduated from high school and only one-fifth went on to college; of one thousand fifth-graders in 1956, two-thirds graduated from high school and one-third went on to college. By 1966 the increase was astounding: of one thousand fifth-graders, three-fourths graduated from high school and almost half went on to college (U.S. Department of Education 14). By the mid-1980s there were more than twice as many students going to college as there were in 1950. Most of this increase has been absorbed by public institutions. Major state universities multiplied and divided into many smaller satellite institutions, some limited to accepting undergraduates not acceptable to parent institutions. It has been at these newer four-year universities and the two-year community colleges that the issue of literacy and its pressure upon writing instruction has been most acute. That's because, in addition to the leap in enrollments in higher education, significant changes have occurred in the composition of student populations.

Census Bureau statistics suggest the alteration in racial makeup of the college-going population. In 1950, of all white students aged 25 to 29 in the United States, only 8 per cent had completed four or more years of college; by 1975, 23 per cent had completed four college years. Contrast this increase with that shown by African-American and Hispanic students: in 1950 only 2.8 per cent had four or more college years, but by 1975, 15 per cent had completed college (Department of Education 1975: 14). While the number of white students finishing college increased three times during that twenty-five year period, the number of African-American and Hispanic students finishing college increased five times. Since 1975, however, such increases have virtually ceased; by 1988 the percentage of minority students completing four years of college stood at 16% (Department of Education 1989: 16).

The proportions of minority students in college also made significant gains in the 1960s and 1970s. Of all students enrolled in postsecondary institutions in 1965, for example, about 5 per cent were African-American students; by 1975 this percentage had doubled to 10 per cent. By the late 1970s, however, these gains leveled off. The proportion of African-American students in postsecondary institutions in 1985 was still about 10 per cent, and the total proportion of African-American and Hispanic students in the general student population—about 15 per cent—was roughly the same in 1987 as it was in 1977 (Department of Education 1989: 197). Nor have minority students been represented equally in the various student populations in the United States. The relatively few black academic institutions offer attractive opportunities for some African-American students. But the urban public universities, some operating on an open-admissions basis, have absorbed the great part of minority students, who in earlier decades might not have considered going to college. The language problems associated with these students' academic efforts have posed several unprecedented challenges to composition teachers untrained in the needs of their universities' new constituencies.

These challenges are all related to the central problem of literacy. First, teachers in schools with large African-American and Hispanic enrollments ask what constitutes literacy: are students competent in a minority dialect—but not in standard English—literate? Second, the widespread use of standardized tests to evaluate language skills raises the question of how literacy may be measured fairly: are such tests a true measure of students' language ability? Third, the increasing numbers of educationally disadvantaged students in schools and colleges have forced teachers and their institutions to develop, quickly and often without adequate instructor training, crash programs in rudimentary literacy instruction. Finally, the introduction of computer technology into the writing classroom and, in many institutions, directly into students' daily academic lives is said by its advocates to offer new possibilities for increasing students' writing abilities. Each of these challenges will be considered separately later in this chapter; first, however, we need to review the relationship between them, with respect to the underlying question, what constitutes literacy in an academic setting?

In America literacy is conventionally viewed as the ability to read and write standard English. And standard English is normally defined as the language of the "educated middle class," that heard in classrooms, public offices, and on radio and television (Wolfram and Fasold 21). Conversely, illiteracy is often defined as the inability to use language appropriate to such settings, or as the inability to make a "competent" score on language aptitude tests or armed forces entry tests. This customary linkage between literacy and standard English has been sharply challenged in recent years. Sociolinguists have argued that defining illiteracy as the inability to read or write standard English is too simplistic for the complex realities of language function. Their arguments center on the social nature of literacy and the "deficit-difference" distinction about language use.

Becoming literate, they say, is not only—for many children not even primarily—a matter of curling up by themselves with a book or a writing pad. It is the outgrowth of a child's total social experience with language: literacy "is a *social* achievement," says researcher Sylvia Scribner, "acquired by individuals only in the course of participation in socially organized activities with written language" (72). For most middle-class children, home and school language experiences reinforce each other; children read and are read to by parents and carry those experiences into their schooling, which extends the activities and values of home language use. For them, reading and writing standard English are behaviors fully reinforced by family and community.

But for countless children, no such integration of home and school exists. For such children, values represented in school experiences conflict with the realities of daily life. Problems arising from the clash between school expectations and the constrictions of poverty are correlated with income, but compounded by race: "Black mistrust and conflict with schools reduce the degree to which black parents and their children can accept ... the schools' goals, standards and instructional approaches," says anthropologist John Ogbu (238). Shirley Brice Heath records a similar dissonance between the aims and methods of schools and the language usages of a rural minority community. For children in these communities, words are not fixed in standard meanings or usages, but are constantly changing as they interact with family groups: "they achieve their meaning as communicators ... through the responses they obtain to their oral language, not in terms of responses in a one-to-one situation of reading a book with an adult" (366). Deborah Brandt argues that because children learn to read and write not in isolation but within family and community contexts, literacy is not a matter of the individual's internalized mastery of pencil and book. Rather, "writers and readers in action are deeply embedded in an immediate working context" and their language activity "finds meaning only in relationship to this ongoing context—a context more of work than of words"(4). Literacy is a process of "learning that you are being written to, and learning . . . that your words are being read"(5). In this perspective, literacy is not merely mastering texts and knowing the codes of written language; it is understanding "how a text relates dynamically . . . to people, place, time and action. . . . *How it relates* is the real challenge in literacy learning" (Brandt 100).

Thus, it may be argued that being able to write standard English is only one sort of literacy—that approved by middle-class social values. Many who study literacy rely on the "deficit-difference" framework to clarify this problem. If a student's low score on an aptitude test can be said to result from a verbal-skills disability, then that student may be said to have a language *deficit*. If the student functions normally within his or her particular language community, and if the low test score is attributable to the inability to use standard English, then the difficulty may be characterized as a language *difference*. Those who take the latter view argue that what some call "incorrect" or "nonstandard" features of language may well be indications of a consistent, functional grammatical system particular to a given language community. Such criticisms of traditional conceptions of literacy have made it difficult to define literacy in our pluralistic society; we must be wary of the reductiveness lurking in any simple formulation.

Because the tests which purport to measure language ability are couched in standard English, the definition of literacy as the failure to score adequately on standardized language tests has been challenged. It is a truth seldom acknowledged that testing is often a way of systematically begging the question: tests shape and define the knowledge they claim to measure. By naming vocabulary and sentence manipulation as testable abilities, for example, the so-called SAT and ACT "language aptitude" tests in effect formulate the language processes they purport to measure. Tests designed to reveal control over a standard written dialect will not necessarily reveal mastery, for example, of an oral dialect like Black English. Thus in the view of those who hold to the "difference" argument, the customary connection in the public mind between test scores and literacy levels damages minority students, who tend to score lower than white students on such standardized "verbal aptitude" tests as the SAT and ACT exams. Minorities' lower scores may not indicate a lack of language ability, it is argued, but rather a mismatch between language strategies required by standard middle-class dialects and those entailed in nonstandard language forms.

The relationship between literacy, testing, and nonstandard dialects is only one facet of the controversy over testing and standards of literacy. The noisiest phase of the controversy occurred as a result of the public notice given the SAT score decline, which began rather suddenly in 1963. One of the first major notices of this decline appeared in 1972 in the impeccably restrained *Change: The Magazine of Higher Learning:* "The Decline of the SAT's," it gently labeled the issue, offering an analysis of the by-then decade-long decline and the persistent correlations between socioeconomic status and test scores (*Change* November 1972: 17). By 1976, however, the decline had become a national disaster in the headlines: *Change* billed it as "THE DECLINE OF LITERACY" in inch-high capitals; a Midwestern newspaper proclaimed an "academic debacle" in reporting on the decline; and *Newsweek* bemoaned the "appalling statistics" which were proving that "the U. S. educational system is spawning a generation of semiliterates" (*Change* November 1976: 13; *Des Moines Register* August 1, 1976: 2B; *Newsweek* December 8, 1975: 57).

In response to this unwelcome media attention, the Educational Testing Service—the company that writes the SATs and many other educational and professional tests—called out a search-and-rescue party in the form of a panel of educators, psychologists, and statisticians to discover reasons for the decline. Their conclusion was that different proportions of nontraditional (by which they meant minority) students in the test-taking population from 1963 to 1970 accounted for some of the drop (Educational Testing Service 44–8). For the continuing decline after 1970 many culprits were named: larger classes in schools and colleges, more TV, lower student motivation, and linguistic confusion in teaching methods, among others. The panel admitted it could not identify any root cause and suggested that the decline may indicate a major shift in the way young people learn in an increasingly media-dominated age.

In the 1980s the decline leveled off, but by 1990 scores began to go down again, particularly the verbal SATs, which dropped to 1980 levels (*Newsweek* 33). Spurred by educators and journalists eager to demonstrate cultural deterioration, the literacy crisis reappeared in headlines and editorial pages. "These kids are just plain dumb," intoned one pundit who sees continued national disaster in the continued SAT-score decline: "for the nation as a whole, the SAT scores represent something of a disaster. But on a personal level, they are a tragedy" (Cohen 8). Predictably, political and ideological capital is made of the continuing decline. Self-appointed prophets point to the score decline as an ominous sign of "cultural deterioration" which can only be halted by adopting a particular intellectual ideology or educational strategy—creating "cultural literacy" by reforming

school and college curricula or channeling access to higher education so that only "qualified" students attend. Like most statistics
about complex social trends, score declines require painstaking
analyses. Unfortunately, our society's penchant for clear and quick
"solutions" to such matters means that they naturally fall prey to
easy explanations and exploitation.

What the score decline may mean for students, teachers and
schools is deeply problematic. Obviously scores on standardized
language tests are lower than they used to be. Does that mean today's
students are less literate, less well read, less capable? Or that these
tests measure things students are not learning and schools are not
teaching? Often educators and politicians make of the statistics what
suits their respective agendas, saying that educational institutions
are failing to make reforms or that governments are failing to support education or that families are failing to nurture their childrens'
learning. In these debates, what is often ignored is the nature of the
tests themselves. In defense of the tests, educational administrators,
pressed to measure the success of public schools or to admit and
place large numbers of students in colleges and universities, have
argued that test scores offer a more equitable way of judging school
achievements and admissions applications than any other available
means. Their argument—and that of ETS—is that standardized tests
are the only consistent measure of what students are learning. ETS
maintains that the SAT measures "developed abilities" for academic
success; and because academic success is officially defined in terms
of gradepoint average, SAT scores can predict moderately well a
student's potential for academic success ("Memo" 1). As we will see
later in this chaper, the statistical basis for confidence in SAT pre-
diction is highly questionable; close examination of the figures has
provoked scepticism, even outrage, from many researchers. As a
result, academic testing, often mystifying to those unfamiliar with its
jargon, has become more visible and more vulnerable in recent years.

The SAT's have proved an especially inviting target. The National
Education Association, the national PTA, and Ralph Nader's research
group have all set upon the Educational Testing Service, accusing
it of creating culturally biased tests which foster the tyranny of the
white middle class in educational decision-making. Because it
attracted considerable attention nationwide, however, the Nader
report deserves particular consideration. Two main criticisms of the
SAT emerge from this report: first, that its predictive potential is
far lower than most users realize (a point we will consider later in
this chapter), and second, that it measures socioeconomic status
much more clearly than verbal aptitude—"class in the guise of
merit" (Nairn 219). Citing the fact that as the socioeconomic

status of test-takers increases, so does their chance of scoring well on the test, the Nader-Nairn report argues that the SAT is an instrument of class oppression manipulated by the educational establishment. The ETS itself is portrayed in the report as an interlocking directorate of class privilege, economic advantage, and academic elitism. The whole matter of the SAT would seem tangential to the concerns of writing teachers were it not that the SAT Verbal test and its sister, the ACT English Usage exam, are used in many institutions for exemption and placement in composition courses. Because these tests are often at the heart of institutional judgments about student writing, we should consider briefly what educators have long known about the relationships between class, race, and test achievement in educational testing.

Scores on aptitude tests have traditionally correlated with income and race. Students from low-income families tend to score lower on such tests than students from higher-income families. There is also a racial aspect to score patterns: black and other minority students tend to score lower on standardized tests than white students (Educational Testing Service 15). Of course, socioeconomic level and race are themselves correlated, since there are larger numbers of racial minorities at the lower socioeconomic levels than at the higher. But the relationships between academic achievement, income levels, and race are not limited to test scores; they hold for other aspects of education as well. Students from lower-income levels don't stay as long in secondary school as other students, fewer of them graduate from high school, and fewer of them go to college. Students from lower-income levels and minority students score lower on IQ tests (see *Digest Of Educational Statistics* [975] 14; also Jencks 77–8). These statistics do not explain "why" such students score less well on standardized tests; they simply suggest that for any number of reasons, a student's class, income, and race influence that student's academic achievement. The scientific community generally has rejected the claim by a few researchers that the heritability of intelligence is proven by such statistics. The majority tend to favor, in Christopher Jenck's words, "environmental explanations" for observed differences in cognitive skills (13). That is, many researchers believe that social and economic conditions blocking minority students' development are so deeply embedded in our culture that they are unable to take advantage of educational opportunities.

The educational establishment has put its faith in the power of schools and government programs—"environmental intervention"—to remedy the conditions that block students' full development. Such faith, for example, has provided the rationale for the increased attention to writing remediation—"basic writing"—in recent years. Low test scores are often taken by schools as primary evidence for basic writing instruction. Remediation is thus directly correlated with testing; both may be seen as systematic responses to the changes in student population in recent decades. While most colleges and universities have added some remedial elements to their writing programs, the largest programs have emerged in places with the most disadvantaged students—i.e., in urban universities with students who score poorly on the tests couched in standard written English. All these developments have their source in the changes noted above in the kinds of students completing secondary education and going on to college. In the rest of this chapter we'll look more closely at three major, closely related issues in contemporary writing instruction: the problem of nonstandard dialects in writing classrooms, the role of language tests in judging language ability, and the nature of remedial programs.

Class, Code and Dialect in Composition

Educators generally define literacy as the ability to understand and use standard written English in school and college work. This is not an entirely stable definition, however, for it has been argued that students required to take a test or write a paper in a standard form of English unfamiliar to them are placed at a disadvantage that masks their actual literacy. Can the concept of literacy be expanded to include writers working in nonstandard dialects? How may we judge the quality of literacy in written forms of English?

The question of linguistic performance within different social and ethnic groups has been addressed in different ways. As we saw in Chapter Two, some researchers in Great Britain have approached sociolinguistic differences through the idea of *code*, which may be defined as a particular form of language use governed by the user's psychological outlook—itself determined by class status. American linguists have preferred the more traditional concept of *dialect* to distinguish between "standard" language forms practiced by the cultural majority, and those "nonstandard" forms used by different minority groups. Code is a class-based concept dependent on distinctions between working-class and middle-class social contexts; it is more narrowly defined than dialect, which is usually related not only to class differences but also to geographical, ethnic, and cultural variations. Code research should be better known to American writing teachers than it now is, because it reflects those social perspectives on writing and reading which have gained major influence in composition study in recent years.

That code research has not gained more ground in the United States suggests the difficulties many researchers encounter in applying a class-based analysis to American society. The basic obstacle to the acceptance of code research by American composition specialists is the difficulty in assigning clear-cut differences in class to separate groups of students (Davis). Bernstein defines his working-class subjects as those educated on a vocational track outside the grammar school and his middle-class students as those with a grammar school preparation (82–3). Since American students cannot be categorized in this way, the research premised on such categories has not been persuasive to American linguists.

Yet interesting connections may be made between elements of code analysis and certain discourse systems influential in American composition studies. The importance of context-based meanings for the restricted code, for example, is analogous to Britton's emphasis upon context in his definition of "expressive" writing. All children, he postulates, begin their mastery of speaking and writing by developing language competence within the context of "close relations" between speaker or writer and audience. Britton defines linguistic growth, in fact, as the child's progress from contextual language to language for generalized, distanced audiences, a capacity Bernstein associates with the elaborated code of the middle class. The issue of context may also be found in *Teaching the Universe of Discourse*, where Moffett argues that "rhetorical distance between speaker and listener" is a crucial determinant of the level of complexity in a communication situation. Britton and Moffett associate the ability to go beyond limited-context communication with individual cognitive growth; Bernstein attributes it to the impact of class status upon the individual.

American sociolinguists generally rely on the concept of dialect to account for differences among American English speakers and writers. Dialect "means a variety of language spoken by a distinct group of people in a definite place"; it "varies in pronunciation, vocabulary, and grammar from other varieties of the same language" (Malmstrom 13). Composition teachers are more interested in written than spoken language, of course, and standardized tests and writing samples require command of written, not spoken, English. But dialectal differences in spoken language do carry over into writing. This is especially true of the most visible nonstandard dialect in the schools, that which dialect specialists call "Black English." In different versions it is used by blacks in urban ghettoes and the rural

South, serving as the main form of oral communication for them. Black English differs in pronunciation, syntax and vocabulary from standard English. Some of its most frequent markers are:

A. Lack of the copula *be:* the use of the invariant *be. He going home. He be going home.*

B. Lack of *d* and *ed* as past tense inflection. *She talk about him yesterday. She walk home by herself.*

C. Lack of s, *es* as third person singular present tense inflection. *He want to read the book.*

D. Lack of suffix s as possessive inflection. *Mary dress be pretty.*

E. Use of multiple negation. *I ain't got no tickets.*

These markers are the most visible differences between black dialect and standard English. Nor are such dialectal variations limited to African-American speakers. The loss of the final r, for example, is characteristic of both Southern and New England regional dialects used by the general population. And double negatives are as typical of nonstandard speech in working class and rural white populations as they are of Black English.

A prescriptive approach to language—with an accompanying insistence that certain ways of speaking are by nature "better" than others—is difficult to defend today. In the words of two linguistic researchers, it is now "axiomatic that language is one form of cultural behavior," reflecting varieties of that culture within its whole language community (Wolfram and Fasold 15). Nowhere has this linguistic relativism been more evident than in the controversy over "bidialectalism," the policy of encouraging nonstandard speakers to learn standard English dialect without abandoning their own dialect. As a way of mitigating nonstandard speakers' difficulties in reading and writing in school, bidialectalism has been encouraged by some educators and damned by others. The fact that Black English is a functional dialect for a large minority of American school children, particularly in urban areas where the minority is often a majority, has made the traditional "deficit" view of nonstandard dialects difficult to defend. Most educators no longer attempt to eradicate Black English in the schools by insisting upon standard English in the classroom; black children often cannot cope with school materials or relate their own experience to schoolwork in standard English. Yet, although "the majority of sociolinguists who have studied social dialects advocate the bidialectalist position," there are great differences among linguists and educators about how standard and nonstandard dialects can actually coexist in schools (Wolfram and Fasold 181). Most teachers, particularly in schools and colleges with high African-American or other minority student populations, are careful not to "correct" students' nonstandard dialect habits, but to help them learn those standard English forms which constitute the governing dialect of business, government and education. Texts and teaching materials in standard and Black English have been introduced in some schools in attempts to help students understand both the linguistic validity of their native dialect and the value of learning the standard dialect also.

One viewpoint hostile to bidialectalism asserts that Black English is best put aside by any speaker of a nonstandard dialect who wishes to become part of the social and cultural mainstream. In this argument, essentially a version of the "deficit" view of dialect, Black English is a corruption of standard English precluding the user from full participation in society; Black English perpetuates the inequalities of race. The political and moral aspects of the dialect question are central to another group of opponents of bidialectalism. In their view, requiring minority students to learn standard English is tantamount to forcing their repudiation of their own culture and self-identity. It is a way of telling black students they must learn the majority dialect because it is the majority, and because that majority is not going to accommodate itself to a minority dialect. "Standard English," says James Sledd—another opponent of bidialectalism— "is a principal means of preserving the existing power structure, for it builds the system of class distinctions into the most inward reaches of each child's humanity: the language" ("Doublespeak" 454). The premise of this argument is that schools—and society in general— ought to nurture individuality, linguistic and otherwise, and encourage communication among dialect groups, not impose a standard dialect upon all groups.

The most controversial argument for bidialectalism comes in the form of a pamphlet entitled "Students' Right to Their Own Language," published in 1974 by the National Council of Teachers of English. Its authority derived from its official sanction by the umbrella organization of all English teachers in the United States; yet the ranks of the NCTE were split by varying degrees of opposition to the document (see Appendix B for some of its crucial sections). After discussing the insights of dialect research mentioned earlier, the pamphlet argued, among other things, that dialectal differences are always superficial and never meaningful, that students ought to be permitted to write in nonstandard dialects, and that students ought to be offered "dialect options" to increase their "self-esteem." Teachers were also urged to acquire a wide range of knowledge about language in order to better grasp the nature of language differences and to tolerate them as expressions of speakers' individual and cultural identities. "Students' Right to Their Own Language" expresses a relativistic view of usage and urges linguistic tolerance on the part of teachers and the society they represent.

Unfortunately, but perhaps inevitably, some of the document's statements blur issues that require clear discrimination by writing teachers. One of its major premises is naive: that sociolingistic insights into nonstandard dialects, particularly Black English, carry over nicely into composition, and have as much relevance to written as to spoken English. This argument has encouraged composition teachers to believe that, if only their attitudes toward nonstandard dialects could change, writing instruction in schools and colleges could include both standard and nonstandard dialect forms. The difficulties of this position, standing against the moral and social justness of dialect tolerance, may not be easily recognized or admitted by supporters of "Students' Right." But they are real and they must be examined closely.

The research precipitating the liberalized attitudes toward dialectal differences has been done by linguists, who by trade are not concerned with writing pedagogy. Teachers of writing may understandably fail to notice what research linguists accept as a given—the fact that Black English in the United States is a spoken, not written, language. Indeed, linguists prefer to rely on speakers of any dialect under investigation because only spoken language is used by all members of the dialect group. Written dialect, where it exists, may often be a codification of oral forms based on the writer's ear for phonetic-scribal equivalence. It is therefore less trustworthy for the linguist interested in the present state of the dialect. Such is the case of Black English. In tracing the history of Black English, linguists have had to rely on written transcriptions of dialect; but since most of these are contained in works of imaginative literature, and were produced by writers laboring without the aid of the phonetic alphabet, most written versions of Black English lack sufficient authenticity for linguistic research. Efforts to establish the rule-governed basis of Black English today focus on speech patterns; little research in linguistics has been devoted to any written—as compared with spoken—versions of Black English.

The actual relationship between spoken and written forms of Black English has never been clearly established. It's easy to assume that oral characteristics are simply reproduced in written dialect, so that the latter may be measured in terms of its faithfulness to the oral form. But there is no research into written Black English comparable to the great body of study of its oral form. There is a sound reason for that: most written versions of Black English are intentional transcriptions of the spoken dialect. Major American black writers have written most of their work in standard English. There are plays, poems, and novels written in dialect by black and white writers, but these are deliberate renderings of spoken Black English. Most fiction couched in Black English involves first-person narration by a dialect-using narrator; Black English poetry artfully renders the voice of black consciousness expressing itself in its own vernacular.

But Black English is seldom put to the purpose of transacting the business, politics, and education of our society. Standard written English has been established by the middle class, black and white, as the "transactional" (James Britton's term seems apt) written dialect of the United States. Black English has no comparable written form. E. D. Hirsch articulates the distinction between dialects (related to region, ethnic culture, occupation, etc.) and a "grapholect," which he defines as a "national written language" that is "transdialectal in character" and "normative" precisely in its "very isolation from class and region" (44). Standard Written English is a grapholect; Black English has never been established as one. This fact, unacknowledged by the committee which prepared "Students' Right" and of minor interest to linguists, has major importance for composition teachers, who must use imaginative prose whenever written models of Black English are desired for classroom use.

The lack of transactional Black English prose severely restricts the availability of prose models for instructors attempting to teach black students "the fundamental skills of writing in their own dialect" ("Students' Rights" 8). Thus composition teachers face crucial choices in dealing with dialects other than standard written English in college writing. Ought the grammatical differences between Black English and standard English be accepted in academic discourse? Are teachers doing minority students a favor by tolerating minority dialect differences, or are minority students better served by having dialect-related usages corrected?

This question is not easily answered. Students attempting to write in a nonstandard dialect like Black English will violate some rules of Standard Written English by using Black English conventions. In the "Students' Right" perspective such violations would be permissible because they are rule-governed choices resulting from dialect habits. However, dialect-using students would also make errors in syntax, idiom, diction, and mechanics which will not be dialect-related. When the differences between dialect-related "nonstandardisms" and errors not dialect-related are systematic and clearly attributable to their respective sources, students may be able to distinguish between them. But often enough these distinctions will be nearly impossible to make, because Black English does not have a normative written form and oral variations among regions and social groups may cover a wide range of nonstandard usages. Free-ing students to use "their own language" will not lead in itself to "clear, forceful writing" ("Students' Right," 8). How are students' native dialects to be respected while they are challenged to develop as writers?

Before some tentative answers to these questions are explored, another related difficulty posed by "Students' Right" should be mentioned. Its authors assert that "differences among dialects in a given language are always confined to a limited range of *surface* fea-tures that have no effect on what linguists call *deep structure*, a term that might be roughly translated as 'meaning' (6)." Here the "Stu-dents' Right" Committee draws upon a distinction in the first phase of transformational grammar theory between deep structure—the so-called "propositional meaning" of a statement—and surface structure—the explicit grammatical form of the statement. One lin-guist defines deep structure as "a system of propositions that express the meaning of the sentence," and surface structure as "these propo-sitions in sentences as they are actually spoken" (Wolfram and Fasold 6). Another says that "transformations do not alter the basic meaning of sentences, [but] they do affect the surface meaning" (Jacobs and Rosenbaum 20). That is, spoken or written sentences are expressions of underlying thought-structures, their shapes closely tied to those structures.

Cognizant of the reluctance on the part of many linguists to assign *all* meaning to deep structure, William Labov suggested in the early stages of the controversy that differences among dialects "are *largely confined* to superficial, rather low-level processes which have *little effect* upon meaning [italics added]" (40). However, where Labov suggested that dialectal differences are "largely confined" to surface features, the authors of "Students' Right" claimed that those differences are "always confined" to surface features. Where Labov suggested that dialect features have "little effect" upon meaning, the "Students' Right" authors insisted that such features have "no effect" upon deep structure, which they apparently equate with the complete meaning of any statement. It appears they read Labov and carefully altered the qualifiers, as though to suggest that meaning is not to some extent inherent in the rhetorical and stylistic elements of writing.

It is important to note, however, that in recent years transforma-tional theory has moved away from confidently-formulated "phrase structure rules," making it more difficult to argue that certain "sur-face" structures are predictable transformations of "deep-structure" meanings. In place of earlier transformation models have come stud-ies of what Noam Chomsky calls "Universal Grammar," a body of theory about innate language knowledge. Such theory applied to the study of English, for example, finds the study of so-called "rules" by which specific sentences are said to be formed less interesting than discovering "a single principle that applies to all rules in English," a principle that would exist as "a state of knowledge" inherent in the human mind (Cook 23). Thus the enthusiasm for detailing specific connections between phrase-structure rules and actual sentences has waned in current transformational theory. As a result, the argument made by "Students' Right" authors enjoys less theoretical support today than it did at the time of its publication.

However, the crucial moral and social issues inherent in the "Students' Right" controversy make it enduringly important for all writing teachers to know about. Teachers often confront writing in which dialect markers are randomly embedded in errors unrelated to dialect conventions. The "Students' Right" position that dialect markers themselves don't affect readability is clearly defensible, but related to this is an equally important countertruth: nondialect-related deviations from standard syntax and mechanics *do* obscure meaning. To afford a closer look at the ambiguous task of dealing with dialect-related *and* nondialect variations in the same writing, let's examine a piece of transactional student writing with just such a blend. Here's an excerpt from an essay comparing Bigger Thomas of Richard Wright's *Native Son* with Maggie of Stephen Crane's *Maggie: A Girl of the Streets:*

> *Bigger Thomas is able to show some freedom of action, while Maggie really*
> 1a   1b   2a
> *haven't no control of her course in society. (What give you a feeling that*
> 2b   3b   3a
> *Bigger is more determined than Maggie) is shown threw Bigger drive to find*
> 4b   4a 5b   6b
> *his idenity in society. Both protagonist are naturalism, (that both are seen as*
> 5a   7b   6a
> *product of their environment.) With this, Wright show Bigger being caught*
> 8b
> *up in this society where blacks have no identity. (Where this is so evident that*
> 7a   9b   8a
> *Wright try somewhat to Bigger seem as a hero,) because even tho he is doom*
> 9a
> *Bigger end up finding his identity.*

Clearly this writer understands the basic distinctions he wants to make between these two protagonists, and he understands a good deal about the concept of naturalism upon which his comparison is based. He is, in other words, an excellent example of the student whose dialect habits have not precluded his understanding literary works written in standard English, or kept him from grasping lectures and discussions about naturalism conducted in standard English. Thus, this student may find it hard to understand why his prose is unreadable, particularly if he has taken to heart the "Students' Right" approval of "vigorous and thoughtful statements in less prestigious dialects" (9), and its disapproval of "finicky correctness in 'school standard' " (8) writing. This student knows that he has understood the material moderately well and that he has made a decent attempt to relate the specific to the general. When the instructor suggests that certain sentences do not communicate meaning, how can the instructor work around the student's predictable assumption that his dialect usage is what's responsible for the teacher's criticism? How can the student be made to see that blurred meaning is a direct result of syntactical strangulation?

Neither this student's writing nor his reading are hampered by his use of Black English. He is already bidialectal in that his nonstandard dialect habits do not interfere with his understanding of standard English. He *is* hampered by his inability to structure standard English sentences in academic discourse, however—and in this his needs are no different from those of standard-English speakers who also need help at the basic-writer level. This student, then, needs to see that style (here in the form of syntactical choices) is part of the meaningfulness of any discourse. In the situation of the sample above, the instructor could begin by numbering the clearly definable dialect markers "1a, 2a, 3a," etc., until all such markers are included in the series (Wolfram and Fasold 205). Then the non-dialect errors may be numbered in a different series "1b, 2b, 3b," etc. The instructor may show the student the causes of the nonstandard usages for each series; such a demonstration clearly will require time, patience, and tact. If the course is at the basic-writing level, an individualized laboratory setting may be available; if the student is "mainstreamed" into a class of mixed abilities and cultural backgrounds, the instructor must find the time to individualize the situation. The sequence of black dialect markers occurs as follows:

1a. Multiple negation; leveling of present tense inflection ("have" for "has").

2a. Lack of suffix -s as third person singular present tense inflection.

3a. Lack of suffix -s as possessive inflection.

4a. Lack of suffix -s as plural inflection.

5a. Ditto.

6a. Lack of suffix -s as third person singular present tense inflection.

7a. Leveling of present tense inflection ("try" for "tries").

8a. Lack of suffix -ed as past participle inflection.

9a. Lack of suffix -s as present tense third person singular inflection.

As the authors of "Students' Right" rightly maintain, such purely dialect-related usages do not affect the passage's meaningfulness or readability. Whether the student is urged next time to use inflections appropriate to standard English depends upon the context and the intentions of instructor and student. Writing teachers who want to encourage students' flexibility in writing might call their attention to the dialect markers, then concentrate on the obvious syntactical difficulties. Indeed, the presence of these markers in this passage clearly reflects the importance of the "difference" perspective—for they suggest that such modest variations from standard English could be acceptable at any but the most formal levels of writing. To acknowledge the legitimacy of Black and Hispanic dialects in speaking and in some kinds of writing is not to threaten the preeminence of Standard Written English for America's formal and published writing. Even Sledd, a radical social critic as well as a linguist, is willing to acknowledge that "Standard English [is] the most useful all-purpose dialect we have" ("Product" 173). What writing teachers must decide for a given piece of writing is, in Sledd's words, "how much variation from whatever norm they choose should teachers of English accept without protest or even encourage," in view of the increasingly multicultural nature of American society ("Product" 173). For English is a remarkably flexible and adaptive language. Teachers can help minority students experience this flexibility by helping them see both standard English's tolerance for rule-governed variation as well as its need for syntactical coherence.

To help students see their language's need for coherent syntactical structure, teachers may analyze a passage like this as follows:

1b. The noun clause "What . . . Maggie," while acceptable as the subject of "is," does not fit idiomatically, because the construction "What gives you [one] . . ." is normally followed by the copula plus a nominative construction, not a copula plus a participle making a passive predicate. Idiomatic English does not permit double predicate constructions linked in this fashion. Traditional handbooks recommend labels like "awk" or "shift" for such errors.

2b. "Determined" is misused here in a semantic rather than syntactical sense. Trying to display his grasp of the concept of determinism, the student uses the word as an unidiomatic modifier. This kind of error results from the student's attempt to apply a regular rule of conversion (from noun of quality to adjective of quality) to a word meaning that cannot be so converted.

3b. A phonetic rendering unrelated to dialect.

4b. A misspelling that could be attributed to any poor speller. It could also be related to the phonological marker of Black English involving lack of final -t, or-d sounds in consonant clusters.

5b. Linking a count, animate noun with a noncount, abstract noun seems outrageous, until we realize that the verb (a form of *be*) is the source of the error. Substitute "exemplify" for "are" and the construction is acceptable; it's the student's lack of vocabulary that causes the difficulty.

6b. The relative clause "that . . . " dangles incoherently and would be so marked by traditional editing. But an "in" inserted before "that" converts the whole phrase to an acceptable structure. Here the student's partial control over a complex, formal idiom ("in that both . . . ") suggests a struggle to express a complex understanding with an inadequate command of standard idiomatic phrases.

7b. The unattached demonstrative pronoun is a common error in all student writing.

8b. The attempted clause "Where . . . hero" is incoherent for several reasons. Again the student leads off with an apparently nominative clause (as in "What give you . . . " earlier), but the verb for which the clause is the subject is absent. The relative "that" attempts to link the initial "where" clause with "Wright try," but fails to do so. The "to" is part of an infinitive whose verb component is also omitted. The student is trying to say that Wright makes Bigger a hero, and that this enhancement of Bigger's stature illustrates (in an "evident" fashion) by contrast the oppressive nature of white society. But the complexity of this literary perception eludes the student's capacity to predicate it.

9b. "Tho" is a colloquial, perhaps phonetic, spelling unrelated to dialect.

To show the student the irrelevance of the dialect markers to the passage's meaning would not be difficult. How extraordinarily difficult it is, by contrast, to clarify the syntactical problems of the passage! Told that he may write "in his own language," the student will be astonished to discover how little "his own language"—defined as his dialect—has to do with the passage's conceptual intentions. It may be argued, that is, that there are elements of two languages in this passage: Black English and what may be called the "interlanguage" of a basic writer trying unsuccessfully to achieve the target language (here, the formal discourse of literary analysis). Some of the nonstandard expressions in the passage follow the rules of Black English; these can be identified in the manner suggested above. Error-analysis of the sort described in Chapter One could also show which of the syntactical difficulties not related to Black English are accidental slips in spelling, usage, or mechanics, and which are deeper intentions gone awry during the writing process.

This student is on his way to becoming literate within the academic community. He appears to know what he wants to say about how the literary text embodies the abstraction "naturalism." The passage yields no examples of black dialect markers themselves blurring the passage's meaning; the paragraph is not disabled by its dialectal characteristics. Yet it is syntactically disabled, too far from its target language—formal written English—to communicate its meaning clearly. Whatever error patterns or interlanguage "rules" may govern the syntax, they are not adequate for articulating meaning within the discourse community this student aspires to.

We may say, then, that a passage with Black English characteristics—or those of other nonstandard dialects—may be quite readable if it conforms to the basic syntactical rules of standard English. It's misleading to students, however, to tell them merely that they may use "their own language"; they may, but only if that language also obeys the rules required by the discourse community reading and responding to their writing. Unfortunately, simultaneous obedience to the rules of both standard and nonstandard English dialects—easy enough for the talented or professional writer—is difficult for most student writers. In particular, a student striving for basic literacy should not be encouraged to seize upon dialect as an excuse for avoiding the task of making readable meaning.

Evaluating Writing Skills

Much of the fuel for the controversy over student literacy has been provided by scores on the standardized verbal aptitude tests (the SAT Verbal and ACT English Usage) given to high school juniors and seniors, which claim to measure general verbal facility, not writing ability. There are other standardized tests, of course, which do claim to measure writing ability, most produced by the Educational Testing Service, and we will consider these shortly. But because scores on the verbal aptitude tests are used in many institutions for exemption or placement in composition courses, we must take a closer look at them.

The SAT:Verbal and the ACT:English Usage are what test-makers call *norm-referenced* tests, in which "raw" scores are put through a formula which ranks students against one another in formulating the reported score. The SAT test is heavily oriented toward vocabulary control; the majority of questions ask students to recognize synonyms, antonyms, and matched pairs of words closely related in meaning. Here's a fabricated example:

> Here is a related pair of words, followed by five lettered pairs of words or phrases. Select the lettered pair that expresses a relationship closest to that of the original pair:
>
> ### 1. DAZZLE: SHIMMER
>
> (A) bright: dull　　　　　　　　　　　(C) polish: glisten
> (B) confuse: clarify　　　　　　　　　(D) glow: gleam
> 　　　　　　　(E) brilliant: tremulous

This question typifies what verbal aptitude tests tend to measure: students' control of a vocabulary available only from written sources. Because many of these words are not commonly used in colloquial speech, only well-read students will be able to answer this question; nonreaders will be baffled by it. The target pair of words describes the production of light; they are descriptions of opposite kinds of radiance. "Dazzle" means to shine directly and brilliantly, while "shimmer" means to shine softly and waveringly. Only E suggests a similar relationship, although between adjectives rather than verbs. While vocabulary control is an important element in both reading and writing, the vocabulary the SAT requires can be learned only from wide reading in formal published writing. Thus the SAT Verbal is actually a measure of whether students have read widely beyond the often modest requirements of most public secondary schools.

On the other hand, the questions on the ACT: English test and the SAT TSWE (Test of Standard Written English) consist of error-recognition in grammar and usage, requiring students to recognize violations of Standard Written English. Here's a typical question of this kind:

> Some parts of the following sentence are italicized and numbered. One of these underlined passages may contain an error in grammar, usage, diction, or idiom. Identify the passage that contains the error.
>
> 　　　　　　1　　　　　　　　　　2　　　　　　　　　　　　　3
> If I *had known* how much you *wanted* to go roller skating, I *would*
> 　　　　　　　　4　　　　　　　　　　　　5
> *of* let you *come with us* last night. No error.

The right answer of course is "3," a choice many students might miss, since young writers often use the spoken colloquialism "of" in

writing as a substitute for "have." That does not mean they misunderstand the tense itself; it means that "of" seems, to many students
unaccustomed to standard written English, an acceptable substitute
for "have." Many of the questions are similar: they test awareness of
literate prose or sensitivity to formal *written* language. So do the
vocabulary questions; they test students' command of words they
will only have seen in writing. Both kinds of questions will tend to
detect students who are wide readers, able to recognize word function within the context of Standard Written English.

Despite their makers' claims to the contrary, these tests sometimes include "errors" which are actually markers of Black Dialect.
Here is an example:

> 1   2
> *Although* he *did not want* to tell his parents, the boy told his teacher
> 3   4   5
> *that* the rock he threw *had broke* a window. No error.

"4" is the answer the test-makers are looking for, since it is the only
portion of the sentence not safely couched in standard English.
Thus the test-makers have been accused of putting minority dialect-
speakers at a disadvantage by presenting nonstandard dialect usages
as "errors." And indeed, minority students do not score as well, on
the average, as other students on these tests. A number of reasons
may account for this fact. Minority students may indeed lack familiarity with the idioms of standard English in which the test questions
are couched. It has been suggested, too, that minority students may
suffer more test anxiety than test-hardened white, middle-class students (see Nairn 113–7). In other words, it can be argued that the
tests' discriminatory potential derives from the culture reflected in
their language and content. To the extent that speakers of Black
English may score poorly because of these factors, white culture may
be said to exert *de facto* bias through tests.

As we have seen earlier in this chapter, differences over the place
of minority dialects in education are expressions of the larger controversies concerning racism. Testing certainly expresses the racial differences that warp our society: because of the consistent correlations
between minority status and low achievement on tests, schooling,
and income, it is clear that minority groups are still far from achieving equality. The entire educational process discriminates in part
simply by depending upon the books, lessons, and the cultural backgrounds of its mainly white teachers educated in standard English.
This, of course, is just the situation addressed by both advocates
and critics of bidialectalism. Some hardliners argue that a minority dialect is culturally disabling and must be totally set aside.

Advocates of bidialectalism argue that speakers of Black English need to learn standard English *in order to* surmount cultural discrimination expressed in language. Others argue the reverse: that speakers of minority dialects should not have to set aside their cultural or ethnic identity in favor of a standard dialect; instead, the larger community should disavow linguistic colonialism by fully accepting minority dialects.

Even by the test-makers' own measures, standardized tests only limitedly measure whatever variables affect how students learn. Test-makers fudge their descriptions of what the tests are supposed to measure with phrases like "developed ability," "learned responses," and "academic development"; such terms, like "intelligence" itself, are defined so variously that they tend to mean something only in the context in which they occur. Many studies have indicated that by themselves ACT and SAT scores can account for 10 to 20 percent of whatever variables affect students' GPAs. Test scores and high school grades together can, at best, account for one-third of GPA variation, according to studies ("Memo" 3). The other two-thirds of the factors affecting academic performance are beyond the ability of any test to measure.

Composition teachers might normally be concerned about SAT and ACT scores only to the extent of their interest in academic admissions policies. But because some colleges and universities use admissions test scores to place or exempt students in writing courses, writing teachers need to understand what such tests can and cannot say about writing ability itself. These tests do not give students an opportunity to write anything.[1] Students who can make accurate choices about sample problems in vocabulary, usage, idiom, and mechanics may not necessarily be able to generate these same choices as they write. They may lack the developed ability to conceive, develop, and revise a coherent essay, or to create a voice appropriate to their audience. While they may be able to detect illogic in a test question, they may not be able to generate a coherent series of sentences on a given topic.

Attempting to gauge writing ability by means of either the SAT Verbal or the ACT English tests is a misuse of both, in light of their dependence solely upon multiple-choice questions. There *are* standardized tests designed to measure the ability to manipulate language in sentence or longer contexts. These tests, of which the ETS', CLEP composition tests are a familiar example, are also used for composition placement and exemption; they are more appropriate to this purpose than are aptitude tests like the SAT and ACT series. Such tests have been designed to "avoid items solely devoted to error recognition." Instead, said their designers when they were introduced in the 1970s, they are intended to "measure students' competency in expository writing skills, following the conventions of Standard Written English," or to measure the "ability to recognize and apply principles of good writing" ("Announcing a New CLEP Exam" 1977). That is, they are intended to measure not only the recognition of good writing but the ability to compose it. The following are among the types of questions found in these tests:

Questions requiring the building of a sentence from given parts. I am an atheist.

I question the existence of a god.

I also question the varying forms of religion.

If you were to combine all the sentences above into one, what is the best way for that sentence to begin?

   A. Because I am an atheist, I question the existence of

   B. The existence of a god and the varying forms

   C. As an atheist, I question both the existence

   D. My being an atheist

   E. Since atheism is my belief, I question

From the test-makers' point of view "C" is the best choice since it most efficiently combines the information of the three base sentences. "A" is wrong because a beginning clause is unnecessary when a phrase will do as well; "B" because it clearly leads nowhere; "D" because the idea of atheism is not the subject here, but the writer's embrace of it; and "E" because the parallel nouns "atheism" and "belief" create needless redundancy.

Questions requiring the ability to perceive and manipulate paragraph structure.

   1. Recent films have set new precedents in explicit anatomical horror. 2 Other films recently have offered their cringing audiences limb amputations by saws, dental surgery with chisels unaccompanied by anesthesia, and mutations of facial features into scarred lumps. 3 The popcorn's not the only thing causing indigestion in theaters these days. 4 One movie offers a blood-spattered closeup of an exploding stomach. *What should be done with sentence 4?*

A. It should be left as it is.

B. It should be combined with sentence 2.

C. It should be placed first in the paragraph.

D. It should be placed between sentence 1 and sentence 2.

E. It should be lengthened to include more explicit detail.

This question is intended to test students' ability to perceive structural coherence in a paragraph of a given number of sentences. They are supposed to recognize that the logical pattern of this paragraph moves from the general to the specific back to the general. They are then expected to sense that, first of all, sentence 4 does not belong at the end or the beginning (choices C & A). They are expected to see also that it has enough detail already (Choice E) and that such detail requires that it go with the other detail sentence. That leaves choices B and D; but students are also expected to see that sentence 2 is already long enough, rendering any combination with sentence 4 impracticable. Finally, they are expected to see that the transitional phrase "other films" beginning sentence 2 indicates that sentence 4 has already offered one film example, and should therefore precede sentence 2 (choice D).

Questions like these make the writing ability tests more than just exercises in error recognition (although there are such questions in them). Students must be able to recognize efficient syntax, logical coherence in sentences and paragraphs, nuances of tone and meaning, and from a limited number of options select the most effective rendering of these qualities. Making such choices does not require generating language; it requires the skilled editing of language. *We might say, then, that a high score on such multiple-choice tests demonstrates that the student is a capable editor of writing.*

But editing is not writing. It is a manipulative skill brought into play in what Britton terms the "rule-governed" phases of the composing process, which Britton suggests follow the "non-rule-governed" earlier phases of "conception" and "incubation" (see Chapter I for Britton's model of the composing process). As editors, student test-takers are showing that they can handle sentence structure, usage, and mechanics. They are not, on multiple-choice tests, able to demonstrate the capacity to devise a focus and shape a piece of writing. Test-makers, sensitive to such critiques, have added essay questions which students may write on and which are returned to the institution for evaluation.

But this convenient adjustment leaves a crucial question unanswered: What exactly do *we*, the teachers of writing, want to measure? When we try to judge language ability, do we want to find out how well our students can manipulate given parts of language, or do we want to discover how well they can generate a whole piece of writing? If we are content to judge their ability to conform writing to its standard written rules, then multiple-choice questions will do the job. But if we want to measure how well students can *write*, then something more than the manipulation of given parts is required. If this is our purpose as teachers, then we must insist on a complete piece of writing (not just one or two paragraphs) that represents the breadth of the student's writing capacity.

An extended writing sample is the most *valid* measure of writing ability. To see why this is so, we need to consider two terms directly related to testing. One is *validity*, the appropriateness of a test to the skill or ability it purports to measure. A writing sample is—on the face of it—the most valid measure of whatever the phrase "writing ability" actually denotes; a piece of writing is the only fruit of writing skill. However, judging writing samples is not always a completely reliable process. *Reliability* is often defined as the consistency with which the same test will yield similar scores for the same test-takers over successive testings. Samples of student writing involve some unpredictable variables. On a given day a student may suffer testing strain, may not think clearly because of fatigue, may not find the topic congenial, or may be trapped in a composing dead-end only to discover there is not time to start over. Reliability may also be defined as the consistency with which different raters will agree as they rate similar writings. Writing evaluation may be strongly affected by variation in the standards of those evaluating the writing. Many professional evaluators, and the testing industry itself, argue that "interrater reliability"—that is, how often two or more raters will agree with each other—is not high enough to justify multiple readings of students' essays as the primary measure of their writing abilities. But there are ways of reducing these differences, as we will see later in this chapter; with such measures, evaluators can make fairly consistent judgments across a wide spectrum of student writing.

Specialists in writing measurement generally agree that extended writing samples are, on the face of it, a more *valid* measure of writing ability than multiple-choice tests, though less reliable than machine-scored, multiple-choice tests. Students' writings are a more valid predictor of how well that student may write in the future than is answering multiple-choice questions about writing. Nor do the standardized scores and percentile ranks offered by national multiple-choice tests give much useful information about the strengths and weaknesses of individual writers or the test-taking population. If they are scored on a particularized scale by institutional readers, writing samples can reveal much about the writers' skills. In some large institutions, of course, enough readers to undertake writing-sample evaluation may be hard to find; evaluating large numbers of writing samples requires many hours of exacting, repetitious labor. For this reason many schools find it expedient to use standardized tests. Yet in so doing they give control over the testing process to the impersonal standardized programs, and lose the advantages institutionally-evaluated writing samples can offer. There are methods by which institutional evaluation can be accomplished.

Evaluating Writing for Placement or Exemption

It is an axiom of testing itself that if a measure of something is not fundamentally valid, no amount of reliability in the testing process can enhance its usefulness. Thus if, as compositionists generally maintain, extended writing samples are more valid than multiple-choice tests, it is vital to strengthen their reliability as much as possible. The first step is to establish a setting for administering the writing samples. Since most placement and exemption decisions concern incoming freshmen, some arrangement must be made to require all students to write for the same amount of time, on the same topic (or on very similar topics), under the same conditions, and with the same test instructions. Enough time must be allowed for students to develop several paragraphs as a fair indication of their capacity to write a focused and coherent piece. For students just entering an academic institution, the only universal topic is probably going to appeal to general adolescent experience: family relationships, peer relationships, education, or a specific issue calling for an evaluative response which a teenager could reasonably be expected to formulate. Students should be told what standards will be used to judge the writing, how it will be read, and what the consequences of the evaluative process will be.

Perhaps the single most important step for any group of writing evaluators is to agree on the evaluative standards to be used. A "rubric" must be established clearly stating the criteria upon which all raters have agreed to base their judgments. The developing of this rubric may take considerable discussion, especially if the raters are not familiar with each others' attitudes and judgments about writing. Articulating a rubric may indeed require negotiation and compromise before all readers agree on the main elements of the rubric. But such negotiation and concurrence must be forthcoming; if different readers consistently favor different criteria, the test will not reflect the commonality of purposes necessary for fair comparison and evaluation of writing samples.

Two kinds of scales for evaluating writing for placement or exemption have emerged as the most workable for writing teachers in schools and colleges: *holistic* and *analytic*. Both combine characteristics of norm-referenced and criterion-referenced tests. That is, both rate students by comparing their scores on a numerical scale (norm-referenced) and by measuring their writing against specific performance criteria (criterion-referenced). The *holistic* or *general impression* method relies on a scale consisting of numbers—1 through 4, for example—each of which represents a level of writing quality. On a four-point scale a 1 would be given any paper appearing to the rater to belong in the lowest fourth of all papers in the group; a 4 would be given any paper belonging to the highest fourth in the group. The larger the range in the scoring scale, the finer the discriminations that can be made. If the only purpose in the process is to select students for exemption, a relatively narrow rating scale will suffice. If placement within two or more composition courses is desired, then a wider scale capable of finer discriminations may be needed.

In this evaluation process, raters read each paper and make an intuitive judgment about the place of that writing among all similar writings from that particular group of students and that particular writing task. Raters base their judgments upon the immediate overall impact the writing makes upon them in terms of the rubric they have agreed to follow. The process of holistic reading requires the following procedure:

1. The writing samples should be randomized (alphabetizing them is one way of accomplishing this) so that those turned in early and late in the test period, or those collected from early-morning and late-afternoon test administrations, or those from different classroom sections which may have had some unknown selectivity in their forming, are all mixed randomly together. No trend or disproportion within the group being tested should be obvious to raters, since either may influence those reading the tests.

2. All raters should be convened in one place and their judgments "calibrated" so that they will consistently give writing samples similar ratings on the basis of the rubric they have accepted. This requires that a number of writing samples exactly like those about to be read be given to each reader, evaluated individually in terms of the scale to be used, and the results compared and openly discussed. The purpose of this exercise is to enhance reliability in evaluation by reducing differences among readers' standards of judgment. Calibration is a crucial first stage in any holistic reading; without it, the scoring may result in some widely scattered numbers that could skew the results.

3. After calibration, readers should immediately begin their work. Each sample should be read by two different readers and the scores added or averaged so as to produce a single total score for each student. If two readers diverge too far (e.g., more than two points on any scale with four to eight points), a third reading should be given and the closest two readings counted. If all three scores are equidistant then the mid-point of the three may be designated as the score. If there are too many samples to be read in one sitting, each successive reading should be preceded by

further calibration to keep readers mindful of collective standards. Readers may be tempted to disperse or take tests home for more convenient reading, but this temptation should be resisted because it can introduce variations of setting and mood into a process whose reliability depends on consistent, unmolested judging.

The other most common scoring scale is an *analytic scale,* which permits a breakdown of writing elements on each paper. Two kinds of scales may be devised: one that permits only a "yes" or "no" checkoff for each element, and one that requires a numerical rating for each standard.

The two-way ("dichotomous") scale might look like this:

	No	Yes
Topic clearly focused		
Organization clear and logical		
Generalizations supported with specific or concrete details		
Sentence structure free of awkwardness and errors		
Spelling and punctuation mostly error free		

A numerical scale could be constructed as follows:

	High	Middle	Low		
Topical focus	5	4	3	2	1
Organization	5	4	3	2	1
Support for generalizations	5	4	3	2	1
Sentence structure	5	4	3	2	1
Punctuation and spelling	5	4	3	2	1

                              TOTAL

Although the standards of judgment are spelled out in the analytic scale, calibration and joint reading are essential to insure consistency in raters' use of the scale. Indeed, collective reading benefits the whole English department by enhancing everyone's awareness of common expectations and standards and strengthening confidence in individual judgments.

Individual writing teachers who ask students to write brief diagnostic essays obviously can't follow all the steps outlined above. But any writing sample (a first-day impromptu, for example) assigned for the purpose of diagnosis should result from a topic students can be expected to handle extemporaneously, and should be evaluated with clear standards in mind. If, for example, reassignment to a remedial class may follow upon the evaluation of an initial impromptu, that sample should allow students to fully demonstrate the skills they do have, and it should elicit the elements of writing that are to be used as a basis for judgment. Impromptu writings are, of course, inherently flawed as examples of what students accustomed to review and revision can do. Students given only a short time to produce a piece of writing will not be able to revise or edit it fully, if they are used to working through a more elaborate composing process. On the other hand, composition researchers like Sondra Perl and Nancy Sommers have concluded that most college freshmen don't know how to revise for anything other than superficial changes in diction and punctuation (see Chapter One). So a truncated writing opportunity is likely to reveal the strengths only of those few students capable of writing fluently under time pressure; it is not likely to reveal capabilities for elaborated composing—which most students haven't yet developed anyway.

It is essential to remember that both kinds of rating methods depend on instinctive judgments of readers as guided by the collective standards of the rubric. The authenticity of this approach draws from what Michael Polanyi calls "tacit knowledge"—our intuitive, unarticulated insights shaped by experience. Readers' standards will be articulated and guided by collaboration under the agreed-upon rubric. One writing measurement researcher points out, however, that despite steps taken to communalize standards of judgment, reliability is a persistent problem in the holistic scoring method: "the importance of reliability is related to the need to generalize test outcomes, to be able to say that success on a particular test insures success on future tests" (Huot 203). Because raters may not actually be consistent with one another in rating writing samples, and because the calibration process may itself skew holistic raters' usual standards of judgment, their reliability must be enhanced with as much collaborative negotiation as possible. It is important to remember that such ratings, like writing itself, are always probationary; they must be viewed as conditional and sensitive to variables often not measurable or accountable.

Evaluating Writing for Progress Assessment and Research Purposes

When writing samples are used for evaluating group progress or the relative efficacy of several teaching approaches, testing procedures must follow specific, well-established guidelines if they are to produce useful information. A group of instructors may, for example, want to compare the writing growth of students in their classes based on certain distinct teaching approaches the instructors have agreed to try. The most important task is to fit the study method to the study goal.

Suppose we want to evaluate the effect upon writing growth of two different kinds of classroom settings, one "innovative" and the other "traditional." An experimental group and a control group should be established, each instructor in the project teaching one of each kind of class, with the experimental class using the "innovative" method and the control class using the "traditional" pedagogy. Comparisons of the writing done by each group of students at the beginning and the end of the semester or quarter (the "pretest" and the "posttest") could provide a means of measuring comparative writing growth. The project must minimize the variables that are not at issue: differences in student attitudes and ability, variations in instructional settings, and differences among instructors' standards and personalities.

Suppose we have collected pretests and posttests; how then should we proceed? Three different methods of evaluation may be used, two of them already discussed earlier in this chapter; each will provide different information about the writing samples under evaluation. All require two steps essential to trustworthy results: the randomizing and the blind reading of all tests. Tests should be coded and entered on a master sheet so that all scores can be collated and results totaled, and all traces of name, class, and other information covered up on the tests themselves. They must then be put into random order to eliminate any pattern discernible to readers. When these steps have been taken, samples may be read by one of these methods:

1. *Holisitic* marking, as described earlier, will produce average pretest and posttest figures for each group, revealing any numerical differences between experimental and control groups. If, for example, the experimental group in the invention project showed an average gain of .7 on a 1-to-4 rating scale, while the control group showed only a .2 mean improvement, that might suggest that the experimental method did result in greater improvement in overall writing achievement than the traditional method. But the general impression method measures only the overall impact the writing makes upon the rater; it does not permit distinctions about text features like logical structure, syntax or usage.

2. The *analytic scale* could allow readers to mark each element of the writing sample, singling out changes in a specific element.

The scale would have to enumerate the various elements of writing in a way that reflected the perceptions of the raters and the goals of the course. With this method the total score could be computed for each separate element and for the whole test, and comparisons made between pretests and posttests.

3. *Primary trait* scoring could be used. This criterion-referenced evaluative method, first widely used in the National Assessment of Educational Progress program, is a way of measuring specific "traits" (not the traditional elements of organization, style, and mechanics) seen as desirable in terms of a preconceived rhetorical framework. For example, in the first round of the NAEP writing assessments "Imaginative Expression of Feeling through Inventive Elaboration of a *Point of View*" was designated a primary trait (Lloyd-Jones 48). The main advantage of primary trait scoring is that it allows such things as point of view, voice, and other aspects of rhetorical context usually difficult to define, to be targeted in a testing situation. The disadvantage of primary trait scoring is the complex, time-consuming training necessary to prepare readers to recognize and evaluate the trait(s) being measured.

Strategies for Basic Writers

A corollary to—in some ways a result of—the widespread emphasis on writing measurement has been increased attention to unskilled, or remedial, or "basic" student writers. The social and educational changes noted earlier in this chapter have required schools and universities to develop programs to help inexperienced writers on a systematic and continuous basis. Such programs involve intensive, often individualized instruction in writing and reading standard English. The pressures felt by schools and colleges as they have formed these programs, however, have generated mutual recriminations. College teachers blame secondary teachers for inadequately preparing students, while secondary instructors in turn accuse elementary teachers of failing to send them literate twelve-year-olds. All teachers join in accusing administrators of failing to support standards of learning and discipline in the classroom; administrators suggest that parents and the community—in the guise of the school board—won't give administrators the money and support needed to run the schools properly. Commentators outside the educational community tend to return the favor by blaming "spineless" administrators and "lazy" teachers. No one sees fit to argue that the young are not wasted illiterates; all seek convenient targets, depending on the direction of their self-interest.

Blame implies guilt, which in turn implies responsibility. A more balanced view of the literacy question, however, suggests that no segment of our society—family, educational institutions, community—has single responsibility for something as complex as literacy. Even if we define literacy very narrowly—as the ability to use standard written English in a school or college setting—it is obviously a function of cultural background, socioeconomic advantage, intensity of preparation, and individual motivation and talent. Although the decline in SAT scores has caused alarm about a "literacy crisis," the small percentage (10 to 20 percent) of overall college performance actually predicted by the SAT scores suggests that whatever the SATs measure (and which has obviously declined) is not crucial in college writing. This university reports enrollment in basic composition up 50 percent from a few years ago; that college claims more of its students need remediation than ever before. What is usually not advertised is that ten years ago *this* university abolished freshman composition as a way of denying support to politically active teaching assistants, while *that* college ten years ago had no remedial program at all. What has changed in education is the *perception* of increased writing problems. And this public awareness results in part from the pressures described earlier in this chapter, related to placing increasing—and increasingly diverse—student populations in writing courses in schools and colleges.

Whether in response to new needs or to long-standing ones newly perceived as important, remediation has become a vital part of writing programs in many institutions. With the coming of open admissions, the needs of basic writers have pushed most institutions far beyond the piety of benign neglect. Basic writers in many universities now must be brought to competency in writing because they *are* the student population. Necessity has generated pervasive institutional efforts to identify and intervene on behalf of those students who without special attention will not succeed academically. And identifying "basic" writing students has become a far more sophisticated and complex process than counting sentence fragments, just as helping such students is now perceived as requiring more than drills on complete sentences and correct punctuation. In the next few pages we'll examine ways to identify students needing help in writing, and discuss strategies for helping them.

The traditional image of the basic writer centers on the puzzled student laboring with a stubby pencil to form a simple sentence on a crumpled piece of paper, like Thurber's football player who cannot name a common mode of transportation until someone whispers "choo-choo." The equally traditional view of remediation for this student includes requiring him to diagram "The boy and his dog ran up the hill" and write twenty-five times, "A sentence expresses a complete thought and ends with a period." This student and his peers sit together in "bonehead English," herded into the noncredit dungeons of the composition curriculum and taught by an instructor struggling with four sections of the remedial course. Underlying this attitude toward the basic writer is the assumption that such students can't write because they haven't learned "grammar" and can't think clearly, since in order to write well one must think clearly and grammatically. Little is expected from such students and often less is gotten, since (in this view) they come to college with such severe disabilities (the fault of previous teachers) that they cannot realistically be expected to do more than scrape by.

This, of course, is caricature, but it does reflect a well-entrenched conviction in academia that remedial students, like the poor, will always be with us, and that institutions should do what they can without hoping for too much. Much basic writing methodology still reflects the conventional antithesis between process and product, primarily because a number of teachers and textbooks cling to the notion that writing teachers' primary mission is to teach "correct" writing through error-avoidance. Whether in classrooms or in writing labs, the traditional, product-oriented approach tends to emphasize a workbook-based, mastery-learning sequence that begins with the study of parts of speech and sentence elements, continues with work on simple, compound, and complex sentences, and includes many drills in error recognition and sentence analysis. Most such texts also cover spelling and punctuation along with drills to drive home these formal mechanics. The emphasis on sentence formation and mechanical control marks the product-oriented view that what basic writers most need to learn is "correctness" of expression at the sentence level before they are challenged with larger prose units. This emphasis upon sentence making and punctuation forces basic writers to labor over discrete, decontextualized writing tasks.

Yet, especially for unskilled writers, language is not a set of pieces they are anxious to assemble more effectively. It's an open process of meaning-making, significant to them only as it has relevance to their struggle to articulate experience. If basic writers are limited to workbook drills, their experience will be "streaked with reductive and discontinuous qualities that cancel the promise of the students' own full literacy" (Meyers 929). The piecework approach may seriously underestimate the capacity of basic writers, for as Mina Shaughnessy points out in her pioneering study of basic writing, it is their language difficulties that most severely hamper their educational progress. "Writing," she says, "is not simply the sum of a number of discrete skills but an expanding work of competencies that interact and collide and finally merge" (289).

But if traditional approaches don't help basic writers, what will? In order to see how writing teachers and scholars today might answer that question, we must first ask who "basic" writers really are. How do they differ from other students? How can they be identified and their difficulties assessed? Some institutions define them as any student whose score falls below a certain level on a standardized verbal aptitude test. But such guidelines are both rigid and reductive, ignoring the real complexity of students' difficulties. Experienced writing teachers prefer to identify basic writers in terms of certain recognizable characteristics. Their sentences and paragraphs often lack coherence, they seem not to be able to shape their writing purposefully, and their editing skills cannot cope with the punctuation and spelling demands of standard written English. And there are more global traits as well: basic writers are repeatedly overwhelmed by regular assignments and expectations, they seem not to progress like their peers, they seem unable to respond successfully to comments, advice, instructions.

Basic Writing: The Cognitive Perspective

While these features give us a general picture of who basic writers are, they do not help us understand why they do not succeed as writers or readers, or how they may be helped. In recent years two perspectives have emerged which may help us understand basic writers. *One view is that basic writers do not understand and cannot utilize the writing process.* In Mina Shaughnessy's words, such students do "not know how writers behave" (79). In this assertion we can see again the influence of the cognitive-process view of writing. Basic writers are unable to fashion coherent sentences and paragraphs because they do not know how to compose fluently, and they cannot edit their writing adequately because they cannot distinguish what should occur in composing and revising from what should happen in editing their work. Their anxiety over editing interferes with successful composing, while their editing efforts often fail to achieve standards of written English. Mike Rose, who has developed large-scale basic writing programs, suggests the usefulness of the process approach to basic writing: "We need ... to make special efforts to change the models of composing our students have internalized. It is possible ... that our remedial classes—at least some significant portion of them—should be very process-oriented. ... [which] means that we should help our students experience the rich possibilities of the writing process" (Rose 117).

Rose's contention that basic writers misunderstand composing—particularly revision—is backed by some compelling empirical evidence. In the late 1970's Nancy Sommers compared the way experienced adult writers and inexperienced student writers revise their writing. While the experienced writers saw revising as "finding form and shape for their argument" and developing "pattern" and "design" in their writing (384), student writers generally saw revision as a "rewording activity" in which they needed to make only lexical and editing changes (382). Thus Rose, building partly on this sense that basic writers do not understand how to exploit the composing process, proposes a classroom strategy requiring students to work and rework writing in response to repeated challenges by the instructor. In his "Revision Scramble," for example, students must take notes on "a five to ten-minute lecture on an academic topic, . . . then must write either a summary or a critical reaction. In the next class they are given a further brief lecture on the same topic but with new information included. They must revise their summary or reaction in ways that account for the new. Thus they come to see that texts can—even must—evolve" (117).

In the process perspective, the nature of error itself also becomes a primary issue: by what cognitive processes do such writers generate faulty discourse structures? The error-analysis strategy described in Chapter One—and best represented by Shaughnessy's influential *Errors and Expectations*—seeks to identify the causes of students' difficulties by analyzing the syntax and structures of basic writing. Its rationale is that when teachers help students discover the kinds or patterns of their errors, students will be able to change their behavior as writers. Instead of simply training basic writers to replace the errors with "correct" usages in writing, "the composition teacher as error-analyst *investigates* error (to discover how a student arrived at the mistake) and then *applies* these insights" (Kroll and Shafer 244). This focus on the conceptual causes of error reflects in yet another way the pervasive influence of cognitive psychology. Psycholinguists argue that since *all* language making is rule-governed, the making of errors must reflect systematic composing behavior. The most important task of the basic writing teacher, in this view, is to help students define for themselves those concepts, or "rules," which create errors, and which if isolated can be changed to generate better writing patterns.

In this definition, the "basic writer" is one who writes poorly in part because of inadequate concepts of sentence-formation. Arguing that forming sentences is the basic activity in generating writing, Shaughnessy identifies several categories of erroneous sentence formation, each reflecting a well-meant intention gone wrong. One category she terms "blurred patterns," which includes sentences "that erroneously combine features from several patterns, creating a kind of syntactic dissonance" (49). A second source of errors for Shaughnessy is basic writers' efforts to "consolidate": "that is, to subordinate, syntactically, some elements of an idea or statement to others and to conjoin other elements that are clearly of equal semantic weight" (51). Basic writers, she says, lack the "command of the language" needed to "bring off the consolidations that are called for in writing" (73). They are not, in this view, careless or lazy writers, but well-intentioned learners struggling to make inadequate sentence strategies bear the weight of complex perceptions. Part of their difficulty is a lack of vocabulary control; they often do "not know the word that would enable [them] to consolidate" sentences (76), or they do not know the appropriate "grammatical form" of the word required by the syntax. Errors may occur, for example, as students try but fail to join parallel elements in a complete sentence:

> The war in Vietnam was a vast waste of human resources. Also an undeclared war and the United States had no business there.

Here the student is trying to make two judgments (the war as waste and as politically illegitimate) and to connect them both with a third and final judgment. Sensing that it's inappropriate to link all three propositions in one independent clause, the student chooses to separate the two initial judgments from the third. This creates what would traditionally be called a sentence fragment; Shaughnessy's "consolidation error" is more accurate because it suggests what the student has actually done—i.e., failed to hold together a series of statements related by a common predicate and an underlying single intention. Another major source of error, identified by Shaughnessy as "subordinate consolidations," includes the traditional dangling modifiers, pronoun reference, and faulty subordination. For example:

> These men left the country of their own accord which I think they should have to face the consequences.

Here the *which* links what is essentially a cause-and-effect sequence (because they left . . . they should have . . .), as the student attempts to yoke the cause to the effect with a relative pronoun which cannot provide the desired connection. Shaughnessy's description helps us see that what the student needs is an explanation of why the chosen form of subordination does not suffice.

Another teaching strategy compatible with the process view of basic writing is sentence combining. Shaughnessy defends it as "perhaps the closest thing to finger exercises for the inexperienced writer" (77). Andrea Lunsford proposes a type of sentence exercise that she argues engages both analytic and synthesizing efforts

("Cognitive Development" 41). Students should first be asked to combine given kernels into specified patterns, then to put their own kernels into patterns which imitate the originals, and then to generate each pattern themselves. She also advocates assignments that build "inferential reasoning" by asking students to compose a paragraph or longer discourse from a list of "data" from which students must infer generalizations that will, in turn, provide the organizational framework for inclusion of the original information. These techniques have the advantage of creating rhetorical contexts within which students must devise tone, voice, and a consistent pattern of meaning for an audience. But sentence combining is only a sophisticated type of drill that does not engage the crucial inventive and organizational phases of composing. Focusing on the manipulation of sentence parts, it does not help students understand writing as engaging with readers in the making of meaning. It should, therefore, be used only on a limited basis for writers whose syntactical control clearly requires such rehearsal.

Basic Writing: The Institutional Perspective

But even as they advocate process-oriented strategies, both Shaughnessy and Rose express serious reservations about whether such strategies fully address basic writers' needs. Among the major characteristics of the basic writer, according to Shaughnessy, is "that the student lacks confidence in himself" and fears writing as exposure; Shaughnessy suggests that anxiety about writing is not just an incidental problem of basic writers, but is a central, disabling trait (85). And this anxiety stems directly from basic writers' feeling of estrangement from the contexts and settings of academic writing. Rose lodges the same warning about diagnosing basic writers' problems exclusively as lapses in their manipulation of composing processes: "in our attempts to isolate and thereby more effectively treat 'basic skills,' we have not only reduced discourse complexity, we have separated writing from reading and thinking" (118).

Basic writers often find that they cannot understand or respond to the analyses, terms, and ways of speaking characteristic of various academic disciplines. That is, finding themselves "outside" the patterns of thought and discourse of many academic disciplines, they are disenfranchised from the various communities that make up academic college life. They cannot write about college-level topics because they have not mastered the language, idioms, and conceptual patterns of academic disciplines. Describing such students, David Bartholomae says that they begin "with a hesitant and tenuous relationship to the materials we put before them, to the terms and imaginative structures that could make that material available, and to the institutional context within which they are required to speak and to write" (*Facts* 8).

This view of basic writers suggests that seeing them simply as students who don't write well is reductive and simplistic. It suggests, instead, that basic writers' difficulties stem as much from institutional alienation as from cognitive sources. *Thus another view of basic writers is that they do not write well because they have not mastered the conceptual patterns, language, and idioms of academic discourse.* In this view, the most important way to improve basic writers' work is to help them internalize the patterns of thought and attitude which constitute academic ways of knowing. Patricia Bizzell argues that the marriage of language and institution is particularly tight in academe, since while "all communities are in some sense language communities . . . the academic community is a community united almost entirely by language" ("What Happens" 296). As a result, she suggests, students struggle to gain entry to this world of formidable linguistic structures by learning "its language-using practices"; thus "basic writers," in her definition, are those least successful in learning "a new dialect and new discourse conventions [in order to discover] a whole new worldview" ("What Happens" 297). In this view, basic writers must master more than syntax and editing codes; they must come to grips with new cognitive perspectives that only new linguistic complexity can make possible.

The most fully-articulated pedagogy based on this definition of basic writers has been proposed by Bartholomae and Anthony Petrosky. Teachers, say these writing theorists, should see basic writers as engaged in a constant "struggle within and against the languages of academic life. A classroom performance represents a moment in which, by speaking or writing, a student must enter a closed community, with its secrets, codes and rituals" (8). They cannot learn to do this by writing only on personal or general topics; they must learn to engage academic texts in order to enter academic discourse as writers. Thus, the basic writing course proposed by Bartholomae and Petrosky asks students to read and write about nonspecialist literary, sociological, and anthropological writings (*The Catcher in the Rye* exemplifies the difficulty level), and to learn the critical vocabulary and methods of analysis appropriate to the ways of knowing enacted by the text. The classes are small and team-taught to ensure personal attention and full recognition of each student's writing and reading problems.

Indeed, a common strategy in any kind of basic writing class is to personalize writing instruction. The most common settings for remediation—the writing lab and the small (usually fifteen or fewer) remedial class—both represent efforts to isolate and individualize basic writing instruction. The frequent contacts between student and instructor in the laboratory arrangement can give students feedback on all stages of the composing process. Getting such feedback can help them gain that understanding of "how writers behave" which, Shaughnessy argues, basic writers need. Writing labs also provide a noncompetitive atmosphere important for those students suffering from writing anxiety. Shaughnessy's diagnosis of the basic writer's "fears that writing will not only expose but magnify his inadequacies" (85) suggests that poor writers fear not only the writing process, but the intellectual inadequacies which their writing may reveal.

It is often difficult for instructors to determine which students need remediation badly enough to warrant placing them in remedial courses, which may not carry credit and are taken before the regular composition requirement. The evaluative strategies described earlier in this chapter will diagnose obvious remedial needs. But often student writers need remediation only in specific areas; some will be able to organize and develop writing but will lack mechanical skills, while others may write error-free prose but be unable to organize coherent paragraphs or develop and support chosen topics. In establishing a successful remedial program, then, instructors must agree on what constitutes remedial needs in their particular school or college. They must define competence and incompetence in the context of their own program and the writing challenges students will face in other areas of their curriculum. And, of course, teachers must accept responsibility for dealing individually with many kinds of remedial needs. Only in this way can students with specific but not overwhelming difficulties make progress within the regular writing courses which provide the foundation for a liberal education.

Notes

1. The Educational Testing Service is considering introducing a writing component as part of the Verbal part of the SAT. It has hesitated because some critics have argued that writing samples will discriminate against minority students even more heavily than do the multiple-choice questions. Urged for years by many writing teachers to add such writing component, ETS, as it finally moves to respond, now finds itself assailed by another set of critics with a different agenda.

Works Cited

Bartholomae, David and Anthony R. Petrosky. *Facts, Artifacts and Counter-facts: Theory and Method for a Reading and Writing Course.* Portsmouth, NH: Boynton/Cook, 1986.

Bernstein, Basil. *Class, Codes, and Control: Theoretical Studies Towards a Sociology of Language.* London: Routledge and Kegan Paul, 1971.

Bizzell, Patricia. "What Happens When Basic Writers Come to College?" College Composition and Communication 37 (1986): 294–301.

Brandt, Deborah. Literacy as Involvement: *The Acts of Writers, Readers, and Texts.* Carbondale, IL: Southern Illinois University Press, 1990.

Breland, Hunter. *The SAT Score Decline: A Summary of Related Research.* Princeton, NJ: Educational Testing Service, 1976.

Cohen, Richard. "These kids are just plain dumb." *The Des Moines Register.* Wednesday, September 5, 1990: 8A.

Cook, V. J. *Chomsky's Universal Grammar.* Oxford: Basil Blackwell, 1988.

Cooper, Charles R. *The Nature and Measurement of Competency in English.* Ed. Charles R. Cooper. Urbana, IL: NCTE, 1981.

Daly, J. A. "The Empirical Development of an Instrument to Measure Writing Comprehension." *Research in the Teaching of English* 12 (1978): 119–26.

Davis, Diana. Language and Social Class: Conflict with Established Theory." RTE 11 (1977): 207–17.

Educational Testing Service. *On Further Examination: Report of the Advisory Panel on the SAT Score Decline.* New York: College Entrance Examination Board, 1977.

Flower, Linda. "Writer-Based Prose: A Cognitive Basis for Problems in Writing." *College English* 41 (1979): 19–37.

Heath, Shirley Brice. *Ways with Words.* New York: Cambridge University Press, 1983.

Hirsch, E. D. *The Philosophy of Composition.* Chicago: The University of Chicago Press, 1977.

Huot, Brian. "Reliability, Validity and Holistic Scoring: What We Know and What We Need to Know." *College Composition and Communication* 41 (1990): 201–13.

Jacobs, Roderick and Peter Rosenbaum. *Transformations, Style, and Meaning.* Waltham, MA: Xerox, 1971.

Jencks, Christopher, et al. *Inequality: The Reassessment of the Effect of Family and Schooling in America.* New York: Basic Books, 1972.

Kintgen, Eugene R., Barry M. Kroll, and Mike Rose. *Perspectives on Literacy.* Carbondale, IL: Southern Illinois University Press, 1988.

Kroll, Barry and John C. Shafer. "Error-Analysis and the Teaching of Composition." CCC 29 (1978): 242–48.

Labov, William. *The Study of Nonstandard English.* Urbana, IL: NCTE, 1977.

Lloyd-Jones, Richard. "Primary Trait Scoring." *Evaluating Writing.* Ed. Charles R. Cooper and Lee Odell. Urbana, IL: NCTE, 1977.

Lunsford, Andrea. "Cognitive Development and the Basic Writer." *College English* 41 (1979): 38–46.

Malmstrom, Jean. "Dialects—Updated." *Black Language Reader.* Ed. Robert Bentley and Samuel Crawford (Glenview, IL: Scott, Foresman, 1973.

Meyers, Lewis. "Texts and Teaching: Basic Writing." CE 39 (1978): 918–33.

Modgil, Sohan and Celia Modgil, eds. *Noam Chomsky: Consensus and Controversy.* New York: The Falmer Press, 1987.

Nairn, Allen. *The Reign of ETS: The Corporation That Makes Up Minds.* Ralph Nader Report, 1980.

Ogbu, John U. "Literacy and Schooling in Subordinate Cultures: The Case of Black Americans." *Literacy in Historical Perspective.* Ed. Daniel Resnick. Washington, DC: Library of Congress, 1983. Rpt. in Kintgen et al. 227–42.

Perl, Sondra. "The Composing Processes of Unskilled College Writers." RTE 13 (1979): 317–36.

Rose, Mike. "Remedial Writing Courses: A Critique and a Proposal." CE 45 (1983): 109–28.

Scribner, Sylvia. "Literacy in Three Metaphors." *American Journal of Education* 93 (1984): 6–21. Rpt. in Kintgen et al 71–81.

Shaughnessy, Mina. *Errors and Expectations: A Guide for the Teacher of Basic Writing.* New York: Oxford University Press, 1977.

Sledd, James. "Doublespeak: Dialectology in the Service of Big Brother." CE 33 (1972): 439–56.

———. "Opinion. Product in Process: From Ambiguities of Standard English to Issues That Divide Us." CE 50 (1988): 168–76.

Sommers, Nancy. "Revision Strategies of Student Writers and Experienced Adult Writers." CCC 31 (1980): 378–88.

United States. Department of Education. *Digest of Educational Statistics,* 1975; 1989.

Wolfram, Walt and Ralph Fasold. *The Study of Social Dialects in American English.* Englewood Cliffs, NJ: Prentice-Hall, 1974.

Chapter Five

Planning the Course
Six Key Questions

Planning next semester's writing courses often sends writing teachers into uneasy—if not agonizing—reappraisals. Have the texts really been useful? Have students used them, or merely lugged them around, to be dumped at the bookstore for a fraction of their cost at semester's end? Did my assignments really work the way I wanted them to? Should I have asked the students to do more academic and less personal writing, since my colleagues think English teachers spend too much time on "flowery" writing anyway? Should I try to use writing groups more often next semester? And perhaps I shouldn't spend so much time talking about dangling modifiers . . . ?

Incompleteness haunts writing courses. Nothing seems really finished at the end of the semester; many students improve their writing, but there are always those who don't seem to have gained skill in writing, despite papers dutifully done and returned. They become frustrated when in paper after paper the instructor seems to find difficulties—sometimes the same ones, but often new ones as old ones are resolved. Teachers may feel the same way, when despite their hours of labor and their faith in the values of revision and editing, some students do not appear to have improved their writing and vent their frustration in their course evaluations.

When we think about it, however, it is not surprising that teaching writing sometimes seems as frustrating as learning it. We saw in Chapter One that writing is an "open" capacity, always susceptible to change and difficult to evaluate. Just as learners continually discover new aspects of writing that require mastery, so teachers may find that appealing, innovative strategies may work very well in some ways, but fail to address other important aspects of writing. New texts, incorporating even the most recent developments in composition theory and touted as the final solution to teachers' needs, seem, after all, not to provide all the answers. Indeed, because writing is so open a capacity, the more a text focuses on one central strategy the less satisfactory it may be as a general text. An unfortunate consequence of such misdirection for teachers can be a retreat into cynicism. When even the best-written texts and methods based on current theories seem not to work well for all our students, why should we continue trying to discover more effective teaching strategies? Wearied by this prospect, we are tempted to recycle our customary course organizations and let the devil take the hindmost as we plan for the next semester.

Yet the openness of writing can make its teaching deeply rewarding precisely because it allows so much latitude for informed, inventive course planning. Though, as we have seen in earlier chapters, writing assessment may produce indeterminate results, we must not be misled into thinking that what we do as writing teachers doesn't matter. Writing is the most deeply personal form of knowledge-making students experience, and writing courses, because they are usually smaller than other courses, offer students uniquely intimate learning relationships with instructors and peers. Students can invest more of their own deeply-felt aspirations in writing courses than in other courses with more formal informational content. Thus, the best defense against twinges of cynicism is serious consideration of what we can expect of students, what they might expect of us, and what strategies may best serve those mutual expectations: in a word, planning. Such planning must begin with an understanding of some basic issues in structuring and administering a writing course.

Some Planning Issues

One thing most compositionists now agree on is that in planning writing courses, writing teachers must design ways to help students *understand the processes of composing.* Teaching language-shaping strategies is one major goal of composition pedagogy today. We have seen in Chapter One that far too much energy has traditionally been spent on grammar drills and editing, when these elements of writing are secondary and tertiary effects rather than primary causes of good writing. Though different writers manifest different processes in their work, composing exhibits the characteristics of a set of dynamic and recursive processes deeply embedded in every writer's behavior. To help students learn how to compose, we writing teachers need now to consider how, in Joseph Comprone's words, we can make writing "intrinsically related to a student's habits of perceiving, thinking, and expressing" (336).

As we saw in Chapter One, teaching conventional formats, grammar, and mechanics conveys the impression that writing can be mastered by adhering to a set of prescriptions. The difference between being able to enact the processes of writing and just knowing language facts is akin to the difference between "knowing how" and "knowing that" described by philosopher Gilbert Ryle. "Knowing that" does not necessarily lead to "knowing how." To illustrate, Ryle argues that if a nonnative speaker only learned the history and theory of English grammar, that speaker would not know how to speak grammatical English as well as an English child whose skills arose from a native competence untutored by any formal language study. Michael Polyani's concept of "tacit knowledge" provides another way of describing those composing processes writing students need to master. Like other forms of tacit knowledge, writing processes are at least partly inarticulate and instinctive; it is not easy to distinguish those processes which can be generalized from those which remain specific and inarticulable in individual writers.

Writing teachers must not only plan how to help students learn to compose; they must also decide how they can help students *situate their writing in terms of purpose, audience, and setting*. As we saw in Chapter Two, recent cognitive and rhetorical perspectives on writing have emphasized its contextual nature. In the cognitivist view, both writing and reading are intentional and goal-oriented; all acts of composing—writing and reading—develop purposefully in response to governing intentions. Frank Smith argues that writers' intentions and readers' expectations can be described in very similar terms, each featuring local and specific acts encompassed by "global," overall intentions (171). All texts are framed by such goal-driven activity, writers projecting their readers as they compose and readers in turn anticipating the writers' purposes as they recompose the text. Rhetorical theorists maintain that just as writers enact their purposefulness by imagining and personalizing the readers they address, so readers anticipate writers' intentions by projecting and personalizing them as they read. All writing is spurred by the intent to say something to somebody; all reading is shaped by the desire to reconstruct those intentions. If communication is saturated with purposefulness, then writing teachers must invest their courses with it; all tasks, discussions and relationships must embody the purposefulness of language.

Writing responds not merely to writers' and readers' purposes, however. It is shaped by the conventions of its form and format, the circumstances of its composing, and the structures of its "production"—the institutional, social, or personal contexts which generate it and within which it has significance. It is an interesting irony that while most teachers view academic as crucial to learning, students themselves tend to see the writing they do in courses as artificial and lacking in any meaningful "real-life" context. They write papers, exams, journals, and reports because they are required to, but would not confuse these writings with those that are genuinely situated in their lives: letters to friends, family, and employers (potential and actual), applications for awards and graduate and professional study, and job-related writings. Students sometimes recognize more quickly than teachers that no "real-world" writing is done merely to show readers that the writer knows a certain subject-matter or can organize certain kinds of knowledge within a fifty-minute time period. Students perceive that much academic writing lacks the purposefulness characteristic of writing in "real" situations, where one writes to and for others with particular goals in mind.

To help students grasp the situated and purposeful nature of good writing, teachers must contextualize their writing assignments. They must formulate writing tasks which require students to identify both writers' and readers' intentions with respect to a given text. Students should be asked to articulate their intentions as writers and to imagine how those intentions match readers' expectations. Some assignments should ask students to write for familiar readers, others for wider audiences. Some strategies are suggested in Chapter Two for helping students activate the "writing self-reading self" relationship and imagine their readers to life. To invest a writing course with these goals, teachers must set strategies for building relationships in the course; students and teachers must become writers and readers of each other.

It is also important for teachers to help students identify their relationships to the discourse communities within which they must think and write. Academic subjects and their departments—history, sociology, physics—are constructed out of communities of scholars and teachers who understand each others' language, attitudes, and methods. Students enter these communities when they enter college, and must learn new ways of thinking, talking, and writing. Writing tasks must be designed to allow students to explore these new fields, and to adapt to the demands of new forms and occasions of writing.

Some Planning Questions

We don't buy a garden spade if we plan to lay a brick wall, or get a mason's trowel if we intend to plant shrubs. Nor do we buy texts before we decide what kind of writing course we're going to teach.

Contrary to the urgent petitions of the book salespeople, many of them former English majors, composition texts cannot shape a course, despite their authoritative tone. Instructors must choose the kind of course to be taught; choosing a text first and trying to organize a course around it is like trying to eat soup in a straightjacket. Deciding the purpose and structure of the course, preparing materials, and devising appropriate teaching strategies are the first priorities in planning. The following questions will help teachers think about these points:

1. What writing purposes and contexts will the course entail?
2. What kinds of writing assignments should I set?
3. How much emphasis should I give to deliberately planned and revised writing? How much to impromptu writing?
4. Should I try to teach grammar in the writing class? What connections are there between formal grammar instruction and writing?
5. Should I use an anthology or other outside source of writing in addition to students' own work in the course?
6. What kind of pacing should I plan for students' writing? How much writing should I require and how often?

These questions, which are by no means exhaustive, will help teachers discover the *what* of their course—its content and pattern. They are not aimed at the *how* of the course, its dynamics; the relative advantages of one-on-one, small-group, and whole-class strategies, discussion methods, and evaluation strategies will be discussed in Chapter Six. And even if the individual writing teacher must plan the course as part of a controlling general syllabus, there remain many choices that only the instructor can make. The discussion that follows is directed primarily towards those choices governed by the needs of the students and the teachers' own preferences.

1. What writing purposes and contexts will the course entail?

We can somewhat arbitrarily divide the kinds of writing students do into two types: personal writing, often reflective and inward-looking, exploring their private experiences of the world (writing that occurs mostly in English composition courses); and academic writing, composed of all the papers, reports, and tests required for academic coursework. Personal writing draws upon students' ready access to familiar audiences and purposes; it offers inexperienced writers opportunities for confidence-building composing. Academic writing, on the other hand, draws students into new discourse groups requiring them to master new forms, styles, and vocabularies. Each kind of writing has important uses; there is a place for both in most writing classes.

Efforts to incorporate personal writing in school and college writing classes have a long history in formal education. Robert Connors suggests that the narrative and descriptive "modes" of writing popularized by nineteenth century rhetorician Alexander Bain brought about "all but complete acceptance" of personal writing topics, with their "narrow/select/develop pedagogy," in schools and colleges by 1900 (177). That popularity remains strong today. Participants in the Dartmouth Conference (see Chapter One for a description of this event in composition history) urged that drama, group interaction, and classroom writing should all be combined in writing classes in order to help students to "a new investment in the experience of writing, and a correspondingly original and personal vision" (Dixon 45). But because such writing does not usually fit the purposes of academic work outside the English department, critics have opposed it as irrelevant and even dysfunctional at the college level. One critic suggests that its intensity and privateness cannot be matched in other writing tasks outside English courses, and consequently it creates false expectations for some students. When the "personal" is made to seem "more real than the objective," or the "reminiscence" more valid than the conjecture, students are ill-served, he argues (Vopat 42).

Britton and others have argued in response that topics drawn from personal experience confer value upon the act of writing for anxious and inexperienced writers. Inexperienced writers are often weak readers. If they are asked to write on a topic drawn from an anthologized essay or some other source outside personal experience (especially in a freshman-level course), the need to digest and respond to strange material compounds the student's difficulties. Inexperienced writers in particular must begin by learning *how* to compose; the forms and topics of personal writing lend themselves to this purpose. Writing anxiety is most acute in poor writers, as Mina Shaughnessy points out: the student needing remediation "lacks confidence in himself in academic situations and fears that writing will not only expose but magnify his inadequacies" (85). Particularly for these students, personal writing requiring narrative and descriptive patterns offers apprehensive writers the readiest starting point.

Unfortunately, faculty in other disciplines sometimes regard personal writing as impractical and unsuitable to the writing tasks students face in most subject areas. Such an attitude can particularly be found among teachers in the sciences, business, and engineering, who traffic in "hard" knowledge empirically derived from "real" things in human life—the nature of matter, the power of money, the observable behavior of human beings. Many of these instructors are convinced that writing in composition courses ought to deal in "real things." They wonder what use could come from a description of a night ride on an Alpine tramway or a narrative of a disagreement over a roommate's insistence on listening to the radio until 3 a.m. They wonder why students should be encouraged to write on such "frivolous" topics when there are so many "substantive" topics that will be required of them: historical or current events, descriptions and analyses of scientific experiments, or critiques of articles and books.

These "substantive" things entail new writing conventions, forms, and audiences arising from various discourse communities across the curriculum. Discourse aimed outside the writer's personal experience comprises the major part of academic writing. Writing of this sort asks students not to inquire into their personal worlds, but to put those worlds aside in favor of new ideas and information gleaned from texts and lectures. It requires the submission of the self to the not-self, that body of thought and experience which society traditionally posits as the content of formal education. Students' obligations to write purposefully for academic assignments is reflected in the admonition in one recent text: "you will find yourself working in broader disciplines, writing reports, gathering information . . . , and, above all, thinking critically," which entails "arguing, proposing solutions to problems, and weighing the value of things" (Kennedy 1).

Inexperienced writers face difficult challenges in academic writing. They must master the formats of academic writing while they struggle to learn the premises, terms, and thought processes of new disciplines. To answer essay test questions or put together a research paper, students must demonstrate knowing *how* to organize and present new ideas and information, just as they are struggling to articulate their knowledge for themselves—knowing *that* it is so. The traditional library research paper is the best example of this, requiring students to master the processes of collecting, analyzing, and documenting information, as well as the process of composing it into a coherent piece of writing. In most schools and colleges, writing teachers must teach these complex, interrelated capacities to students of widely divergent abilities. As we will see, a carefully planned syllabus must try to integrate these purposes and keep the fault lines between them from serious fractures.

Perhaps the most formidable challenge faced by writing teachers is that of helping students learn to use language as a way of knowing in a wide variety of fields. Writing courses are often seen institutionally as "service" courses: they are expected to empower students with language skills for virtually every other discipline. It is never put so baldly in curriculum guidelines or college catalogs, which tend to innocuous phrases like "the importance of communication in human culture" or "the necessity for clarity in our thoughts and actions." But parents, administrators, other faculty, and employers all expect English teachers to give students skills fitted to their own respective preferences. Parents expect students to be able to write letters to grandparents; administrators expect them to score well on language tests; other faculty expect them to write coherent exams and reports; and employers expect them to enter the company ready to dash off letters, memos, and reports. The marshaling and analysis of facts and ideas on essay tests, research papers, and reports will be their main writing chore in non-English courses. Comparing and contrasting, analyzing and synthesizing, relating the specific to the general—skills that make it possible to learn and communicate course content—will be essential to the academic uses of writing.

The development of writing-across-the-curriculum programs in many schools and colleges in recent years has helped writing teachers understand the forms and contexts of writing in other disciplines, and has sensitized teachers in many disciplines to the power of writing as a means of learning. Such programs tend to take one of two forms: either writing teachers build courses within the English department around writing tasks appropriate to other disciplines, or teachers in other disciplines, guided by experienced writing teachers, build their own writing-intensive courses within their respective departments. In recent years a number of writing teachers have developed ways of teaching cross-disciplinary writing tasks in their composition courses. Their first task, suggests one team of writing teachers, is to explore the conventions of writing applicable to various fields of knowledge: teachers must understand and teach their students how "three relationships—of writer and reader, of writer and writers, of writer and field of written discourse" comprise those conventions that govern writing in any discipline (Moore and Petersen 468). In preparing writing assignments applicable to fields ranging from history and literature to anthropology, these teachers read journals and books in these fields and discussed writing conventions with both faculty and students as they prepared tasks specific to these fields. Another teaching team takes a different approach, devising "a small repertory of expository forms" which could be applied "flexibly in a variety of academic situations" (Kiniry and Strenski 191–2). This set of forms embodies "eight basic 'schema' . . . that all of us use to process information and make meaning": listing, definition, seriation, classification, summary, comparison/contrast, analysis and argument (192–4). Each "schema" is embodied in a specific writing task which, taken together, form a set of assignments appropriate to almost any field of knowledge.

Such wide-ranging writing tasks can help prepare students for the demands other academic fields will make on them. Yet the power of such tasks to draw students into unfamiliar discourse situations should not blind teachers to the very real value of personal writing. It offers students the chance to articulate their own experiences for a disciplined audience of instructors and peers capable of genuinely educative feedback. This does not necessarily mean that students will change their lives because they must write discriminatingly about their own experience. It does mean that they will take the act of writing about themselves more seriously because they perceive that others will—indeed are obliged to by the nature of the course context. And taking writing seriously is the first step in the student writer's discovery that writing is purposeful human activity, not just academic labor. Personal writing subjected to serious inquiry and feedback will take on value for writers themselves, as a reflection of its value for others. Causing writing about personal experience to take on reflexive significance for students can, in turn, give unique significance to that experience.

It is difficult to separate personal from academic implications in any given assignment, since some personal awareness may grow out of any writing task, in addition to its potential for placing the student writer within a particular academic discourse field. The experience of many writing teachers is that strategies for teaching writing can be appropriate to a wide range of academic areas. For example, teachers may want to assign journals in addition to other writing tasks, but may hesitate because journals appear to serve only the personal writing goals in a curriculum that emphasizes practical writing purposes in—for example—a scientific field. But journals may well seem to students the most interesting, personally engaging kind of writing asked of them. Journals offer students opportunities to digest and summarize lectures, articulate responses, formulate questions for class and topics for writing assignments, and evaluate their own progress. Writing journals, may, in other words, bring home to students the essential power of writing to create learning and build knowledge. Indeed, any writing task that can help students discover writing as a way of giving meaning to experience will justify and centralize itself in students' lives.

2. What kinds of writing assignments should I set?

Making up writing assignments is the most important part of planning a writing course. Writing assignments determine the way in which students will perceive the course, the amount and seriousness of their labor, and the attitude toward writing they will carry into their work. We have already seen that small-scale, uncontextualized writing tasks—sentence and paragraph exercises or error-correction exercises—can easily fill up class time and be assigned as homework. But students will perceive such labor as makework, typical "English course" activity. For where outside the writing classroom do we correct a list of twenty sentence errors or rearrange paragraphs? Indeed, a major reason why students do not write effectively, or regard writing as serious work, is that they are not asked often enough to *do* genuine writing in school. They have filled in countless workbooks, written out spelling and definition lists, and diagrammed endless sentences. But they have not done much writing. Here is where writing teachers who want to make a difference in students' lives can do so: they can build a sequence of significant writing assignments, and help students see, perhaps for the first time, that writing is essential human activity.

The basis of a good writing course is a sequence of purposeful writing tasks with both *topical* and *situational* dimensions. Each task should bring together a clear topical focus and purpose and a projected reader or audience in a well-defined situation. The series of tasks can be organized in several ways: by means of the writer's logical processes, or in terms of a sequence of topics, or as a sequence of different rhetorical situations, or as a combination of such elements. For inexperienced writers, theorists like Elbow and Park have argued, developing the subject matter often takes precedence over audience-awareness. Student writers often need to discover *what* they have to say about a topic before they are able to envision *how* they can adjust their styles to different audiences. That is why inexperienced writers sometimes produce what Linda Flower calls "writer-based prose," writing which primarily reflects student writers' attempts to master unfamiliar material and adapt it for other readers. The backbone of an effective writing course for inexperienced writers, therefore, should be a carefully planned sequence of tasks challenging them with gradually more complex contexts and differentiated audiences.

Ann Berthoff argues that as they compose topics, writers must see "relationships of parts to wholes, of items in a sequence, of causes and effects; composition is a matter of seeing and naming relationships, of putting the relationships together, ordering them" (71). In the language of the cognitive perspective we explored in earlier chapters, this connecting and ordering could be said to represent the development of more complex "schemas." Establishing hierarchies of the general and the specific and the abstract and the concrete is essential to virtually every writing task college students may face, from laboratory reports to poetry. Finding relationships entails movements of mind that range from the particular and the immediate to the universal and speculative—from "he's mad" to "people get mad." But grasping the interaction between universal and particular requires the experience of it *in language*, in something we say or write. When teachers are tempted to write "muddy thinking" in the margin of a text, it is an assertion of the wedded bond between thinking and composing.

Effective introductory writing courses must help students see how language enables them to articulate and manipulate their ways of knowing themselves and their world. For inexperienced writers in particular, articulating ways of seeing will begin most readily out of personal experience. All students have memories of specific experiences that can be particularized in description and narration, even though such experiences may not have been rationalized or reflected upon. Thus, early writing tasks for inexperienced writers should include descriptive and narrative patterns as ways of rendering particularity in language. As student writers begin to reflect on what has happened, to compare one experience with another, to classify an encounter in terms of other encounters like it, or to find reasons why it occurred, they are moving beyond telling about experience (which gives life to particulars) into the modes that connect particulars to form general patterns. In such writing students are obliged to recognize particularity and manipulate it into patterns that reveal general and abstract meanings. They will be able to do this effectively only to the extent, however, that they have come to recognize the language of the particular and the language of the general as the two interact to make meaning. Such recognition must be taught carefully and thoroughly if students are to master these languages for their own purposes.

There are several types of assignment sequences which can further this developmental pattern. One entails a movement from "inner worlds to outer worlds"—that is, from concrete personal experience to the more impersonal subject matter of various academic disciplines. Acknowledging the influence of Piaget and the concepts of developmental psychology, Stephen Judy [now "Tchudi"] describes a sequence falling into three phases: the first featuring descriptions and narratives of personal experiences, the second a variety of forms collected in a class "magazine," and the third a series of academic writing tasks. Another writer describes a sequence based on repeated treatments of personal experiences (Katz). The first assignment asks students to describe a geographical place and discuss its meaning for them. Later assignments ask students to describe and analyze a relationship with someone else, an internal conflict, and an experience that left them with a strong opinion. The final task is the traditional research paper requiring discovery of knowledge beyond students' personal experience. Each assignment except the research paper is rooted in students' personal experience, but requires making general, speculative statements about that experience.

Another way of organizing writing tasks is by means of a sequence of writings examining and re-examining a general idea or issue; William Coles is a well-know progenitor and proponent of this approach. This method requires the instructor to build into each topic the logical and rhetorical strategies desired. Students are asked to write a series of papers, each developing an aspect of the central topic, and each emerging from previous papers and class discussions. The entire focus of the course is the students' writing generated in response to the sequence of topics. Little outside reading is required and class discussions center on students' own writing and issues raised in it. A variation on this pattern has been termed an "epistemic" approach, featuring assignments that ask students to reflect repeatedly upon themselves as writers. Quoting John Dewey on experiential learning, one proponent of this approach asserts that "a typical epistemic writing assignment . . . directs students to follow the experience of composing with some 'reflective review and summarizing' of what they have been doing" (Dowst 75). Though assignments differ in topic and reference, they are cumulatively recursive and revisionary, consistently asking students to reexamine their roles as writers and learners. Yet another kind of topical writing sequence may ask students to draw upon outside readings in addressing a central theme. A series of assignments exploring, for example, "The Anti-Hero in Literature" could draw from literary and nonliterary readings and require students to go beyond their own experience in defining the writing topics. Such a sequence would, of course, be limited primarily to expository purposes, as students respond to thematic issues by defining, comparing, classifying, and analyzing.

But a topical, reading-based sequence need not be limited to exposition; it can encompass a variety of purposes and forms. One proposal offers a reading based series of assignments that asks students to understand published writers "as writers" and to write in ways that represent "an essential component of a particular writer's performance, a component that the writer used often, and with variety, throughout the piece in question" (Moran 2). Students in this course wrote descriptive analyses on a geographical place (representing Cather's technique in *Death Comes for the Archbishop*) and stream-of-consciousness meditations within a moment of time (embodying Virginia Woolf's strategy). Such exercises are intended to enlarge students' awareness of context in writing, and facilitate "the transfer of technique from the reading to the writing" (27). Another, more traditional proposal suggests the use of literary contexts for the routine sequence from autobiography to the library research paper. The major writers in the British canon are surveyed and writings derived from the students' responses to literature. The first assignment is an autobiographical meditation on how the student has experienced literature in the past; other assignments ask students to write a character description after Chaucer and to compose an argument over the value-conflicts in *The Rape of the Lock*. Such tasks presume some literary sensitivity on the students' part and, obviously, the teacher's tolerance for inexperienced writers' exaggeration of effect. But both these strategies leave students free to explore, develop, and articulate their own experiences within the discipline of specific forms and styles.

But writers do not compose in a vacuum; they shape topics in terms of the situation within which they write. Writing assignments must establish meaningful contexts for student writing. Unfortunately, the assignment sequence implied in many big-selling texts relies primarily on modes or discourse forms as the basis for framing assignments. Textbook discussions of purpose and form are often followed by assignment suggestions that are formal and without rhetorical context. Implied in this conventional handling of writing tasks is that composing begins with a sense of form. The practical result is often a series labeled "a description paper," "a comparison and contrast paper," "an argument," and so on. The absence of content and context means that students must devise a topic without seeing any connection with what they may have written previously, or what they may write about later. The lack of rhetorical context encourages "writer-based prose," or at best a piece aimed at what students have discovered about the teacher's expectations. Above all, the task will strike students as just another exercise in doing what is expected of them, in which dutifulness—rather than inventiveness, uniqueness, or any form of risk-taking—is the supreme virtue. They know perfectly well that no one writes simply to compare and contrast things, or classify things, or argue with a shadowy audience about some abstract issue—except, of course, in a classroom.

Telling students to "define *politics*" or "compare and contrast roommates" or "argue for gun control" will not do. Such tasks lack both coherence and self-justifying significance for student writers. Packaged in a semester's syllabus as a series of jobs students must perform to get the reward of a good grade, such assignments confirm students' sense that academic writing is like lab experimentation in basic science courses. Students know that the teacher knows what to expect: there are "more right" and "less right" responses. Students (particularly the best ones) quickly learn to divine the teacher's wants and write to them. This is writing as academic gameplaying; from it students learn that writing is just another form of test-taking. Like taking tests, writing papers requires a canny judgment about the teacher's biases and a dutiful attempt to do what is asked. If the job is done with a modicum of care, the reward will come in the form of an A or a B. But, of course, this is not writing, any more than drawing up a lab report on the structure of a daisy is real botanizing. For neither activity has real consequences; they are merely training exercises. Of course, botany students need to learn how to dissect and classify flowers in the lab, but only in order to be able to go into the field and botanize in a way that makes a difference to someone somewhere. And this, finally, is what genuine writing instruction must encourage: composing and writing that makes a difference, that exists within a context students perceive as fraught with consequences beyond merely good or bad grades.

Writing in the "real world" always bears consequences. A feasibility report may launch or kill a new venture. A performance evaluation may do the same for a career. A legal brief may impress a judge and help a client, or muff the job and lose the case. An article by a research engineer may present the research and its results persuasively and change the state of the art, or garble the facts and their interpretations so badly that the work has no impact. "Real world" writing always has an outcome, always makes some difference, even if only for the writers themselves. But writing that emerges from an assignment to "compare your values to those of your parents" has no significance for the student writer unless it is engendered by the writer's genuine need to make such a comparison, to address some issue that lends importance to the effort.

What attributes, then, should an effective assignment sequence—the backbone of the writing course—possess? It should at all costs avoid a mere stringing together of modal or generic tasks. Each assignment should have some rhetorical context: a clear topic, a distinct readership (even if only the student writer herself), and an underlying purpose that makes certain structures and styles appropriate. And a good assignment should also encourage the writer to compose and recompose, and set the duration of the task to make that possible. The assignment must be planned so that even if it is an impromptu assignment, students should have a liberal amount of time for the recomposing and revising that alone produce readable texts. Thus, the scope of the task should be adjusted to the setting within which students are asked to write.

But sometimes, even when assignments have all these things, students may still perceive them as mere exercises, the more so as elements of the assignment appear remote or unfamiliar. An essential aspect of writing assignments is their genuine significance for the writer: something that gives discourse the promise of a meaningful outcome. Take, for example, that assignment requiring students to match their values or attitudes with those of an older generation. Most students will have engaged in some dialectic on this general theme for years with their parents. But simply writing a paper explaining their disagreements is not a natural writing purpose; it's a laboratory formulation only. Suppose instead that students were asked to write a letter to a younger brother or sister having similar conflicts with the parents; the letter should explain the writer's perceptions of the conflict and offer some suggestions to the reader about coping with conflict, based on the writer's longer perspective. Or suppose students were asked to imagine themselves as 65-year-olds writing a family history, in the course of which they find it necessary to trace a family conflict, clarify their youthful role in it, and assess its impact upon decisions made at the time. The audience in this case would be—aside from immediate family members—an uncertain future readership quite unlike the sibling audience of the previous assignment. Both such assignments have a rhetorical context; one requires a descriptive analysis for a familiar audience, the other an analysis for a more distant audience seeking understanding rather than advice.

The topic of value conflict is part of the dialectic of maturation present in all our lives. Neither of the assignments just described would necessarily reconcile the generations, though either one might help the student writers change their feelings about themselves or their parents. From such tasks students would articulate their experiences more fully, learning a bit more about shaping experience in and through language. But they will not experience the genuine power of effective writing until they are given the chance to see its consequences as more than merely the gaining of a certain mark. The instructor can make this possible by establishing writing tasks that students must take seriously. Family relationships are only one part of students' lives; any topic, private or public, provided it has context bears some implications for students, can call out their seriousness and invite them to discover the power of writing.

3. *How much emphasis should I give to deliberately planned and revised writing? How much to spontaneous, impromptu writing?*

The emphasis upon composing and revising now appears as a matter of course in writing texts. The models of composing described in Chapter One suggest prewriting activities that may include a systematic heuristic or discovery process which can frame random ideas into organized sequences (Burke's "pentad," for example).

The assumption behind this emphasis upon careful composing is that revision is essential to good writing. However, this assumption has been challenged by some well-known teachers. Such influential writers as Ken Macrorie and Peter Elbow have emphasized free-writing and other kinds of informal writing as ways of enhancing students' ability to compose and become more fluent as writers. Macrorie urges students to "write for ten minutes as fast as you can, never stopping to ponder a thought. Put down whatever comes to your mind" (8). Macrorie wants students to write so rapidly and freely that they won't have a chance to use that stock of clichés he labels "Engfish." He argues that students often labor diligently to write pretentious and overwrought prose in order to please the English teacher; freewriting is an intensive experience in generating writing in the student's own voice—writing that is "telling." He points out that freewritten prose is not "fully realized" writing (10), however, and must undergo revision and reworking. Peter Elbow argues the other side; brief freewritten pieces, he says, can be "less random, more coherent, more highly organized" than deliberately composed writing because the writer's intention is intensively focused to achieve an "integration of meanings" (8). However sponta-neous writing may be justified, its immediate effect is clear: it delib-erately telescopes the normal phases of composing into brief, intensive spurts. It prevents young writers from reflecting on those phases as they pass through them in their writing. Macrorie and Elbow argue strongly—but from different standpoints—that this tele-scoping helps counteract bad habits and gives students confidence as writers. The largest danger in impromptu writing, of course, is that in shortcircuiting deliberate composing and revising, it conveys to stu-dents that this is how effective writing is normally generated—a notion that belies the conclusions of all recent research into the composing process.

In the 1970s, under the influence of strong advocates like Mac-rorie and Elbow, there was widespread interest in removing con-straints from students' writing tasks. Impromptu writing seemed to many teachers the best way to encourage writing growth. However, spontaneous writing allows students to circumvent the revising and reworking which the cognitive-process view of writing has main-tained is essential to successful writing. Such composing may, as wise advocates like Macrorie suggest, be used as a carefully arranged loosening-up exercise. But other studies—as well as common sense—suggest that students participating in an array of planning, composing, reviewing, and revising activities will become more reflective, self-directed, and fluent writers. One recent study reports that younger students deliberately taught an awareness of com-posing processes, reader expectations, and context, as well as various text patterns and conventions, "did improve their writing as well as show enhanced metacognitive awareness" of the psychological and situational elements of writing (Raphael et al. 377). This study proposes that students whose writing—and whose understandings of themselves as writers—are both targeted for intensive study produce better writing than those who merely write and do grammar and editing exercises. This study adds that the students also found these aspects of writerly self-awareness applicable to writing in courses other than writing classes.

Indeed, the need to help students understand and gain control of their writing behavior has been thoroughly documented in recent years. Researchers Donald Murray and Nancy Sommers have demonstrated that a major weakness of inexperienced writers is their failure to understand what genuine revision is. Murray divides the revising process into "internal revision," in which writers "discover and develop what they have to say, beginning with the reading of a first draft," and "external revision," which is "editing and proofreading" (91). He points out what we have already seen in Chapter One—that writing texts tend to emphasize "the etiquette of writing" (91) rather than the essential work of discovering meaning, form, and voice. Sommers extends this argument by showing that student writers generally have a far narrower grasp of the revision process than "experienced adult writers," largely because the students have been taught that revising is putting commas in the right places and spelling correctly. Experienced writers in Sommers' study saw revision as a way of "finding form and shape for their argument" (384), and making stylistic and tonal choices appropriate to their audience. They saw revision as re-seeing and re-shaping, not merely as the fixing of grammar and punctuation errors.

4. Should I try to teach grammar? What connections are there between formal grammar instruction and editing?

The split between "knowing *that*" and "knowing *how*" is sharp and clear in these questions. We saw earlier that knowledge of the nature of language has not been shown to help students become better writers. Yet some teachers still believe grammar is necessary to help students learn to write. For example, defending transformational grammar as offering "meaningful explanations for what traditional grammars ignore," Elaine Chaika argues that the focus of "new grammar" is on "the creative process itself" and is useful in helping students learn to compose sentences. Writing teachers should select only texts with a transformational basis to its grammar material, she concludes (771). Some widely-used texts still urge the study of grammar both as a way of exploring sentence structure and as a means of identifying and repairing syntactical errors.

Opponents of grammar in the writing class argue that forcing students to learn grammatical notations does not help them learn to write. As Frank O'Hare notes, a number of experiments have shown no useful relationship between grammar and the improvement of writing skills: "Study after study tested the hypothesis that there was a positive relationship between the study of grammar and . . . composition. Result after result denied this hypothesis" (5). Those arguing that grammar is not needed for writing often argue by analogy. Do children need to know the laws of physics in order to learn to swim? Do they have to grasp the principles of optics to learn to read? Is an understanding of the principles of internal combustion needed by student drivers? O'Hare himself, arguing that "grammar study is in disrepute at the present time largely because it has failed to help students write any better," offers a sentence-combining strategy that "does not necessitate the study of a grammar, traditional or transformational" (30). James Moffett also argues strongly against grammar in the writing classroom. "Poor punctuation, illogicality, ambiguous pronoun reference, run-on or rambling sentences, inaccurate vocabulary, lack of transition or coherence or subordination"—problems often lumped under the heading of "grammar"—are not grammar problems at all, says Moffett, but questions of usage and mechanics having nothing to do with the grammaticality of sentences (Moffett and Wagner 19). "Can anyone seriously believe," he asks, "that theorizing about habits as deep and automatic as those of speech will alter practice?" (21). Poor writers, Moffett suggests, may generate ungrammatical sentences, but knowing what a subject or a finite verb is will not guarantee their being able to write one. Only making sentences—i.e., writing—will improve students' skills in making sentences: "the best way to improve grammar is to practice discourse in all its forms," he concludes (464).

But teachers still must find effective ways to help students learn to edit their writing. As we saw in Chapter Four, there is a standard written dialect or "grapholect" of American English, with its conventions of syntax, usage, punctuation, and spelling. At some point in every writing class, those students who lack editing skills must be asked to confront their deficiencies. A student text may show well-ordered intentions, focused thinking, and clear organization, but without careful editing it will lack effectiveness and irritate readers. Indeed, violations of the so-called "surface" features of the standard dialect are often more immediately visible to many readers than the elements of focus, logic, and voice. The key to helping students learn crucial editing skills is to contextualize these skills. That is, rather than trying to teach students to edit by using formal exercises based on either part-of-speech or transformational grammar, all editing instruction should occur within the context of a shaped text. One way to accomplish this is for teachers to distinguish sharply between early and final drafts, and expect carefully edited writing only on the last draft to be submitted. Many teachers, however, are uncomfortable with this somewhat arbitrary effort to divide writing into distinguishable draft stages, each with its own characteristics; they tend to see composing as a continuous process of reseeing and reworking, in which careful editing ought to be an ongoing effort. Whatever pattern teachers find appropriate, however, they should help students recognize the wholeness of discourse—the importance of standard conventions of syntax, idiom, punctuation and spelling in the whole process of constructing meaning through language.

5. Should I use an anthology or other outside sources of writing in addition to students' own work in the course?

To question the need for readings is to threaten the profitability of great publishing houses and send tremors through the academic cottage industry of anthology-making. Yet readings should be chosen only after the teacher has asked a fundamental question: do students need to read as well as write in a writing course? Ann Berthoff argues strongly that they do: "reading and writing, I believe, should always be taught together. . . . composing is best nurtured by interpreting texts as well as [interpreting] experience" (10). On the other hand, Peter Elbow maintains that teachers should focus attention in class on students' own work, the only writing "the members of the class can take seriously" (20). Published writing may seem remote to inexperienced writers, who will despair of their own writing as it contrasts with polished work. They may read such writing with interest but find little in it that they can absorb into their own composing.

Contemporary cognitive-process researchers, discourse theorists, and rhetoricians agree that writing and reading are interdependent activities. Acceptance of this general principle has influenced the way many writing teachers plan their courses; they agree that teaching writing necessarily entails teaching reading: "We explain reading to understand writing," says Susan Miller, because "writers actually and figuratively read *and* write" (18). Arguments for the use of readings in writing courses draw in part from cognitive-process theory, which postulates three kinds of interrelationships between writing and reading (as we saw in Chapter Two):

1. Writing and reading are both intentional acts of composing in which writers and readers purposefully "represent" or construct meaning.

2. Writing and reading are both predictive activities; writers and readers "compose" texts under the influence of goals and expectations.

3. Writing and reading are both dependent on context for meaning; the composing of writers and readers is shaped by the conventions of situation and circumstance.

As writers write and readers read, they have in common the activity of constructing meanings. A writer composing a text is also a reader of that text as it emerges; all writers are simultaneously readers. The "reading self" continuously reciprocates the "writing self," interpreting and recomposing the meanings intended by that other self. In this sense, all writing courses are inherently reading courses as well, and therefore should include some attention to students' reading habits and skills.

One important benefit of readings for writing students can come from discussions of the composing situations from which texts emerge. Teachers can help demystify professional writing by clarifying the composing processes experienced writers use, analyzing their ways of signalling their intentions in texts, and outlining the contexts and circumstances within which the texts are produced. Published writing can be examined in terms of the stages of its composition (John Ciardi's essay on Frost's labor with "Stopping by Woods" is an example); teachers can also show their own composing methods in pieces they may be working on. Another way to help students grasp the variety and force of traditional genres of writing is to ask them to utilize its forms and contexts as represented in published texts. From its beginnings, rhetorical training has asked students to shape their own voices and styles out of the best traditional models of established writers and speakers. One proponent of this strategy for writing students suggests that students can be "acculturated" to the demands of academic writing by first composing letters, dialogues, and essays in the manner of earlier practitioners of those forms (Prince). Students are asked to write a sequence of letters, dialogues, and formal arguments on "increasingly difficult topics" until they are prepared to write an "argumentative essay" for a general audience on a complex academic topic. Reading letters of Jack London and Vincent Van Gogh, students compose similar writings for their own familiar readers as they gradually learn to summarize and argue the issues raised by such writers as Ralph Waldo Emerson and Walter Lippmann.

Reading published writing can spur students' interest in discovering their own attitudes and values. The often decontextualized contents of anthologies are not the only—often not the best—source of topical material for students. Newspapers, magazines and journals, and films can all be used as sources for writing in all modes, from narrative descriptions of sensational murder cases to reviews of current films. Another kind of collateral material emphasizing cultural and social experience outside academe is fieldwork, wherein students are required to develop a project exploring some person, profession, or situation in the community outside the academic institution. Even nonverbal materials can provide the subject matter of composition, such as paintings and photographs whose interpretations offer challenging writing tasks.

Readings can also help students understand how, in a given writing situation, personal motives and intentions interact with institutional and public occasions and conventions. Analyses of the implicit intentions and settings of texts can help students understand how experienced writers take up roles engendered by their participation in a writing situation. Reading may thus be presented as a kind of dramatics, a way of understanding writing roles by playing those roles. Students know intuitively, Jonathan Culler argues, that "to read is to play the role of a reader and to interpret is to posit an experience of reading" (*On Deconstruction* 67). Linda Brodkey suggests that "as teachers we need to learn how to 'read' the various relationships between writer, reader, and reality that language and discourse . . . produce" (125), so that we can help students understand how these relationships define a variety of writing situations. Unfortunately, in too many highly visible prose anthologies touted for use in writing courses—containing some of inexperienced writers' first reading experiences at the college level—writing is presented in simplified, noncontextual fashion. Selections are excerpted, stripped of context, and categorized under abstractions like "theme" or "mode," and offered as discrete, unconnected reading experiences. Such experiences do not represent reading as it really is: complex role-playing dependent on the interplay between writer, reader, and context.

Readings must be designed to help students understand how writing is embedded in personal, institutional, and public contexts. Teachers can direct attention to the writer by asking "what do you understand about the writer and his or her goals and circumstances?", leading students to examine and articulate the roles played by that writer with respect to that text. Or teachers can direct students' attention to the text by asking "what sort of reader does this text want you to be?" and "how do your own expectations shape your responses to the text?" These questions can help students understand the interactive, reciprocal nature of writing and reading, and encourage collaborative explorations of writing intentions and responses. Reacting to such questions will require students to recognize the contextual and textual cues that define writing and reading roles.

Reading assignments must, in other words, help students articulate the situatedness of texts, writers, and readers. Students must be shown that writing and reading are governed by the genres, situations, and conventions out of which all texts emerge. They must be helped to understand that writers never compose, nor readers respond, in a vacuum. To help students understand context, teachers must insure that readings are always presented within the contexts that give them significance. If Virginia Woolf's "If Shakespeare Had Had a Sister" is assigned, it should not be merely as an "analysis" or as a token example of feminist writing. To play the role of the reader required by this essay, we must grasp some of the major issues in the feminist tradition which it attempts to address, and the circumstances of Woolf's own life. The enduring appeal of this essay simply can't be fathomed by students encountering only a truncated version wedged in between George Will and Richard Wright (as one popular anthology presents it).

Similarly, for example, if students in a composition class are asked to read Orwell's popular "Shooting an Elephant," it cannot be merely as the unintroduced lead entry under the "Politics and Government" section (as another anthology presents it). It is crucial to readers' responses to this piece that they understand something about the genre of anti-colonial writings, especially colonialism's socialist critiques, and Orwell's personal experiences that led him to this essay and to *Burmese Days*, composed in the same creative period. Why is the reader inclined to read this narrative as a parable about the death of colonialism? What are the links between intention and response here, given the times and Orwell's own background? Inexperienced readers will find textual cues to these ambiguities necessary but not sufficient; a satisfactory reading of this essay depends on the reader's contextual understandings.

Not the least of all, teachers can help students experience the pleasure of reading, that sense of delight which accompanies the personal play of responding and building representations of texts.

Teaching reading in the writing class can be a way of empowering students to make the most of their experiences of a text.

6. What kind of pacing should I plan for students' writing? How much writing should I require and how often?

Perhaps the dominant tradition in composition courses is to plan regular writing tasks of limited length—500 or so words every week or two. This standard has some obvious advantages for the student and the instructor. It is short enough to allow students to develop, write, and revise within a few hours, about as long as the average student is likely to spend on one assignment. And it is long enough to permit the development of two or three major points in some detail. Moreover, such length allows peers and instructors to read and respond with reasonable time commitments. Training students to write within a 500-word scope is nothing more than developing their artfulness in exploiting a given form as fully as possible. What James Britton terms "transactional" writing in most disciplines (and in most business settings) occurs within just such limited formats demanding conciseness as a primary virtue. Nor is it the brevity (or length) of assigned writing that brands it as routine school writing. As we saw earlier in this chapter, that stigma results from the lack of situatedness and context in assignments. Indeed, brevity is the governing condition of much "real world" writing—most of it shorter even than 500 words. Learning to establish and develop all that can be said within a stated limit is a valuable composing skill in many contexts, and assignments of various lengths can help develop it.

Smaller and more frequent assignments can help students focus on writing at the paragraph level, and can offer inexperienced writers in particular a necessary sense of freedom within attainable limits. The advantage of small-scale assignments is the narrow focus it permits upon specific strategies, and the immediate feedback to the students available in the classroom setting. The disadvantage is the effect of small assignments upon the students' need to push beyond a paragraph or two if a topic calls up their interest and draws them into the situation more intensively. Larger writing tasks afford scope for inventing and developing topics, for creating larger rhetorical units, and for composing more complex logical patterns. For the average freshman composition student, somewhere between 500 and 1000 words is the limit to ask on a weekly or biweekly basis. Some students could produce more without strain, but inexperienced writers cannot cope with a larger regular writing task without at some point abandoning planning or revision and simply putting down words as fast as possible. Most students will feel too badgered by other academic and social commitments to put in sufficient time for longer writing tasks on a weekly basis. Meanwhile, instructors teaching two (or more) writing courses who want to respond personally to each assignment or draft will face many hours of reading per week, in addition to preparation for class meetings and student conferences. As we will see in Chapter Six, however, writing teachers need not be limited to the conventional editing-plus-terminal-comment routine.

For too many students, however, all assigned writing is an imposition regarded with an equal measure of fear and loathing. There are ways to avoid setting particular tasks for students who might flourish on a more independent basis: some teachers have found success requiring regular writing of no set length, while others simply ask students to write a certain number of pages on no fixed schedule. While writing on a fixed schedule gives students freedom to write as they wish under the discipline of a deadline, writing without a deadline throws them back squarely upon their own self-directedness. This freedom of output can result in high satisfaction for students with sufficient self-motivation. Indeed, students' delight in work they alone have generated is a natural advantage of such an assignment pattern. But are the benefits of regular deadlines worth sacrificing for the increased pleasure some students may find in setting their own pace?

Undoubtedly a few well-motivated students thrive under such freedom; they enjoy seeing how far their abilities can take them. The majority, however, cannot use the freedom because they do not have the discipline. They discover that some kind of pressure—pressure of the task itself, peer pressure, grade pressure—is essential to motivate them into regular effort. And if these covert pressures do not stimulate poorly-motivated students, their gradually increasing guilt could alienate them from the course and ultimately from themselves. They will have confirmed themselves failures. The course that has no specific assignments or deadlines also creates difficulty in the feedback process. The student who puts off writing for weeks or months at a time and then turns in a mass of work as make-up will fail to get the regular attention that might have enhanced his critical awareness of his own work. Able students may flourish under a regime of freedom; but poor or even average students, lacking the discipline of structured assignments or deadlines, may fall short of their own capacity for growth because it has not been called up in them sharply enough. These students need the challenge of regular assignments.

There is a popular assignment pattern that stops short of absolute deadlines and a required number of writings, but offers more intrinsic structure than the "open" course. This is the "contract" course that matches certain totals and types of written work with specific grades, so that students know what and how much they must write in order to get a certain grade. The psychological basis of this course pattern is a deliberate, forthright correlation of work and reward. Students see clearly that "achievement" is a relative term, depending on realistic goal-setting, and that their own persistence as much as their writing ability will determine how far they go. Especially for students whose fear of writing is based on unhappy previous experience, a course that requires drive and ambition as much as skill is highly attractive. Any task that promises to yield to effort, rather than to be totally dependent upon an ability doubtful in the holding, will attract students with even modest motivation. One "contract" system sets forth several levels of achievement based on the number of papers completed, and evaluated on a graduated scale of polish and complexity, so that an "A" grade represents eight successful writings judged by increasingly rigorous standards, a "B" six writings judged by the same incremental standards, a "C" four writings (Knapp). Other contract patterns may involve more (or fewer) papers, may require experimentation with a variety of situations and topics, or may allow for students to select several of what they judge to be their best writings for final evaluation. However administered, the contract pattern offers an attractive blend of discipline and freedom. Students may legitimately be asked to write in a variety of modes, use a wide range of rhetorical strategies, and still be offered their own choice of how much work they will do and what reward they are willing to settle for. Few other courses in school or university can provide such self-fulfilling latitude within a structured situation.

Planning a writing course requires imagination; teachers must think ahead about how their students may respond to the tasks and situations in the course. The purposes of the course, its writing assignments, the connections between writing tasks and readings, and the amount and pacing of work should be established at the outset so students clearly understand them. A syllabus that ends halfway through the semester or is filled with blank spaces invites students to disregard it. Even with careful planning, however, unanticipated difficulties may come to light as the course unfolds, requiring teachers to improvise new tasks or realign learning relationships. Students will accept changes if they see that they are necessary to the direction established for the course in the beginning; without the innate purposefulness of a clearly developed course plan, however, changes may appear arbitrary or counterproductive. A deeply-embedded sense of purpose can help make a writing course a memorable learning experience for students.

Works Cited

Berthoff, Ann E. *Forming/Thinking/Writing*, 2nd ed. Portsmouth, NH: Boynton/Cook, 1978.

Brodkey, Linda K. "On the Subjects of Class and Gender in 'The Literacy Letters'." *College English* 51 (1989): 125–41.

Chaika, Elaine. "Grammars and Teaching." CE 39 (1978): 770–83.

Coles, William E. Jr. *The Plural I—and After*. Portsmouth, NH: Boynton/Cook, 1988.

Comprone, Joseph. "Burke and Teaching Writing." *College Composition and Communication* 29 (1978): 336–40.

Connors, Robert. "Personal Writing Assignments." CCC 38 (1987): 166–83.

Culler, Jonathan. *On Destruction: Theory and Criticism After Structuralism*. Ithaca, NY: Cornell University Press, 1982.

Dixon, John. *Growth through English Set in the Perspective of the Seventies*. London: Oxford University Press, 1975.

Donovan, Timothy R. and Ben W. McClelland, eds. *Eight Approaches to Teaching Composition*. Urbana, IL: NCTE, 1980.

Dowst, Kenneth. "The Epistemic Approach: Writing, Knowing, and Learning." Donovan and McClelland 65–86.

Elbow, Peter. *Writing Without Teachers*. New York: Oxford University Press, 1973.

Judy [now Tchudi], Stephen. "The Experiential Approach: Inner Worlds to Outer Worlds." Donovan and McClellan 37–52.

Katz, Marilyn. "From Self-Analysis to Academic Analysis." CE 40 (1978): 288–92.

Kennedy, X. J. and Dorothy M. Kennedy. *The Bedford Guide for College Writers*. 2nd ed. Boston: St. Martin's Press, 1990.

Kiniry, Malcolm and Ellen Strenski. "Sequencing Expository Writing: A Recursive Approach." CCC 36 (1985): 191–202.

Knapp, John. "Contract/Conference Evaluation of Freshman Composition." CE 37 (1976): 647–53.

Macrorie, Ken. *Telling Writing*. 4th ed. Upper Montclair, NJ: Boynton/Cook, 1985.

Miller, Susan. *Rescuing the Subject: A Critical Introduction to Rhetoric and the Writer*. Carbondale, IL: Southern Illinois University Press, 1989.

Moffett, James and Betty Jane Wagner. *Student-Centered Language Arts K-12*. 4th ed. Portsmouth, NH: Boynton/Cook, 1992.

Moore, Leslie and Linda H. Peterson. "Convention as Connection: Linking the Composition Course to the English and College Curriculum." CCC 37 (1986): 466–77, 488.

Moran, Charles. "Teaching Writing/Teaching Literature." CCC 32 (1981): 21–29.

Murray, Donald. *"Internal Revision: A Process of Discovery."* Research on Composing, ed. Charles R. Cooper and Lee Odell. Urbana, IL: NCTE, 1978. 85–103.

O'Hare, Frank. *Sentence Combining: Improving Student Writing Without Formal Grammar Instruction.* Urbana, IL: NCTE, 1973.

Park, Douglas. "The Meanings of Audience." CE 44 (1982): 247–57.

Polanyi, Michael. *The Tacit Dimension.* New York: Doubleday & Co., 1966.

Prince, Michael B. "Literacy and Genre: Towards a Pedagogy of Mediation." CE 51 (1989): 730–749.

Raphael, Taffy E., Carol Sue Englert, Becky W. Kirschner. "Students Metacognitive Knowledge about Writing." *Research in the Teaching of English 23* (1989): 343–79.

Ryle, Gilbert. *The Concept of Mind.* London: Hutchinson House, 1949.

Shaughnessy, Mina. *Errors and Expectations: A Guide for the Teacher of Basic Writing.* New York: Oxford University Press, 1977.

Smith, Frank. *Understanding Reading: A Psycholinguistic Analysis of Reading and Learning to Read.* Hillsdale, NJ: Lawrence Erlbaum Associates, 1988.

Sommers, Nancy. "Revision Strategies of Student Writers and Experienced Adult Writers." CCC 31 (1980): 378–88.

Vopat, James. *"Uptaught* Rethought: Coming Back from the Knockout." CE 40 (1978): 41–5.

Chapter Six

Teaching the Course

In Dickens' *Dombey and Son,* during the search for a school for little Paul Dombey, Dr. Blimber's establishment is recommended: in it, remarks one character, "there is nothing but learning going on from morning to night." Adds Mr. Dombey, "And it's very expensive." In short, it is wonderfully fitted to Mr. Dombey's predilections about education and capitalism. Efficient in the delivery of its product—learning—and prestigiously expensive, Dr. Blimber's establishment would suit an administrator of today perfectly; it embodies faculty and physical plant in continuous use, and makes a comfortable profit. The fact that Dr. Blimber's faculty is badly paid and works day and night further enhances profitability, for learning is produced in the largest possible quantity at the lowest possible cost. Needless to say, such logic is no fiction even today for many faculty whose professional lives are beset by budget and enrollment pressures.

Illustrating the contemporary relationship between education and capitalism are the findings of a study typical of one sort of composition research. The authors describe an experiment which attempts to measure the relative improvement in writing skills of a group of students taught tutorially, on a one-to-one basis, and a group of students taught primarily in the classroom (Butz and Grabar). Their conclusion is that those taught primarily in large groups showed significantly greater improvement than those taught primarily through weekly conferences with the instructor. Although the article did not say so explicitly, it would appear from the conclusion ("we are all going back to the classroom") that the underlying issue is the familiar argument about the relative desirability of cost-effective classroom teaching over labor-intensive individualized teaching.

193

Teachers of writing nurture a faith in the value of personal contact; for since writing is so personal, its demands and rewards so inner-directed, must its teaching not also be personal? In college and university English departments, administrators and teachers often battle over the size of the composition class and the number of sections assigned to each instructor. Do writing teachers want a moderate three sections per semester with no more than twenty students per section (the position taken by the National Council of Teachers of English)? Impossible, says administration; faculty must teach at least four sections each semester with twenty-five students per class. But look at our load, cries faculty; we cannot adequately teach that many students. What can we do? blusters administration; we haven't the money to hire more teachers. If you don't want one hundred writing students, we know some unemployed teachers and short-order cooks who'd step over your bodies to get them. Course loads for secondary writing teachers can be even more oppressive. High-school and middle-school English teachers can have a total load of 150 students or more. Using the same arguments based on costs of staffing, school administrators often argue that funding constraints require such loads, and that the tax-paying public has not proved itself willing to fund schools at a level permitting lower teaching loads.

So the stakes are high in this game. If classroom methods work more "efficiently" than individualized methods, then the perpetual clamor for smaller classes may be quieted. And those who keep insisting on the need for smaller and fewer writing sections may find their pleas silenced. All who have taught writing in schools or colleges divided between the desire for smaller classes and the push for larger enrollments know that institutional pressures for more large-scale writing instruction remain very strong. What many administrators and budget-makers do not perceive, of course, is that writing is so complex an activity that generalizations about it are almost always reductive and oversimplified. Writing progress depends upon so many complex variables that both large-group and individual case-study research projects can only assess a few variables at a time. But many studies based on group comparisons in recent decades do in fact seem to indicate that different kinds of writing instruction yield measurably different results, and that writing instruction does make a difference to students' other academic work. Given the inherent ambiguity of writing and of research into writing, however, we must be judicious about claims made on behalf of various teaching strategies in writing.

Experienced writing teachers would probably agree that differences among strategies and techniques are less important in the effective writing class than the thoroughness of the commitment made by students and teachers alike. However, it has often been shown that different teaching situations do carry inherently different experiences with them, real enough for the student though not always measurable by the conventional educational assessments. Thus, experienced teachers also agree that students do not necessarily feel the same way, behave identically, or learn in the same way in one-on-one situations as they do in small groups. How differently are students likely to respond in one-on-one or tutorial settings, as opposed to classrooms or small groups? In what ways are student-teacher relationships different from student-student relationships? How are students likely to feel about peer responses and evaluations as opposed to those from their instructors? Can different aspects of writing development flourish in different settings? To address the questions, we must explore various kinds of learning relationships in the teaching of writing.

Many who have opinions about the teaching of writing today tend to characterize its practitioners as one of two sorts of pedagogues: those who insist that teaching writing entails teachers "putting something into" submissive students, and those who believe it entails teachers interacting with students in a reciprocal relationship. The "banking concept" of education critiqued by Paulo Freire (see Chapter Two) is often cited as the implicit teaching theory of those who insist seeing students as passive recipients of knowledge. Freire argues that such teaching is oppressive because knowledge is seen as a commodity which teachers "deposit" in students. Teachers are the "experts" whose command of the desired knowledge authorizes them to imprint it upon their students. Yet if writing emerges from interactive relationships between writers and readers, then teachers should see themselves as facilitators rather than depositers. They will find it necessary to develop mutual relationships which nurture students' growth as writers. Such teachers will not consider themselves authorities possessed of special knowledge, but rather as experienced readers whose interest is in empowering students to join wider circles of discourse.

Most writing teachers today would agree that students must be active participants in any writing-learning relationship. Another issue is more often contested: that is, whether writing is best taught as an individual enterprise between student and teacher, or as collaboration among students and teachers. Which are more important: students' individual relationships with teachers (as experienced writers), or students' collaborative interactions with peers (mostly inexperienced writers)? The former is an individualistic model, the latter a social and collective one. Some teachers have noted the implications of the stimulus-response-reinforcement (SRR) model of learning behavior for the teaching of writing. They argue that while reinforcement or "feedback" is crucial to this model, such feedback may consist of any number of reinforcing behaviors, such as "reward, punishment . . . knowledge of results, encouragement, prompting, or information" (Ellson 150). Feedback will come from the instructor, but it will also emerge from students' interaction with their peers and, most importantly, from their own assessments of their progress.

Relationships are the heart and soul of the writing class: such is the implicit theme of much of what we have read in earlier chapters. Whether we see writing and reading from an individualist or a collective viewpoint, students' relationships will play the telling role in their development as writers. The pedagogy of the one-on-one student-teacher relationship rests on the concept of individual empowerment. Writing and reading are seen as separate acts carried out by individuals. And individuals learn their powers and come to terms with their experiences differently, as a function of their distinct and separate personalities. Such a perspective derives in part from our Western intellectual tradition. The slaveboy in the *Meno* discovers through Socrates' patient tutoring that he is not really being "taught" but is able to "recollect" knowledge through the power of his "soul's" memory; goaded by his acute self-awareness, Descartes concludes that because he thinks, he is; Michael Polanyi argues that "tacit knowledge"—unarticulated knowledge which can strongly shape the "focal knowledge" upon which we usually act—also feeds the idea of learning as individual empowerment. Writing, that most personal and idiosyncratic form of knowing and doing, seems ideally suited to an individualist pedagogy.

But if a strong case can be made for teaching student writers as individuals, an equally convincing case can be made that learning to write is a collaborative, social process. Just as we are empowered separately as we learn, so too are we empowered collectively through relationships with family, community, and culture. One analogy for this process might be the condition of the citizen-voter; though we retain individual rights as citizens, when we participate in the electorate we sign over some rights to others as we integrate our needs with those of the community. Losing some individuality is in fact an enfranchisement; we pluralize our own experiences by absorbing and being absorbed into others' perspectives. Though we often prefer to think we learn through private acts of reading and writing, many psychologists and discourse theorists argue that our very notion of "self" is constructed by the networks of family, community, and culture within which we are nurtured. Language itself—by which we articulate our experience—is in this view an inescapably social force.

Writing Relationships and Their Settings

One-on-One: Students and Teachers

Grounding the teaching of writing in the one-on-one relationship between student and teacher means that although the setting may vary from classroom to conference, students write for the teacher, receive feedback from the teacher, and set goals and measure success within the teacher's orbit. The teacher's authority governs students' self-assessments and sense of progress. At its most conservative this model entails the teacher acting in what James Britton's research team calls the role of "examiner," with the majority of school writing falling into the "pupil to examiner" mode (Britton et al. Chapter 10). In this pattern, students write for teachers and measure their progress against their teacher's responses. Such a relationship keeps students directly in touch with an experienced reader who can help them see their goals, structures, styles, and editing strategies with more experienced eyes.

"Tutorials. . . ." The term sounds faintly elitist, evoking the image of a tweedy, pipesmoking instructor conferring with a student about the weekly paper across a polished table. It implies a low student-teacher ratio, a leisurely, student-oriented faculty, and highly-motivated, intellectually independent students. Such a fantasy seems ill-suited to the pressures of today's universities, where most students do not burn with commitment to the life of the mind, and the professoriat finds itself driven to teach, publish, and often perish all at once. Yet the teacher-student tutorial has emerged as a complement—sometimes even an enticing alternative—to the classroom arrangements typical of schools and colleges. The reason for its popularity and the source of its effectiveness is the potentially strong relationship between teacher and student.

Students will be strikingly vulnerable to the teacher's immediate influence in a one-on-one conference between teacher and student. Even before the first piece of writing is brought to the teacher, students will begin to meditate on this authority to whom they must submit, without the customary group of peers around them in the classroom. No matter how humane the teacher may wish to appear, students may be at first fearful of revealing weaknesses to the instructor, even perhaps resenting the instructor's authority. Yet despite their anxieties upon confronting a close, exacting relationship, the very intensity of the tutorial setting can develop into a strongly task-oriented partnership rapidly if conditions are right. Reciprocity is the crucial element in such a partnership. The expectations brought to it by teacher and students can shape a personal interaction with major advantages for the learning process, and with certain dangers as well.

Indeed, the flexibility and intensity of the one-on-one conference have led some teachers of writing to urge it as a method of choice for all writing instruction. Yet learning theorists disagree on just how it creates learning, and just how its advantages should be weighed. One such disagreement concerns whether personal contact with the instructor or the learning activity itself is the key to the tutorial's effectiveness. The importance of a close, caring relationship in helping students learn has most forcefully been argued by psychotherapist Carl Rogers. The qualities of personal relationships that Rogers emphasizes—"prizing" and empathy—have frequently been cited by those who feel that the important thing in writing instruction is a caring relationship between instructor and student. Rogerians assert that teachers must project themselves into their students' feelings, accept those feelings, and nurture them into the positive self-regard that Rogers argues is essential to genuine learning. The teacher's ability to empathize, to leave her own standards at bay in the act of seeing the tasks she has set for the student as the student sees them, is in this point of view crucial to the writer's growth. However, some critics have questioned the value of the personal relationship itself in teaching writing. Not enough measurable connection between feelings and cognitive development can be shown, argues one critic, to justify the belief that there is "magic in individual attention" (Ellson 133). Rather, says this researcher, "the significant variable in producing effective tutoring is the tutoring program—what tutors do" (137). Nevertheless, tutorial methods have been strongly advocated by teachers convinced that personal relationships are essential to real writing growth.

The one-on-one pattern has been variously implemented. Roger Garrison's widely influential model is based on the teacher's conferencing briefly with individual students during a given class period. He insists that while "the *least* effective method is the regular class meeting," "the *most* effective teaching method is one-to-one tutorial, or editor-to-writer"(69). Garrison's premise is that students best learn to write by writing with the instructor's "creative intervention in [their] work process" (69). Garrison urges that the classroom be turned into a workshop in which the instructor gives rapid, sharply focused attention to fifteen or twenty students per class hour, so that students' work can be evaluated in early and finished stages as the revision process goes on. A teacher who practices Garrison's method points out that it takes some time for writing teachers to master its time-intensive demands: "getting quickly into and out of a paper, learning to focus on its strengths and its most immediate problems, . . . and giving them specific directions" for change are skills that take time to master (Simmons 228). It takes less time, maintains Garrison, to teach one hundred writing students tutorially than in the classroom, because direct contact between instructor and student provides necessary editorial advice more efficiently than the laborious written commentaries often ignored by students when writings are returned after being read separately the the teacher.

Another teacher describes a method which places all contact time in regular conferences, during which the teacher evaluates students' work by reading it with them to demystify the evaluation process and enhance "on-going communication" about their work (Knapp 649). The tutorial method takes no more total time than a classroom arrangement, and "three hours of conference time is, in quality, as well as in practical necessity, worth almost twice as much time as the other method" (653). The assumption here is that the directness of tutorial interaction shapes students' writing growth more efficiently than the more distant, less controlled interactions of the classroom. But this will happen, in the view of one composition scholar, only if teachers see themselves in a sharing rather than a dominant relationship with students: understanding "is forged out of an ongoing dialogue, an endless sequence of transactions between . . . one reader and another" collaborating to make meaning (71). Thomas Newkirk maintains that in conferencing "the teacher must balance two opposing mandates: on the one hand . . . to evaluate, to suggest possible revisions and writing strategies; and on the other to encourage the student to take the initiative, . . . to make decisions, to take control of the paper" (317). Furthermore, he points out, "both student and teacher need to come to a meeting of minds fairly early in a writing conference; they need to set an agenda, agree to one to two major concerns that will be the focus of the conference" (318). Another proponent of one-on-one teaching draws on practical psychology and speech communication to outline the conference as a planned sequence of steps from "engagement" to "termination" (Arbur 338). Though she sees the conference only as an adjunct to classroom work, she urges the value of particularized feedback in conferences.

Advocates of student-teacher conferencing emphasize the instructor's control over feedback the student receives. If students do not see why the paper's focus is too broad, they can be brought to recognize paragraph by paragraph where it wanders and where it can be trapped and held onto. If they cannot recognize sentence difficulties, they can work through sentences with the instructor, leaving the conference with specific instructions to practice needed sentence variations. Perhaps most importantly, with oral feedback the instructor can avoid the intimidating simultaneity of written comments on returned papers. When papers are returned, students may read whatever final evaluation is on them before, or in place of, reading marginal comments which focus on particular parts of the text. In the tutorial the instructor can begin at whatever point seems fitting, and then deal with other matters in the order and at the speed appropriate to the student. All these advantages carry the virtues of immediacy and appropriateness in the feedback process.

Whether part of a classroom experience or in place of it, the successful tutorial depends upon a routine of conferencing, writing, and revision. If students are to be met regularly, a consistent meeting time should be set so that they may pace their writing and revision. The teacher may choose not to read students' work ahead of conference time, preferring to read quickly at the outset of each meeting. But in-conference reading requires concentrated attention by the instructor while the student waits anxiously for the verdict. This strategy primarily benefits the teacher by saving the time required for pre-conference reading. A large teaching load may justify it, particularly if it makes conferences possible where they might not otherwise be feasible. But all writing teachers recognize how difficult it is to see a text's problems and possibilities in a quick reading. Requiring that writing be submitted in time for the instructor's prior reading will make it easier to appraise the writing's problems and its potential. To engineer a situation requiring rapid, immediate reading of student work is to risk overlooking crucial elements needing comment and negotiation.

The pitfalls of a one-on-one teacher-student relationship have been intensively studied in recent years, and all writing teachers need to be fully aware of them. One is that when the real audience for students' writing is limited to the instructor, students have little choice but to defer to the unmediated authority of the teacher-reader. James Britton points out that while some teacher-student relationships in schools are based on a "teacher-learner dialogue," most of them are not dialogical but "pupil-to-examiner" in nature (209). The heart of the matter is the "power relationship between the student-writer and the teacher-reader," in the words of one writing teacher (Onore 240). In a classic critique of the authoritarian character of the teacher-student relationship, Lil Brannon and C. H. Knoblauch describe students' uncertainty in a teacher-student setting. Writing for teachers, they argue, obliges inexperienced writers to yield control of their writing choices to the inherent authority of the teacher, who envisions an "ideal text" against which the efforts of the student are measured : "far from controlling the responses of an intended reader, [students writing for teachers] are forced to concede the reader's authority and to make guesses about what they can and cannot say" (159).

What remedy is there for what these critics see as the inherently stifling effect of the teacher's omnipresence in the student-teacher relationship? "The teacher's proper role," argue Brannon and Knoblauch, "is not to tell the student explicitly what to do but rather to serve as a sounding-board enabling the writer to see confusions in the text" (162). In this view, teachers must give power back to student writers by freeing them to make writerly choices on their own authority, and by responding seriously to student writers' total efforts. Later in this chapter we will explore some ways in which teachers' responses in a one-on-one relationship can empower inexperienced writers to take the risks necessary for real growth as writers.

Another criticism of the one-on-one student-teacher relationship is the constricted range of audience it offers student writers. A number of writing theorists have maintained that students need to learn to write for different kinds of readers in different contexts. The discourse systems proposed by Britton and by James Moffett emphasize the need for inexperienced writers to encounter a variety of readers and writing situations. Moffett's "abstractive scale" of writer-audience relations suggest students' need to understand the rhetorical demands of audiences ranging from "interpersonal" to "impersonal," the latter a "large anonymous group" such as the readership of a published article or book (33). The progression from expressive writing into "broadly differentiated kinds of writing" urged upon all writing students by Britton also supports the view that inexperienced writers should write for a range of audiences, to nurture flexibility in the use of voice and tone (10). The one-on-one student-teacher relationship does not provide the diverse readership offered by a classroom group, nor does it offer the supportive responsiveness of a small peer group. A student taught only by tutorial conferences may lack opportunities to be challenged by a variety of audience expectations and feedback.

Another possible disadvantage lies in the potential loss of objectivity in an exclusively mentorial relationship. In a close tutorial setting, instructor and student alike may forget that a certain distance is needed for objective evaluation and feedback. The tutorial relationship, in other words, is not necessarily a friendship; criticism must be given and received without constraint. If the student sees the instructor primarily as a friend, then criticism may come to be perceived as betrayal; or the teacher may begin to overlook weaknesses or lack of progress as the student betrays the stresses all students face as the semester proceeds. A genuinely caring relationship requires the instructor to maintain a balance between support and needed criticism if the student is to derive full value from the tutorial.

Writing Together: Student-to-Student

Much attention has been given recently to the nature and value of student collaboration in the process of learning to write. Chapter Two explores the social-constructionist view of knowledge which underlies the increasing attention paid to collaborative learning in many fields. The constructionist view of meaning-making is encapsulated in the suggestive word "conversation." In this view, knowledge-making is a social enterprise enacted by collective human activity—conversation—and our thoughts are to a great extent internalized conversations. Because it is "community life that generates and maintains conversation," Kenneth Bruffee says, "we must seek to understand and cultivate the kinds of community life that establish and maintain conversation that is the origin of . . . thought" (640). Basing his argument on this collective view of knowledge-making, Bruffee claims that "writing teachers . . . must [be committed to] engaging students in conversation among themselves" as often as possible (642). That is, writing teachers must replicate the conditions of knowledge-making among their students as often as possible. And to draw students fully into the responsibility that knowledge-making requires, they must in their collaborations be challenged to make their own truths rather than simply to find preselected answers targeted as appropriate by the teacher.

Those who prize student-on-student collaboration tend to describe its benefits as the inverse of the student-teacher relationship's disadvantages. If student-teacher relationships make students vulnerable to the teacher's domination, then—it is argued—student-student relationships foster equality, thus enfranchising students as agents of their own learning. "Intensive peer review," argue Martin Nystrand and Deborah Brandt, "works largely because it establishes reciprocity between writer and reader," accomplishing this, moreover, "in a way that is not always possible . . . when students write exclusively for the teacher" (210). When students write with and for each other, they can—with appropriately open-ended tasks given them by the teacher—discover an unfamiliar sense of responsibility for bringing about their own successes. Working directly with each other, with the teacher playing only a task-setting and facilitating role, students will find themselves free to control both their own responses and ways of reading. Other writing teachers argue that "both writing and knowing . . . are from beginning to end collaborative: they are things we do with others" (Reither and Vipond 856–7). To make knowledge with others, they maintain, requires that students be empowered to work together to do more than find the "right answers" or merely to help each other find ways to improve a given text. The primary goal of a writing group, they suggest, should be to nurture the long-term growth of its members as writers, including their successes and their failures with particular texts.

Student collaboration is most often established through what Anne Ruggles Gere calls "school-sponsored writing groups," those formed within the supportive framework of writing classes. The key to establishing class-based student writing groups is to cede to those groups as much autonomous authority as possible within the framework of the course organization. Only with such freedom will students develop what Gere calls the necessary "commitment" to make groups successful: "instructors who claim belief in writing groups give life to that statement by the kind of authority they pass on to the students" (106). Proponents of student-student collaboration maintain that collaborative learning requires freedom for students to direct their own learning. With authority over their own collaborative processes, students will be more likely to develop the commitment necessary to making those processes succeed. Group work in writing classrooms has received much attention in recent years; we must now look carefully at its uses in the teaching of writing.

Given the right conditions, writing groups can give students more direct control over their own writing than any other kind of learning situation. But several things can affect the success with which they give appropriate feedback to students. Writing ability may vary widely in classes, yet instructors' attempts to balance skilled and unskilled writers in the same group may prove counterproductive. Inexperienced writers may resent being counseled by their peers, however skilled. Good student writers may not be able to communicate what they know about writing, or be psychologically prepared to share their experience with others. Some students may find self-disclosure to a small group as threatening as disclosure to the whole class. Indeed, students can easily fear exposure to one another more than they flinch at direct contact with the teacher, who fills a familiar authoritarian role in their experience. Adolescent sensitivities may well have created a vulnerability that will resist group sharing. An ethos of trust may develop in a peer group, but only when that group fulfills certain basic conditions for success.

Forming and Maintaining Student Writing Groups

Bruffee has described the learning that can result from the properly administered small-group experience: in giving each others' writing sympathetic, nonjudgmental hearings, students can provide an "astute and demanding audience" that will detect "lack of clarity, organization, logic, and substance" in each others' work

("Collaborative Learning" 55). However, inexperienced writers will lack both the ability to recognize effective prose and the vocabulary to communicate their perceptions. The teacher must help students develop these skills before groups can function. The "showing" reactions which Peter Elbow, for example, prescribes for his peer-group feedback may be interesting as metaphors—"drizzling," "foggy" "gusty," "forested," "hilly," etc.—but they provide little explicit direction to the student about how to make foggy writing clear or hilly writing smooth (*Writing Without Teachers* 90).

The first step in forming student groups is not to divide students up and ask them to start talking; it is to introduce students to the nature of collaborative work itself. Feedback helpful to students will not emerge immediately in group work at the beginning of the course. For weeks in the course's beginning, the instructor must help students learn how to respond to each others' writing. "What students need," says Karen Spear, "is information about the nature of collaborative interaction and opportunities to practice it" (57). Some "salient features of group interaction" outlined by Spear include "sustained, goal-directed discussion" and "decision-making by consensus or merit, not by authority" (58). These qualities are not developed in most students by our present school and college methodologies; they must be taught and nurtured. Gere is specific about the training students must receive before collaborative groups are formed and set at their tasks:

> If students are to read drafts aloud and receive oral comments, they should be told how time is to be divided among group members, the number of times a selection should be read, the form of note taking that will aid effective response, how authors should introduce their writing, and whether authors should receive written comments in addition to oral ones (109).

Gere also suggests students need to learn the roles of "timekeeper, attendance taker, convener, arbitrator, and recorder," and the writing of "group reports" summarizing progress made during group meetings (109). Teachers may want to ask students to begin the semester by collaborating in preparing an outline or manual of procedures to follow, detailing what groups are to do and how they are to do it.

Small groups may be created either within the framework of regular class meetings or in independent work-groups meeting on their own schedules. Working with what he terms a "parceled classroom," Thom Hawkins pictures the teacher as a "floating resource" who sorts students into groups and establishes tasks for each group. These tasks include generating topics for student writing, discussing collateral readings, working rhetorical and grammatical exercises, and most importantly, responding to each others' own writing. One day a week is devoted to the latter task, at the end of which the teacher collects students' writing and adds his own responses to those of the group. Nearly every class day of the semester will be given to one of these group tasks; the groups themselves retain the same membership through the semester. The basic advantage of such "group inquiry," says Hawkins, is that "it's more fun to work through problems together with other students your own age than to work in isolation under the direction of someone from a different generation" (640). Peter Elbow's "teacherless writing class" goes further by rejecting advice from teachers as a major contribution to writing growth: "to improve your writing you don't need advice about what changes to make; you don't need theories of what is good and bad writing" (77). What the student does need, he argues, is a committed, stable, caring audience for his writing, so that he can "see and experience his own words *through* seven or more people. That's all" (77). Both models assume that peer support plays a crucial, even predominant role in students' writing growth, and that what is lacking in expertise can be made up for in the value of the freedom and responsibility offered.

Once familiarized with techniques for successful group interaction, students may be organized into their working groups. Particularly with inexperienced writers, teachers need to build writing groups carefully. A student group must be the right size—"the smallest one that contains all the skills required for the accomplishment of the group task," says one researcher (Gall and Gall 176). A pair of students (or "dyad") may be appropriate if one-to-one peer feedback is desired; a rough-draft or editing workshop for the class may use dyads, with students paired so that each has some skills that can help the other. A group of three offers a comfortably small size but with limited possibility of divergent judgments about work under discussion. Groups of four or five offer more varied viewpoints for the group size, but are more vulnerable to fragmentation in sharing the work load and focusing on the task. In forming small groups, the teacher should strive to include a mix of these abilities in each group:

A. *Willingness to take responsibility* for convening, organizing, assigning group tasks. Though collaboration and a division of labor will characterize the successful student group, some students will bring more initiative to these responsibilities than others. At least a couple of students in each group should have demonstrated a sense of responsible other-directedness strong enough to draw less committed students into participation in group work.

B. *Self-confidence in group discussion.* Some students in each group should have the self-confidence to announce opinions about writing. Such students may not be the best writers in the group, but they can stimulate discussion, even dispute.

C. *Mediating tactfulness.* One or two students should have some instinct toward moderation, be uncomfortable with negative comments and eager to sympathize with and defend others.

If these characteristics exist in some mixture in the group, there should be enough heterogeneity to create momentum in discussion, along with sufficient cohesiveness to pursue tasks set by the instructor.

Leadership in each student group may be set in various ways. One way is to assign leadership roles—as well as other roles such as recordkeeping—on a rotating basis to group members in order to disseminate opportunities for responsibility as widely as possible. The leader of any small group, whatever the task, has some or all of the following responsibilities:

A. Clarifying the group's goals.
B. Asking exploratory questions.
C. Using responses to generate other responses.
D. Mediating disputes.
E. Summarizing viewpoints of group members.

One researcher has suggested that a major function of group leaders is to cope with the indifference, reserve, or hostility of group members by preventing "such a negative buildup, or bring it within control if it begins. . . . [The group leader] must be able to cope with the most dominant and negative members, but he must not be too dominant or negative himself" (Bales 216). The measure of the group leader's success is the extent to which the group members work together as listeners and responders.

Another leadership model features each student as a discussion leader. Each in turn becomes the leader when his or her writing is discussed by the group. "In successful groups," suggests one teacher, "the writer nearly always begins and encourages discussion" (George 323–4). Placing the writer in the role of discussion leader gives the initiative to the student with the largest investment in the discussion. The writer, seeking responses by which to gauge the need for revision, will be more likely than a third party to push her peers into giving specific, detailed feedback, thus focusing the group's interests on the writer's expressed needs. If this model is to succeed, however, the writer/discussion leader must distance herself from her writing, controlling the natural urge toward defensive self-justification ("that's not what I meant!") in favor of questions which objectively elicit her peers' responses to her writing. The instructor can facilitate this process by helping students prepare a set of guidelines specifying what questions are to be asked or avoided by the leader, and what kinds of comments are appropriate from readers.

Some experienced writing teachers maintain that teachers must set explicit goals for student writing groups if real gains are to be made in those groups: "the success of the collaborative model," asserts Harvey Wiener, "depends primarily upon the quality of the initial task students must perform in group. Hence, the instructor's role as tasksetter" is crucial in establishing what goals the groups are to work toward (54). But what sort of goals should a student group be asked to pursue in a writing class? Should groups be given the primary task of reaching agreement as to what to say to each writer in the group? Most experienced writing teachers would agree that that's an impossible, even illogical, goal. Students' responses to each others' writing-in-process are likely to be as disparate as their readings of unfamiliar published texts. If their task is to reach "consensus" about a given text, so that the text's writer may have some clear guidelines for revision, how is such consensus to be defined, much less achieved?

The meeting of minds in a collaborative group is a utopian goal that actual groups in real settings cannot achieve, argues John Trimbur. Social constructionist arguments, he maintains, have led to a misunderstanding about the nature of consensus. Collaboration seldom leads to the kind of general agreement we are accustomed to call "consensual"; rather, most group discourse reaches toward what Trimbur calls "dissensus": "consensus does not reconcile differences . . . , [but] structures differences by organizing them in relation to each other" (610). We must redefine collaboration so that groups reach toward an understanding, not of how people agree, but "of how people differ, [and] where their differences come from" (610). But if the most student groups can do is articulate differences among their responses to each others' work, wouldn't the lack of a clear, authoritative voice prevent them from leading each other toward needed changes in their writing, changes which require clear, directed feedback?

This question obliges us to confront those disquieting ambiguities about writing and writers discussed in earlier chapters: the tacit, unarticulated dimensions of writers' knowledge about themselves; the elusiveness of any one text (is it "finished"? "right"?); and—most disturbing for writing teachers—the difficulty in proving that writing instruction can have a substantial effect on students' growth as writers. These problematic elements in the teaching of writing must be anticipated and confronted, and students' expectations set at an appropriate level. If teachers ask students to help each other as writers, then students must be given workable advice about what can be achieved for the "improvement" of a given text on a given day. Some student writers will hear little that will strike them as useful from their peers; they may so distrust their fellow students' responses that they discount them entirely. Others may concede so much authority to peers' judgments as to lose their control over their own work. Carol Berkenkotter records both difficulties in groups she has observed, suggesting that "students who write for peer readers as well as their teacher might not necessarily reap the advantages we'd like to imagine" (318). The diversity of student attitudes and abilities in a given writing group make it sometimes difficult for students to receive constructive feedback.

Only if students are strongly encouraged to see writing as always conditional, and writing "progress" as recursive and reiterative rather than neatly sequential, will they feel empowered enough to benefit from each others' feedback. "Inquiry is not possible," says Cynthia Onore, "without contraries, conflicts, and tensions. Chaos, then, is a categorical feature of the inquiry process just as it is a categorical feature of the composing process" (240). Some days, in some group discussions, students will be more frustrated than enlightened. But if students understand that some texts can never be satisfactorily "improved" or "finalized," they will be more accepting of their own and others' failures and more willing to continue taking risks as writers. All composing and revising, whether or not it reaches satisfactory short-term resolution, deepens the experience of the writer: "if we value the growth of an individual text . . . over the growth of a writer, we may unnecessarily inhibit the development of writing abilities" (Onore 246). Student writers must be nurtured in ways that keep them willing to continue risking themselves to write and read for others.

In well-grounded writing groups, students may discover their own resources and gain perspective on the infinite ways to come at a piece of writing by listening to others discuss their labors. Finding what they want to say can get a strong stimulus from small-group discussion. "I was trying to write about my roommate," one student may say, "but I just couldn't seem to say what I really thought about her." Why not, others ask. What's she like? What does she do? The speaker is thus encouraged to separate her feelings about her roommate from her observations of the roommate's behavior, and to discover concrete elements of appearance and behavior that can clarify the roommate's essential qualities. Another group member may say "I wanted to tell how great my fraternity is, but I just seemed to get stuck on the stuff we learned in pledge week." What did you do in pledge week? others ask. How did it make you feel? What's so great about your fraternity brothers? The instructor could ask such questions in class or conference, but when the writer hears other students asking them out of genuine curiosity, he senses the power of his own words to make others feel and see as he does. The small-group bull session becomes for him an important heuristic.

A cohesive small group will help its members understand the social dimensions of writing. It is just as important for students to witness each others' failures as it is for them to admire their successes. Reading their work to small groups of their peers, students can enjoy praise if the work is liked, or come to understand how the piece does not satisfy other readers. Neither the tutorial conference nor the classroom group can provide quite the same nurturing that the small-group atmosphere offers the frustrated, struggling student. Such nurturing is essential for students to carry themselves over what John Dewey calls the "dead places" in their progress as learners. Without the small-group presence, the student will seek its supportive benefits elsewhere, in places like the dorm where specific task-orientation may be lacking. Peer groups offer students an opportunity that cannot be provided by other settings. But they require a great deal of effort by both teacher and students. It is up to the instructor to provide the stability of routine that will sustain the group's vitality and enable it to give its members the kind of responses that will encourage their growth as writers.

Teacher-to-Students: The Whole Class

If the instructor's relationship to individual students is monopolistic and intense in the one-on-one tutorial setting, in the classroom it is unpredictable. Classroom interaction seldom stays on a direct line of exchange, but varies as the instructor speaks specifically to certain students, and students reply to the instructor or to each other. The extent of a student's participation in lecture-discussions may vary widely from day to day, depending on the student's knowledge, interest, or feelings. Recently an educational researcher measured the rate of retention by students over the course of a sixty-minute lecture (MacLeish 262). His findings suggest that students will remember what has been discussed best in the first and last minutes of a lecture only, and that retention moves in roughly inverse proportion to the passage of time. Clearly, an entire class hour devoted only to the teacher's lecturing can bring few benefits to students struggling to learn an activity as complex as writing. Yet there are some things to be said in favor of a whole-class setting for teaching writing.

In the classroom, for example, the teacher can demonstrate various ways of responding to texts. In tutorial and student-group arrangements, students' actual time with the instructor will be limited. Thus, the classroom student will hear far more explanation and analysis than the tutorial student, directed at a few students and their work but witnessed by the whole class. Discussions of collateral reading, for which there will be no time in the tutorial setting, may be introduced into the classroom setting. Texts may be discussed at length from student and professional writing, with the aid of handouts, blackboard, or overhead projector. The classroom is an efficient forum for general discussions of composing and responding.

But the classroom offers the least effective setting for insuring that students absorb new strategies into their own writing behavior. No class of twenty-five students meeting three hours a week can target each student's writing for discussion with the thoroughness of the small-group or tutorial sessions. Student writing (reproduced prior to class) may be discussed by the whole class, but only a few pieces can be covered in an hour of class time. In the classroom, students may benefit from the diversity of responses, but the instructor cannot control the impact of those responses upon the student. Nor will class discussion necessarily benefit poorer writers who need it most, because large groups tend to inhibit the less verbal student. For those basic writers who cannot progress at the same rate as their more skilled peers, points about grammar, logic, and mechanics may need repeating again and again. This repetition may well be crucial to the success, even the survival, of some students; yet a restless classroom group may easily deter the instructor from clarifying by repetition. Classroom groups, by virtue of their mass, resist the teacher's efforts to provide that specific, individualized feedback that some students require.

The challenge for the teacher of a classroom-based writing course is to create systematic, appropriate feedback for each student, within the constraints of a classroom setting. One way to direct classroom feedback to individual students is to organize the whole class into a teacher-led writing group. Teacher-guided readings of student work by the whole class have distinct benefits: they confront student writers with a readership larger and more diverse than the instructor alone can offer, while at the same time student responses are shaped and directed by the teacher's participation. W. E. Coles, Jr. has developed an influential model for a semester's writing program in which every class meeting is devoted to a discussion of unidentified student writing, which is the sole subject matter of the course; there are no rhetoric handbooks and no outside readings. General classroom discussions of some students' work each week means that, over a quarter or semester's time, all students in the class would receive feedback not only privately on each returned paper, but several times publicly in company of their peers. Coles' model makes each class meeting a series of whole-class discussions of individual papers, taking advantage of the diversity of viewpoints within the classroom. Each class period is devoted to the work of a different group of students whose writings are sometimes reproduced for distribution in class, and sometimes prepared with transparencies for use with an overhead projector.

However, some students may find such public exposure of their work painful. For inexperienced writers particularly, sharing writing may be perceived as a violation of individuality, even when anonymity is preserved. When we share written work with a group of peers, says one teacher, we think immediately "of what they directly or indirectly say we are, and are reminded of what we are not— our failures, misplaced commitments, erroneous assumptions, self-delusions, and misguided intentions" (Bales 217). Students whose work is under discussion may only half listen to what is said about the writing itself. They will be acutely aware of their instructor's and peers' voices, and of the possibility of implied judgments about themselves. Comments that might appear calm and disinterested to an uninvolved listener may sound negative or hostile to the sensitive student. To minimize this threat, instructors must attune themselves to the tone of the discussion, judge its effect on students whose work is under discussion, and manipulate that discussion so that its impact on student writers is supportive and helpful without being judgmental.

So done, classroom sharing can strongly benefit student writers. Their intense awareness of exposure may impress upon them, as private conferences cannot, the "realness" of writing, its power to elicit responses as a genuine act of communication. In other words, public sharing of writing can sharpen students' respect for writing as a means of power. It can also help students learn how to participate in larger group interactions and how to respond to feedback from larger audiences. But a classroom wholly given over to discussion of student writing omits other, equally useful activities. Perhaps most seriously, there will be no time for dyads or small groups, in which students interact with one another *without* the immediate presence of the instructor.

No test has yet been devised that can accurately measure the differing results of tutorial, small-group, and classroom settings. But some likely effects of these different settings may be enumerated. Regular weekly tutorial sessions insure that students will have the chance to participate in a strongly task-oriented partnership which can provide them with consistent, particularized feedback from an experienced writer. Such a partnership can help students learn rapidly the discipline of constant revision as an essential part of the writing process. On the other hand, small-group collaboration can offer students the kind of direct and supportive feedback available only from a group of peers. Student writers sharing their work in a cohesive small group can develop a sense of responsibility for their own and others' work that confers an empowering freedom unmatched by other pedagogical settings. Then, finally, in a writing-reading course which requires students to read and respond to writing from a variety of unfamiliar disciplines and genres, the whole-class setting offers the fullest context within which a wide range of responses can be articulated. Full discussions of such material can best occur in classrooms, with their diversity of responses. We might say, then, that conference-taught students may come to discover particularly well their own writing needs, and gain the disciplined ability to revise in accordance with a growing perceptiveness about the writing process. That awareness will lack scope, however, if it hasn't been enriched by a classroom discussion. But only in small-group settings will students fully experience the communality of the act of writing, and benefit from the constructive tensions of writing with and for others.

Responding and Evaluating

Writing comments on drafts is the most prevalent method by which teachers respond to and evaluate student writing. But if classroom discussion often fails to make a point jell for a student, written comments on returned papers may be unread or misunderstood, unless they are carefully planned and organized to capitalize on students' attentiveness to feedback. It is not that teachers can't write wise and witty comments or that students always ignore them. Rather, developing writing fluency requires students' continuous incremental translation from the conceptual to the practical, from theory to practice. If comments written by teachers or by peers are ambiguous or do not match the declared goals of the course, it will be hard for students to translate such feedback into their practice as writers.

It is crucial for writing teachers to differentiate between *responses* that encourage more productive writing behavior and more effective texts, and *evaluations* that fix a text with a final judgment—a grade. Once a young teacher returned some papers to a class that included an aggressive male student who thought well of his own abilities. He rushed up to the instructor as the class ended and shouted, "What is this, giving me a D? I don't get grades like that!" The instructor, taken aback, asked him if he wanted to talk about it in his office. "No," muttered the cooling student, "there's no point in talking about it. It wouldn't do any good." The student's anger, boiling up and then subsiding, gave that instructor a sharp lesson in the pressures involved in grading. Students recognize that the only evaluation that "counts" is the grade which goes on their transcript. They may accept the teacher's verbal assessments of their work, but the grade is the crucial item. They may have enjoyed the class, they may believe they have learned in it, they may see how it has helped them grow, but if the grade is not what they expect, the whole experience is soured. The writing teacher faces an especially acute problem. The act of writing is bound up in students' egos, its product tied to their self-identity more deeply than most other academic efforts. It is therefore especially important for writing teachers to make sure their students understand the processes of response and judgment towards which students' efforts are directed. When students are asked to submit work that is still in progress, teachers' and peers' responses must be directed toward the ongoing process of composing and revising. When students are asked to submit work for which no further revision will be possible, they need to understand the relationships between the responses that have helped shape the drafts and those final evaluative comments which will justify the grade.

1. What is the relationship between responding and evaluating?

Certainly writing has to be evaluated, it might be said; how else will the student know what he's doing wrong, and thus improve? Yet this is not the idle question it seems, nor is the answer so obvious. As we have seen in earlier chapters, theorists from a wide range of disciplines have maintained that only a supportive, caring atmosphere can create the psychological freedom within which students can grow as writers. Evaluation, it is argued, inhibits development of this freedom by implying criticism, which stifles the student's willingness to experiment with words and risk failure. For example, one teacher has proposed a "low-risk, affirmative" experience which avoids "inadvertent put-downs" and permits only positive feedback from peers, with "exclusive concentration on strengths," so that every paper the student submits to the class is an "experience of success" (Denman 44). The teacher is limited to devising positive situations in which "desired behavior" in writing is elicited and reinforced through supportive group interaction. Such a system emphasizes the importance of psychological factors in writing growth and the beneficial power of peer nurturing.

As much as students may fear criticism and welcome feedback that dwells on their strong points, however, students need to know how effective instructor and peers perceive their writing to be. If students are told only that their work has certain strengths which may perhaps be improved, they'll grow restless. For most students recognize, if only from seeing other students' work, that some writing seems to be more effective and convincing than theirs. Most students also grasp the self-evident truth that unless they learn how to organize their essays clearly, unclutter their syntax, make their paragraphs cohere, and edit their work adequately, they will not be able to perform successfully in their coursework. Grades on essays and written tests will not improve. Perhaps the strongest argument against providing only positive feedback is that it may create a fool's paradise of students who love their own writing so much they will be devastated when somebody criticizes it later. To give feedback which is too positive, too vague, or too late is to lose the unique opportunity afforded every writing teacher to improve the single most important ability students require for success.

But teachers may respond to students' work, giving helpful commentary and reactions, without formally evaluating it for a grade. The process of responding itself necessarily contains an important evaluative or judgmental element; but such responding can—and must—be directed towards changing the process rather than merely assessing it by some fixed grading scale. Responding to drafts must be a crucial part of a writing course and must always precede the final step of a graded evaluation. Teachers must ensure that students understand the provisional and recursive nature of writing itself, and nurture their willingness to trust their own instincts as they struggle to shape their texts.

2. Who should respond to student writing?

Students will see the teacher's responses as bearing crucial authority. As we saw earlier in this chapter, the tutorial setting offers the widest scope and specificity for the teacher's feedback to individual students. But even in a classroom setting teachers, through classroom interaction and comments in writing on students' work, can strongly shape students' writing attitudes and behavior. By responding clearly and thoroughly to some student writings, both in class and in a one-on-one situation, teachers can positively nurture students' confidence as writers. Aware of their dominance in the conventional teacher-student relationship, however, many teachers urge students to include their peers in their sense of audience. But Thomas Newkirk warns that when writing teachers urge students to write not only for the teacher but also for other students in their class or writing group, teachers may unwittingly encourage inconsistency in students' reader-awareness. Teachers must be "fully aware of the criteria that the peer audience applies to students' writing," and they must insure "that those criteria are consistent" with the goals set for the students' writing, and by which they are being judged by the teacher ("Direction and Misdirection" 309). To create some consistency between students' and teachers' responses, the teacher should—even in a class organized primarily around small-group collaboration—discuss responses to various student writings with full class participation. Only when responses are shared and developed collaboratively will both students and teachers feel some partnership in shaping each other's efforts.

The instructor's unavoidable dominance in the teacher-student relationship, some argue, can hinder the student from feeling free enough to risk failure in experimenting with various voices and styles. Advocates of peer feedback and self-evaluation argue that the teacher's responses are sometimes too cursory, detached, and unsupportive to nurture the proper risk-taking attitudes in their students. "A teacher," says Elbow, "tells you what he thinks the weak and strong points were and suggests things you should try for. But you usually get little sense of what the words actually did to him—how he *perceived* and *experienced* them" (77). Only small, cohesive peer groups, say their advocates, can offer this kind of response to student writers—evaluation that is descriptive rather than judgmental, clarifying *what* the writing does to the audience, not how well it may carry out rhetorical or grammatical rules.

For these reasons, students often find peer feedback less threatening than their teachers' judgments, making it easier for them to accept such feedback for themselves and offer it to others. One peer-evaluation strategist urges that students be trained to "assume more control" of the evaluative process, moving from more structured to less structured sessions as they learn how to make more discerning analyses of each others' work (Beaven 150). This progression assumes interaction between two learning processes. Students begin working in pairs and then in larger groups as they learn the interpersonal skills needful to cooperative work; they also begin evaluating each others' writing using "highly structured rating scales" (148), moving to less structured evaluations after they have gained experience. Such a graduated system of peer evaluation "helps student writers find their voices, develop a sense of audience, and experiment with revision strategies" (153). Self-directed feedback may also force students to take responsibility for their own writing growth, and internalize writing standards that may carry over into later writing efforts. In the beginning of the course they could, for example, be asked to write a narrative description of the writing process by which they shape their early writing tasks. Gradually, as they learn to be readers of others' writing, they will also gain the ability to judge the effectiveness of their own writing. Despite its potential for making students more responsible for their own progress, self-evaluation requires careful nurturing and support from instructors. It also demands that students be made to feel that their evaluations of themselves actually count—that the teacher will pay attention to their self-evaluations in determining a final grade.

3. How and when should feedback be directed to students?

Effective feedback must be appropriate and carefully directed. Teachers must write comments which help students "know what is the most important problem in the text and what problems are of lesser importance," says Nancy Sommers (151). That is, comments on early drafts should be directed toward those processes most involved in early composing stages; those directed towards later drafts should address those processes appropriate to final revision stages. "We need to develop an appropriate level of response for commenting on a first draft, and to differentiate that from the level suitable to a second or third draft," she continues, in order to show students "why new choices would positively change their texts, and thus to show them the potential for development implicit in their own texts" (155–6). Teachers' comments should be seen as flowing naturally from standards already shared with students in conferences and groups; such comments should represent the group's collective ownership of such standards.

Some teachers devise a specific checklist of priorities embodied in written comments, while others find it more appropriate to articulate such priorities differently for each student and text. "Response to a preliminary draft of a student paper should . . . engage a student in revision *activities* that significantly improve that particular piece of work," say two teachers who advocate teachers' carefully planned sequence of responses to student drafts (Mallonee and Breihan 221). They also urge that teachers measure their responses to student drafts by means of a "checklist" of response categories fully shared with students in the beginning of the course. In addition, they suggest that when commenting on drafts, teachers should minimize marginal—and thus intrusive—comments, and "prepare a summary end comment that schedules revising activities," in order to offer students a plan for further reworking of the text (224). Students should be able to see a match between the stages of their composing and the kind of responses they receive.

Given the pressures of a typical semester's or quarter's writing course, students need to have both regular and timely responses. One basis for supporting timely feedback lies in the stimulus-reinforcement behavioral model described earlier in this chapter. In terms of composition pedagogy, this model asserts that the more quickly the evaluator responds to the writer, the more acutely subsequent writing behavior will be influenced. The longer the time elapsing between submission and return of a given text, the more students' awareness of its issues and difficulties will be crowded out by new and changing tasks. Ineffective and counterproductive writing strategies are hard for most students to change; persistent and patient responses are needed to bring about improvement. The snowball effect of unchanged composing strategies in writing can grow very quickly when feedback is delayed beyond a reasonable point.

Regular, consistent feedback in writing is crucial, but it should be balanced with a brief cooling-off period between the writing of the paper and its evaluative response. As the anecdote described earlier suggests, students who, hot and expectant from writing papers, get immediate evaluations may lack sufficient distance to accept them. Timing in evaluation is really a matter of proportion; delays of longer than a week allow them to forget the intentions they may have had and sentence them to repeat errors and to be ignorant of their strengths in their next assignment. One of the most dispiriting experiences for a student is to submit a piece of writing within a deadline (perhaps at some cost to other courses) only to have weeks go by before the instructor returns it. Not only does such delay short-circuit the feedback cycle, it also violates the implicit contract of good faith which gives the writing course its unique humaneness on the college campus.

4. How should evaluation and grading be done?

Clarifying the standards by which students' work will be graded is a difficult and often thankless task for teachers. Teacher and students may agree on the characteristics of "good writing," and students may convince themselves that they expect to be evaluated according to such characteristics. But some students may resist the instructor's standards from the outset of the course, if those standards threaten the student's self-image or the grade. Other students who struggle to meet the teacher's demands at the beginning may perceive the teacher as intransigent if they continually fail to meet the teacher's standards or if these standards appear to change as the semester proceeds. The latter situation may well emerge if the teacher feels it proper to expect more from students as the semester goes by, or when students submit one or more revisions of the same work. Problems hidden at first reading may be resolved in the first revision, only to be superseded by further, legitimate criticisms of remaining difficulties.

Teachers must engage students in dialogues that result in clear and mutually acceptable evaluative standards. If revisions or papers written later in the semester are to be evaluated more stringently than earlier ones, students must be helped to understand the basis for such progressive expectations. They should be encouraged to see that their awareness of their own writing behavior and their ability to manage it should evolve during the course, so that their composing, revising and editing become increasingly effective. But instructors should not impose their standards *ex cathedra* upon students. Evaluative standards which students do not understand or accept will produce no real growth in writing skill and will inevitably lead to confusion and unhappiness as the course proceeds. General agreement on writing standards can best be achieved by teacher-shaped class discussion focusing on student writings which illustrate varying levels of effectiveness. Such discussion will make students more aware of the openness and complexity of the very idea of "good writing" and will make them feel collectively responsible for the formulation of standards. Student writing rather than professional work should be used in discussing the actual standards to which students will be held, for students know they cannot write at the level of anthology prose, though they may well recognize the techniques embodied in that prose. On the other hand, they will often feel challenged by effective writing produced by their peers.

After the classes and conferences, the writing, the reading and rewriting comes the final, inevitable evaluation that must result in a grade for the course. Such decisions can tax teachers as they try to decide whether a student's work has been strong enough for an A, or just a B+; a B, or just a C+; nor are decisions any easier if they must pick Honors, Pass, or Fail. All the semester's work comes to this last reduction of labor and hope to a single letter. Teachers may simply average all the grades awarded to the student's work in the semester—if individual writings have been graded—and leave it at that. But many writing teachers would argue that a more appropriate strategy is to grade on the basis of students' progress through the various writing tasks of the course. There are variations of the "progress" strategy: students may at course's end submit what they think are their best writings; or the grade may be assessed on all work as a whole, perhaps in conference with the student. Or the instructor may devise a grading system depending on several variables, including actual written work, willingness to revise, class or group participation, and attendance. If a contract has been formed between instructor and student, such as that described earlier in this chapter, the final grade will depend on the extent to which the contract has been fulfilled. The basic necessity in any of these grading patterns, of course, is that students should have understood clearly the basis upon which their work is to be evaluated.

But what of the complaint that Ms. X gives B's or C's to work which Mr. Y gives A's to? Is there any way to avoid the inherent subjectivity of grades on writing, measure-resistant as it is? Some teachers suggest a "portfolio system" of final evaluation that employs the instructor's colleagues in disinterested judgments of students' work (Ford and Larkin). After students select what they judge to be their best work at the end of the term, this "portfolio" is given a pass-fail evaluation, not by the teacher, but by a colleague. The outside reader's pass-or-fail judgment, based on department-wide standards, is final unless the original instructor strongly disagrees, in which case the matter may be appealed. Final evaluation by a disinterested party, it is argued, makes the students "more willing to accept the teacher in the role he or she actually fulfills, the friend and mentor who has a great stake in preparing the student to pass the portfolio" (952). Such a system requires cooperation among all writing teachers, a working together which can benefit all participants by developing a clearer cross-departmental consensus about standards.

Indeed, how can individual instructors be confident that their judgments represent the same standards their colleagues use? As they read volumes of student essays over the years, experienced writing teachers tend to form an intuitive sense about where a piece of writing falls on a scale of effectiveness. Usually the scale is structured along the A to F range required by the standard grading system; variations such as Honors-High Pass-Pass-Fail scale or the like allow the same sort of hierarchical scale. Nor is it difficult to articulate the differences in levels of such a scale. Most experienced readers can describe an "A" paper, a "B" paper, and so on down the scale, relying on degrees of effective organization, style, support, mechanics and usage, and tone, for example. It is in the application of the reader's intuitive scale to particular papers that the rub usually comes. What one teacher perceives as an "A" paper may appear to another as a "B−", not because they disagree on what an "A" paper is in the abstract, but because they perceive a particular writing differently. For an infinite variety of reasons, individual pieces of writing may cause sharp disputes among instructors who share the most serene theoretical agreement about standards of effective writing. New writing teachers especially may use inconsistent evaluative standards; they may be unprepared for the enormous variation in student abilities or for the complex mixture of strengths and weaknesses in a single piece of writing.

Evaluative standards can be harmonized among teachers, however. A crucially important activity can help: periodic, department-wide readings of student writing during which teachers' evaluations are openly discussed, compared, and adjusted if too far afield from the consensus. This "calibration" of grading standards (described in Chapter Four) can help new and experienced teachers both. It can help new writing teachers articulate their standards and form a sense of where particular essays may fall on their personal evaluative scales. Experienced teachers may gain trust in their judgments by having them confirmed in public discussion and by articulating more clearly the reasons for them. If a teacher's judgments depart frequently from the judgments of colleagues, a change in his or her own evaluative scale may be needed. The joint reading must be followed by an open discussion among all participants. This process, by serving the writing teacher, ultimately serves the student: fairer and more consistent evaluations of student work will result from collaborative openness.

Works Cited

Anson, Chris M. *Writing and Response: Theory, Practice, and Research.* Urbana, IL: NCTE, 1989.

Arbur, Rosemarie. "The Student-Teacher Conference." *College Composition and Communication* 28 (1977): 338–42.

Bales, Robert. "Communication in Small Groups." *Communication, Language and Meaning.* Ed. George A. Miller. New York: Basic Books, 1973.

Beaven, Mary. "Individualized Goal Setting, Self-Evaluation, and Peer Evaluation." *Evaluating Writing.* Ed. Charles R. Cooper and Lee Odell. Urbana, IL: NCTE, 1977.

Berkenkotter, Carol. "Student Writers and Their Sense of Authority Over Texts." CCC 35 (1984): 312–19.

Bleich, David. *The Double Perspective: Language, Literacy, and Social Relations.* New York: Oxford University Press, 1988.

Brannon, Lil and C. H. Knoblauch. "On Students' Rights to Their Own Texts: A Model of Teacher Response." CCC 33 (1982): 157–66.

Britton, James et al. *The Development of Writing Abilities* (11–18). London: Macmillan Education, 1975.

Bruffee, Kenneth. "Collaborative Learning and the 'Conversation of Mankind'." CE 46 (1984): 635–52.

Butz, Judith and Terry Grabar. "Tutorial vs. Classroom in Freshman English." CE 37 (1976): 654–66.

Coles, William E. Jr. *The Plural I: The Teaching of Writing.* New York: Holt, Rinehart and Winston, 1978; rpt. Portsmouth, NH: Boynton/Cook, 1988.

Denman, Mary. "The Measure of Success in Writing." CCC 29 (1978): 42–46.

Elbow, Peter. *Writing Without Teachers.* New York: Oxford University Press, 1973.

Ellson, Douglas G. "Tutoring." Gage 130–65.

Ford, James E. and Gregory Larkin. "The Portfolio System: An End to Backsliding Writing Standards." CE 39 (1978): 950–55.

Gage, Nicholas, ed. *The Psychology of Teaching Methods.* Chicago: National Society for the Study of Education, 1976.

Gall, Meredith and Joyce P. Gall. "The Discussion Method." Gage 166–216.

Garrison, Roger. "One-to-One: Tutorial Instruction in Freshman Composition." *New Directions for Community Colleges* 2 (Spring 1974): 55–84.

George, Diana. "Working With Peer Groups in the Composition Classroom." CCC 35 (1984): 320–26.

Gere, Anne Ruggles. *Writing Groups: History, Theory, and Implications.* Studies in Writing and Rhetoric. Carbondale, IL: Southern Illinois University Press, 1987.

Hawkins, Thom. "Group Inquiry Techniques for Teaching Writing." CE 38 (1976): 637–46.

Knapp, John V. "Contract/Conference Evaluations of Freshman Composition" CE 37 (1976): 647–53.

MacLeish, John. "The Lecture Method." Gage 252–301.

Mallonnee, Barbara C. and John R. Breihan. "Responding to Drafts: Interdisciplinary Consensus." CCC 36 (1985): 213–31.

Moffett, James. *Teaching the Universe of Discourse.* Boston: Houghton Mifflin, 1968.

Newkirk, Thomas. "Direction and Misdirection in Peer Response." CCC 35 (1984): 301–11.

Nystrand, Martin and Deborah Brandt. "Response to Writing as a Context for Learning to Write." Anson 209–30.

Onore, Cynthia. "The Student, the Teacher & the Text." Anson 231–60.

Probst, Robert E. "Transactional Theory and Response to Student Writing." Anson 68–79.

Reither, James and Douglas Vipond. "Writing as Collaboration." CE 51 (1989): 855–67.

Rogers, Carl. *Freedom to Learn.* Columbus, OH. Merrill, 1969.

Simmons, Jo An McGuire. "The One-on-One Method of Teaching Composition." CCC 35 (May 1984): 222–29.

Sommers, Nancy. "Revision Strategies of Student Writers and Experienced Adult Writers." CCC 31 (1980): 378–87.

Spear, Karen. *Sharing Writing: Peer Response Groups in English Classes.* Portsmouth, NH: Heinemann Boynton/Cook, 1988.

Trimbur, John. "Consensus and Difference in Collaborative Learning." CE 51 (1989): 602–16.

Wiener, Harvey. "Collaborative Learning in the Classroom: A Guide to Evaluation." CE 48 (1986): 52–61.

Appendix A

Text of
"Teaching Composition:
A Position Statement"
—NCTE Commission on
Composition, 1985

The Act of Writing

Writing is a powerful instrument of thought. In the act of composing, writers learn about themselves and their world and communicate their insights to others. Writing confers the power to grow personally and to effect change in the world.

The act of writing is accomplished through a process in which the writer imagines the audience, sets goals, develops ideas, produces notes, drafts, and a revised text, and edits to meet the audience's expectations. As the process unfolds, the writer may turn to any one of these activities at any time. We can teach students to write more effectively by encouraging them to make full use of the many activities that comprise the act of writing, not by focusing only on the final written product and its strengths and weaknesses.

The Purposes for Writing

In composing, the writer uses language to help an audience understand something the writer knows about the world. The specific purposes for writing vary widely, from discovering the writer's own feelings, to persuading others to a course of action, recreating experience imaginatively, reporting the results of observation, and more.

Writing assignments should reflect this range of purposes. Student writers should have the opportunity to define and pursue writing aims that are important to them. Student writers should also have the opportunity to use writing as an instrument of thought and learning across the curriculum and in the world beyond school.

The Scenes for Writing

In the classroom where writing is especially valued, students should be guided through the writing process; encouraged to write for themselves and for other students, as well as for the teacher; and urged to make use of writing as a mode of learning, as well as a means of reporting on what has been learned. The classroom where writing is especially valued should be a place where students will develop the full range of their composing powers. The classroom can also be the scene for learning in many academic areas, not only English.

Because frequent writing assignments and frequent individual attention from the teacher are essential to the writing classroom, writing classes should not be larger than twenty students.

Teachers in all academic areas who have not been trained to teach writing may need help in transforming their classrooms into scenes for writing. The writing teacher should provide leadership in explaining the importance of this transformation and in supplying resources to help bring it about.

The Teachers of Writing

Writing teachers should themselves be writers. Through experiencing the struggles and joys of writing, teachers learn that their students will need guidance and support throughout the writing process, not merely comments on the written product. Furthermore, writing teachers who write know that effective comments do not focus on pointing out errors, but go on to the more productive task of encouraging revision, which will help student writers to develop their ideas and to achieve greater clarity and honesty.

Writing teachers should be familiar with the current state of our knowledge about composition. They should know about the nature of the composing process; the relationship between reading and writing; the functions of writing in the world of work; the value of the classical rhetorical tradition; and more. Writing teachers should use this knowledge in their teaching, contribute to it in their scholarly activities, and participate in the professional organizations that are important sources of this knowledge.

The knowledgeable writing teacher can more persuasively lead colleagues in other academic areas to increased attention to writing in their classes. The knowledgeable teacher can also work more effectively with parents and administrators to promote good writing instruction.

The Means of Writing Instruction

Students learn to write by writing. Guidance in the writing process and discussion of the students' own work should be the central means of writing instruction. Students should be encouraged to comment on each other's writing, as well as receiving frequent, prompt, individualized attention from the teacher. Reading what others have written, speaking about one's responses to their writing, and listening to the responses of others are important activities in the writing classroom. Textbooks and other instructional resources should be of secondary importance.

The evaluation of students' progress in writing should begin with the students' own written work. Writing ability cannot be adequately assessed by tests and other formal evaluation alone. Students should be given the opportunity to demonstrate their writing ability in work aimed at various purposes. Students should also be encouraged to develop the critical ability to evaluate their own work, so they can become effective, independent writers in the world beyond school.

Appendix B

Partial Text of "Students' Right to Their Own Language"

IV. Why Do Some Dialects Have More Prestige Than Others?

In a specific setting, because of historical and other factors, certain dialects may be endowed with more prestige than others. Such dialects are sometimes called "standard" or "consensus" dialects. These designations of prestige are not inherent in the dialect itself, but are *externally imposed*, and the prestige of a dialect shifts as the power relationships of the speakers shift.

The English language at the beginning of its recorded history was already divided into distinct regional dialects. These enjoyed fairly equal prestige for centuries. However, the centralization of English political and commercial life at London gradually gave the dialect spoken there a preeminence over other dialects. This process was far advanced when printing was invented; consequently, the London dialect became the dialect of the printing press, and the dialect of the printing press became the so-called "standard" even though a number of oral readings of one text would reveal different pronunciations and rhythmic patterns across dialects. When the early American settlers arrived on this continent, they brought their British dialects with them. Those dialects were altered both by regional separation from England and concentration into sub-groups within this country as well as by contact with the various languages spoken by the Indians they found here and with the various languages spoken by the immigrants who followed.

At the same time, social and political attitudes formed in the old world followed to the new, so Americans sought to achieve linguistic marks of success as exemplified in what they regarded as proper, cultivated usage. Thus the dialect used by prestigious New England speakers early became the "standard" the schools attempted to teach. It remains, during our own time, the dialect that style books encourage us to represent in writing. The diversity of our cultural heritage, however, has created a corresponding language diversity and, in the 20th century, most linguists agree that there is not single, homogeneous American "standard." They also agree that, although the amount of prestige and power possessed by a group can be recognized through its dialect, no dialect is inherently good or bad.

The need for a written dialect to serve the larger, public community has resulted in a general commitment to what may be called "edited American English," that prose which is meant to carry information about out representative problems and interests. To carry such information through aural-oral media, "broadcast English" or "network standard" has been developed and given precedence. Yet these dialects are subject to change, too. Even now habit patterns from other types of dialects are being incorporated into them. Our pluralistic society requires many varieties of language to meet our multiplicity of needs.

V. How Can Concepts from Modern Linguistics Help Clarify the Question of Dialects?

Several concepts from modern linguistics clarify and define problems of dialect. Recent studies verify what our own casual observation should lead us to believe—namely, that intelligence is not a factor in the child's acquisition of a basic language system. In fact, only when I. Q. is at about fifty or below does it become significant in retarding the rate and completeness with which children master their native spoken dialect. Dialect switching, however, becomes progressively more difficult as the speaker grows older. As one passes from infancy to childhood to adolescence and to maturity, language patterns become more deeply ingrained and more a part of the individual's self-concept; hence they are more difficult to alter.

Despite ingrained patterns characteristic of older people, every speaker of a language has a tremendous range of versatility, constantly making subtle changes to meet various situations. That is, speakers of a language have mastered a variety of ranges and levels of usage; no one's idiolect, however well established, is monolithic and inflexible. This ability of the individual speaker to achieve constant and subtle modulations is so pervasive that it usually goes unnoticed by the speaker and the hearer alike.

The question, then, is not whether students can make language changes, for they do so all the time, but whether they can step over the hazily defined boundaries that separate dialects. Dialect switching is complicated by many factors, not the least of which is the individual's own cultural heritage. Since dialect is not separate from culture, but an intrinsic part of it, accepting a new dialect means accepting a new culture; rejecting one's native dialect is to some extent a rejection of one's culture.

Therefore, the question of whether or not students *will* change their dialect involves their acceptance of a new—and possibly strange or hostile—set of cultural values. Although many students *do* become bidialectal, and many *do* abandon their native dialects, those who don't switch may have any of a number of reasons, some of which may be beyond the school's right to interfere with.

In linguistic terms the normal teenager has *competence* in his native dialect, the ability to use all of its structural resources, but the actual *performance* of any speaker in any dialect always falls short of the totality implied by competence. No one can ever use all of the resources of a language, but one function of the English teacher is to activate the student's competence, that is, increase the range of his habitual performance.

Another insight from linguist study is that differences among dialects in a given language are always confined to a limited range of *surface* features that have no effect on what linguists call *deep structure*, a term that might be roughly translated as "meaning." For instance, the following groups of sentences have minor surface differences, but obviously share meanings:

Herbert saw Hermione yesterday.
Herbert seen Hermione yesterday.

Mary's daddy is at home.
Mary's daddy is to home.
Mary daddy home.

Bill is going to the circus.
Bill, he's going to the circus.
Bill he going to the circus.

Preference for one form over another, then, is not based on meaning or even "exactness" of expression, but depends on social attitudes and cultural norms. The surface features are recognized as signs of social status.

VI. Does Dialect Affect the Ability to Read?

The linguistic concepts can bring a new understanding of the English teacher's function in dealing with reading and writing skills. Schools and colleges emphasize one form of language, the one we called Edited American English (EAE). It is the written language of the weekly newsmagazines, of almost all newspapers, and of most books. This variety of written English can be loosely termed a dialect, and it has pre-empted a great deal of attention in English classes.

If a speaker of any dialect of a language has competence (but not necessarily the ability to perform) in any other dialect of that language, then dialect itself cannot be posited as a reason for a student's failure to be able to read EAE. That is, dialect itself is not an impediment to reading, for the process of reading involves decoding to meaning (deep structure), not decoding to an utterance. Thus, the child who reads

Phillip's mother is in Chicago.

out loud as

Phillip mother in Chicago.

has read correctly, that is, has translated the surface of an EAE sentence into a meaning and has used his own dialect to give a surface form to that meaning. Reading, in short, involves the acquisition of meanings, not the ability to reproduce meanings in any given surface forms.

Reading difficulties may be a result of inadequate vocabulary, problems in perception, ignorance of contextual cues that aid in the reading process, lack of familiarity with the stylistic ordering, interference from the emotional bias of the material, or combinations of these. In short, reading is so complicated a process that it provides temptations to people who want to offer easy explanations and solutions.

This larger view should make us cautious about the assumption that the students' dialect interferes with learning to read. Proceeding form such a premise, current "dialect" readers employ one of two methods. Some reading materials are written completely in the students' dialect with the understanding that later the students will be switched to materials written in the "standard" dialect. Other materials are written in companion sets of "Home" version and "School" version. Students first read through the "dialect" version, then through the *same* booklet written in "school" English. Both methods focus primarily on a limited set of surface linguistic features, as for example, the deletion of -ed in past tense verbs or the deletion of -r in final position.

To cope with our students' reading problem, then, we cannot confine ourselves to the constricting and ultimately ineffectual dialect readers designed for the "culturally deprived." We should structure and select materials geared to complex reading problems and oriented to the experience and sophistication of our students. An urban eight-year-old who has seen guns and knives in a street fight may not be much interested in reading how Jane's dog Spot dug in the neighbor's flower bed. Simply because "Johnny can't read" doesn't mean "Johnny is immature" or "Johnny can't think." He may be bored. Carefully chosen materials will certainly expose students to new horizons and should increase their awareness and heighten their perceptions of the social reality. Classroom reading materials can be employed to further our students' reading ability and, at the same time, can familiarize them with other varieties of English.

Admittedly, the kinds of materials we're advocating are, at present, difficult to find, but some publishers are beginning to move in this direction. In the meantime, we can use short, journalistic pieces, such as those found on the editorial pages of newspapers, we might rely on materials composed by our students, and we can certainly write our own materials. The important fact to remember is that speakers in any dialect encounter essentially the same difficulties in reading, and thus we should not be so much interested in changing our students' dialect as in improving their command of the reading process.

VII Does Dialect Affect the Ability to Write?

The ability to write EAE is quite another matter, for learning to write a given dialect, like learning to speak a dialect, involves the activation of areas of competence. Further, learning to write in any dialect entails the mastery of such conventions as spelling and punctuation, surface features of the written language. Again, native speakers of any dialect of a language have virtually total competence in all dialects of that language, but they may not have learned (and may never learn) to punctuate or spell, and, indeed, may not even learn the mechanical skill of forming letters and sequences of letters with a writing instrument. And even if they do, they may have other problems in transferring ease and fluency in speech to skill in writing.

Even casual observation indicates that dialect as such plays little if any part in determining whether a child will ultimately acquire the ability to write EAE. In fact, if speakers of a great variety of American dialects do master EAE—from Senator Sam Ervin to Senator Edward Kennedy, from Ernest Hemingway to William Faulkner—there is no reason to assume that dialects such as urban black and Chicano impede the child's ability to learn to write EAE while countless others do not. Since the issue is not the capacity of the dialect itself, the teacher can concentrate on building up the students' confidence in their ability to write.

If we name the essential functions of writing as expressing one-self, communicating information and attitudes, and discovering meaning through both logic and metaphor, then we view variety of dialects as an advantage. In self-expression, not only one's dialect but one's idiolect is basic. In communication one may choose roles which imply certain dialects, but the decision is a social one, for the dialect itself does not limit the information which can be carried, and that attitudes may be most clearly conveyed in the dialect the writer finds most congenial. Dialects are equally serviceable in logic and metaphor.

Perhaps the most serious difficulty facing "nonstandard" dialect speakers in developing writing ability derives from their exaggerated concern for the least serious aspects of writing. If we can convince our students that spelling, punctuation, and usage are less important than content, we have removed a major obstacle in their developing the ability to write. Examples of student writing are useful for illustrating this point. In every composition class there are examples of writing which are clear and vigorous despite the use of nonstandard forms (at least as described by the handbook)—and there are certainly many examples of limp, vapid writing in "standard dialect." Comparing the writing allows the students to see for themselves that dialect seldom obscures clear, forceful writing. EAE is important for certain kinds of students, its features are easily identified and taught, and school patrons are often satisfied when it is mastered, but that should not tempt teachers to evade the still more important features of language.

When students want to play roles in dialects other than their own, they should be encouraged to experiment, but they can acquire fundamental skills of writing in their own dialect. Their experiments are ways of becoming more versatile. We do not condone ill-organized, imprecise, undefined, inappropriate writing in any dialect; but we are especially distressed to find sloppy writing approved so long as it appears with finicky correctness in "school standard" while vigorous and thoughtful statements in less prestigious dialects are condemned.

VIII. Does Dialect Limit the Ability to Think?

All languages are the product of the same instrument, namely, the human brain. It follows, then, that all languages and all dialects are essentially the same in their deep structure, regardless of how varied the surface structures might be. (This is equal to saying that the human brain is the human brain.) And if these hypotheses are true, then all controversies over dialect will take on a new dimension. The question will not longer turn on language *per se*, but will concern the nature of a society which places great value on given surface features of language and proscribes others, for any language or any dialect will serve any purpose that its users want it to serve.

There is no evidence, in fact, that enables us to describe any language or any dialect as incomplete or deficient apart from the conditions of its use. The limits of a particular speaker should not be interpreted as a limit of the dialect.

Just as people suppose that speakers who omit the plural inflection as in "six cow" instead of "six cows" cannot manipulate the concept of plurality, so also some believe that absence of tense markers as in "yesterday they *look* at the flood damage" indicates that the speaker has not concept of time. Yet these same people have no difficulty in understanding the difference between "now I *cut* the meat / yesterday I *cut* the meat," also without a tense marker. The alternative forms are adequate to express meaning.

And experience tells us that when speakers of any dialect need a new word for a new thing, they will invent or learn the needed word. Just as most Americans added "sputnik" to their vocabularies a decade or more ago, so speakers of other dialects can add such words as "periostitis" or "interosculate" whenever their interests demand it.

IX. What Is the Background for Teaching One "Grammar"?

Since the eighteenth century, English grammar has come to mean for most people the rules telling one how to speak and write in the best society. When social groups were clearly stratified into "haves" and "have-nots," there was no need for defensiveness about variations in language—the landlord could understand the speech of the stable boy, and neither of them worried about language differences. But when social and economic changes increased social mobility, the members of the "rising middle class," recently liberated from and therefore immediately threatened by the lower class, demanded books of rules telling them how to act in ways that would not betray their background and would solidly establish them in their newly acquired social group. Rules regulating social behavior were compiled in books of etiquette; rules regulating linguistic behavior were compiled in dictionaries and grammar books. Traditional grammar books were unapologetically designed to instill linguistic habits which, though often inconsistent with actual language practice and sometimes in violation of common sense, were intended to separate those who had "made it" from those who had not, the powerful from the poor.

Practices developed in England in the eighteenth century were transported wholesale to the New World. Linguistic snobbery was tacitly encouraged by a slavish reliance on rules "more honored in

the breach than the observance," and these attitudes had consequences far beyond the realm of language. People from different
language and ethnic backgrounds were denied social privileges, legal
rights, and economic opportunity, and their inability to manipulate
the dialect used by the privileged groups was used as an excuse for
this denial. Many teachers, moved by the image of the "melting pot,"
conscientiously tried to eliminate every vestige of behavior not sanctioned in the grammar books, and the schools rejected as failures all
those children who did not conform to the linguistic prejudices of
the ruling middle class. With only slight modifications, many of our
"rules," much of the "grammar" we still teach, reflects that history of
social climbing and homogenizing.

Further Readings

The following titles are, for the most part, in addition to those named in the "Works Cited" lists. A few works of special importance are listed both here and at the end of one or more chapters.

Some Basic Books for Writing Teachers:

Donovan, Timothy R., and Ben W. McClellan, eds. *Eight Approaches to Teaching Composition*. Urbana, IL: NCTE, 1980. Describes types of writing courses based on different settings, assignment patterns, psychological perspectives and readings.

North, Stephen. *The Making of Knowledge in Composition: Portrait of An Emerging Field*. Portsmouth, NH: Boynton/Cook Publishers, 1987. Clearly-written analyses of various sources of thought in composition: "scholars" studying the history and philosophy of writing, "researchers" doing case-study, classroom and ethnographic research, and "practitioners"—teachers whose insights have influenced the teaching of writing.

Ponsot, Marie, and Rosemary Deen. *Beat Not the Poor Desk*. Portsmouth, NH: Boynton/Cook, 1982. Lively descriptions of classroom methods for creating active, responsive relationships among students and teachers. Useful for secondary and college writing classes.

Shaughnessy, Mina. *Errors and Expectations: A Guide for the Teacher of Basic Writing*. New York: Oxford University Press, 1977. The classic study of inexperienced and basic writers and their difficulties. One of the first major efforts to articulate the psychological and social problems inherent in these students' encounters with institutional expectations.

Tate, Gary and Edward P. J. Corbett. *The Writing Teacher's Sourcebook*. 2nd Ed. New York: Oxford University Press, 1988. Reprints a variety of influential articles covering more than two decades of writing study, covering such areas as "writing and learning," "the composing process," "audience," style," "basic writing" and "responding to writing."

White, Edward M. *Teaching and Assessing Writing*. San Francisco: Jossey-Bass, 1985. Urges holistic evaluation for assessing writing progress, but warns against inherent ambiguities in all writing assesseent; gives detailed suggestions about measurement strategies.

Chapter One: Teaching Writing: Tradition and Change

The Handbook Tradition

Applebee, Arthur N. *Tradition and Reform in the Teaching of English: A History*. Urbana, IL: NCTE, 1974.

Berlin, James A, and Robert P. Inkster. "Current-Traditional Rhetoric: Paradigm and Practice." Freshman English News 8 (Winter 1980): 1–4, 13–14.

Finegan, Edward. *Attitudes Toward English Usage*. New York: Teachers College Press, 1980.

Joos, Martin. *The Five Clocks*. New York: Harcourt, Brace and World, 1961.

Pooley, Robert C. *The Teaching of English Usage*. 2nd ed. Urbana, IL: NCTE, 1974.

The Rhetorical Tradition

Bereton, John, ed. *Traditions of Inquiry*. New York: Oxford University Press, 1985.

Bizzell, Patricia, and Bruce Herzberg. *The Rhetorical Tradition: Readings from Classical Times to the Present*. Boston: Bedford Books, 1990.

Corbett, E. P. J. *Classical Rhetoric for the Modern Student*. New York: Oxford University Press, 1965.

Covino, William A. *The Art of Wondering: A Revisionist Return to the History of Rhetoric*. Portsmouth, NH: Heinemann, Boynton/Cook, 1988.

Ehninger, Douglas. "On Systems of Rhetoric." *Philosophy and Rhetoric, 1* (Summer, 1968): 131–44.

Kennedy, George A. *Classical Rhetoric and Its Christian and Secular Tradition from Ancient to Modern Times*. Chapel Hill: University of North Carolina Press, 1980.

Scaglione, Aldo. *The Classical Theory of Composition from Its Origins to the Present: An Historical Survey*. Chapel Hill, NC: University of North Carolina Press, 1972.

Period Histories of Rhetoric

Murphy, James A. *A Synoptic History of Classical Rhetoric*. New York: Random House, 1972.

Murphy, James. *Rhetoric in the Middle Ages: A History of Rhetorical Theory from St. Augustine to the Renaissance*. Berkeley: University of California Press, 1974.

Clark, Donald L. *Rhetoric and Poetry in the Renaissance*. New York: Columbia University Press, 1963.

Howell, Wilbur Samuel. *Logic and Rhetoric in England, 1500–1700*. Princeton: Princeton University Press, 1956.

Berlin, James A. *Writing Instruction in Nineteenth-Century American Colleges*. CCCC Studies in Writing and Rhetoric. Carbondale, IL: Southern Illinois University Press, 1984.

Golden, James and E. P. J. Corbett, eds. *The Rhetoric of Blair, Campbell and Whately*. New York: Holt, Rinehart and Winston, 1968.

Howell, Wilbur S. *Eighteenth-Century British Logic and Rhetoric*. Princeton: Princeton University Press, 1971.

Murphy, James J., ed. *The Rhetorical Tradition and Modern Writing*. New York: Modern Language Association, 1982.

Freedman, Aviva, and Ian Pringle, eds. *Reinventing the Rhetorical Tradition*. Conway, AR: L&S Books, 1980; rpt. Urbana, IL: NCTE, 1980.

Schilb, John, and Patricia Harkin, eds. *Contending with Words: Composition and Rhetoric in a Postmodern Age*. New York: MLA, 1991.

Rhetoric and Teaching

Berlin, James A. "Rhetoric and Ideology in the Writing Class." College English 50 (1988): 477–94.

Connors, Robert J. "The Rise and Fall of the Modes of Discourse." CCC, 32 (December, 1981), 444–55.

Knoblauch, C. H., and Lil Brannon. *Rhetorical Traditions and the Teaching of Writing*. Portsmouth, NH: Boynton/Cook, 1984.

Miller, Susan. *Rescuing the Subject: A Critical Introduction to Rhetoric and the Writer*. Carbondale, IL: Southern Illinois University Press, 1989.

Psychology and Writing

Donahoe, John W., and Michael Wessels. *Learning, Language, and Memory*. New York: Harper & Row, 1979.

Ginsburg, Herbert, and Sylvia Opper. *Piaget's Theory of Intellectual Development*. Englewood Cliffs, NJ: Prentice-Hall, 1969.

Golman Eisler, F. *Psycholinguistics*. London: Academic Press, 1968.

Jakobson, Roman. "Linguistics and Poetics." In *Style and Language*, ed. T. A. Sebeok. New York: John Wiley, 1960.

Putnam, Hilary. *Mind, Language and Reality*. New York: Cambridge University Press, 1975.

Whitehurst, Grover J., and Barry Zimmerman, eds. *The Functions of Language and Cognition*. San Francisco: Academic Press, 1979.

Composing and Revising

Berthoff, Ann E. *The Making of Meaning: Metaphors, Models, and Maxims for Writing Teachers*. Portsmouth, NH: Boynton/Cook, 1981.

Cooper, Charles R. and Lee Odell. *Research on Composing: Points of Departure*. Urbana, IL: NCTE, 1978.

Emig, Janet. *The Web of Meaning: Essays on Writing, Teaching, Learning, and Thinking* Portsmouth, NH: Boynton/Cook, 1983.

Flower, Linda and John Hayes. "Problem-Solving Strategies and the Writing Process." CE, 39 (1977), 449–61.

Kneupper, Charles. "Revising the Tagmemic Heuristic: Theoretical and Pedagogical Considerations." CCC, 31 (1980), 160–67.

Koch, Carl, and James M. Brazil. *Strategies for Teaching the Composition Process.* Urbana, IL: NCTE, 1978.

Larson, Richard. "Discovery through Questioning: A Plan for Teaching Rhetorical Invention." CE, 30 (1968), 126–34.

LeFevre, Karen Burke. *Invention as a Social Act.* Carbondale, IL: Southern Illinois University Press, 1987.

Mohr, Marian M. *Revision: The Rhythm of Meaning.* Portsmouth, NH: Boynton/Cook, 1984.

Chapter Two: Writing and Reading, Writers and Readers

Individualist Perspectives

Dyson, Anne Haas, ed. *Collaboration Through Writing and Reading: Exploring Possibilities.* Urbana, IL: NCTE, 1989.

Flower, Linda S. "The Construction of Purpose in Writing and Reading." CE 50 (1988)

Kirsch, Gesa, and Duane H. Roen. *A Sense of Audience in Written Communication.* Newbury Park, CA: Sage Publications, 1990.

Murray, Donald. *Expecting the Unexpected: Teaching Myself—and Others— to Read and Write.* Portsmouth, NH: Boynton/Cook, 1989.

Social and Political Perspectives

Bullock, John, and John Trimbur. *The Politics of Writing Instruction,* Vol. II. Portsmouth, NH: Boynton/Cook, 1990.

Bizzell, Patricia. "Foundationalism and Anti-Foundationalism in Composition Studies." PRE/TEXT 7 (Spring-Summer 1986) 37–56.

Clark, Gregory. *Dialogue, Dialectic, and Conversation: A Social Perspective on the Function of Writing.* Carbondale, IL: Southern Illinois University Press, 1990.

Cooper, Marilyn, and Michael Holzman. *Writing As Social Action.* Portsmouth, NH: Boynton/Cook, 1989.

Crowley, Sharon. *A Teacher's Introduction to Deconstruction.* Urbana, IL: NCTE, 1988.

Fox, Tom. *The Social Uses of Writing: Politics and Pedagogy.* Norwood, NJ: Ablex, 1990.

Handa, Carolyn. *Computers and Community: Teaching Composition in the Twenty-first Century*. Portsmouth, NH: Boynton/Cook, 1990.

Hill, Carolyn Erickson. *Writing from the Margins: Power and Pedagogy for Teachers of Composition*. New York: Oxford University Press, 1990.

Neel, Jasper. *Plato, Derrida, and Writing*. Carbondale, IL: Southern Illinois University Press, 1988.

Shor, Ira, *Critical Teaching and Everyday Life*. Boston: South End Press, 1980.

Chapter Three: Discourse Systems

Burke, Moffett, Britton

Comprone, Joseph. "Kenneth Burke and the Teaching of Writing." CCC, 29 (1978): 336–40.

Heath, Robert L. "Kenneth Burke on Form." *Quarterly Journal of Speech*, 65 (1979): 392–404.

Keith, Philip. "Burke for the Composition Class." CCC, 28 (1977): 348–51.

Kinneavy, D'Angelo

Harris, Elizabeth. "Applications of Kinneavy's *Theory of Discourse* to Technical Writing." CE 40 (1979): 632–52.

Knoblauch, C. H. "Intentionality in the Writing Process: A Case Study." CCC, 31 (May, 1980): 15 3–9.

O'Bannion, John D. "*A Theory of Discourse*: A Retrospective." CCC, 33 (1982): 196–201.

Other Treatments of Discourse Theory

Coe, Richard M. *Toward a Grammar of Passages*. Carbondale, IL: Southern Illinois University Press, 1988.

DeBeaugrande, Robert. "Psychology and Composition." CCC, 30 (1979): 50–57.

Larson, Richard L. "Language Studies and Composing Processes." *Linguistics, Stylistics and the Teaching of Composition*. Ed. Donald McQuade. Akron, OH: University of Akron, 1979. 182–90.

Weathers, Winston. "The Rhetoric of the Series." CCC 17 (1966): 217–222.

Sentences

Arena, Louis A. *Linguistics and Composition: A Method to Improve Expository Writing Skills*. Washington: Georgetown University Press, 1975.

Christensen, Francis, and Bonniejean L. *A New Rhetoric*. New York: Harper & Row, 1976.

Faigley, Lester. "Generative Rhetoric as a Way of Increasing Syntactic Fluency." CCC 30 (1979): 176–81.

————. "Names in Search of a Concept: Maturity, Fluency, Complexity, and Growth in Written Syntax." CCC 31 (1980): 291–300.

Gibson, Walker. *Tough, Sweet and Stuffy*. Bloomington: Indiana University Press, 1966.

Kerek, Andrew. "Bibliography on Sentence-Combining: Theory and Practice, 1964–1979." *Rhetoric Society Quarterly* 9 (Spring, 1979): 97–111.

Maimon, Elaine P., and Barbara F. Nodine. "Measuring Syntactic Growth: Errors and Expectations in Sentence-Combining Practice with College Freshmen." *RTE* 12 (1978): 233–44.

Ohmann, Richard. "Use Definite, Specific, Concrete Language." CE, 41 (1979): 390–97. Rpt. in *The Writing Teacher's Sourcebook*, 353–60.

Paragraphs

Braddock, Richard. "The Frequency and Placement of Topic Sentences in Expository Prose." RTE 8 (Winter 1974): 287–304. Rpt. in *The Writing Teacher's Sourcebook* 341–52.

Halliday, M. A. K., and Ruquaiya Hassan. *Cohesion in English*. London: Longman, 1973.

Karrfalt, David. "The Generation of Paragraphs and Larger Units." CCC 19 (1968): 211–17.

Shearer, Ned. "Alexander Bain and the Genesis of Paragraph Theory." *Quarterly Journal of Speech* 58 (December 1972): 408PK1>17.

Stern, Arthur. "When Is a Paragraph?" CCC 27 (1976): 253–57.

Warner, Richard. "Teaching the Paragraph as a Structural Unit." *CCC 20 (1979): 152–5.*

Chapter Four

Literacy, Social Change and Testing

Bloome, David, ed. *Classrooms and Literacy*. Norwood, NJ: Albex, 1989.

Cross, K. Patricia. *Beyond the Open Door: New Students to Higher Education*. San Francisco: Jossey-Bass, 1971.

Farr, Marcia, and Harvey Daniels. *Language Diversity and Writing Instruction*. Urbana, IL: NCTE, 1986.

Gere, Anne R. and Eugene Smith. *Attitudes, Language and Change*. Urbana, IL: NCTE, 1979.

Grommon, Alfred H., ed. *Reviews of Selected Published Tests in English*, Urbana, IL: NCTE, 1976.

Moffett, James. *Coming on Center: English Education in Evolution.* Montclair, NJ: Boynton/Cook, 1981.

Mosteller, Frederick, and Daniel P. Moynihan, eds. *On Equality of Educational Opportunity.* New York: Random House, 1972.

NAACP Special Contribution Fund. *NAACP Report on Minority Testing.* New York: NAACP, 1976.

Tuman, Myron C. *A Preface to Literacy: An Inquiry into Pedagogy, Practice, and Progress.* Tuscaloosa: University of Alabama Press, 1987.

Weaver, Constance, with Diane Stephens and Janet Vance. *Understanding Whole Language: From Principles to Practice.* Portsmouth, NH: Heinemann Boynton/Cook, 1990.

Class, Code and Dialect

Bolinger, Dwight. *Aspects of Language.* New York: Harcourt Brace Jovanovich, 1968.

Dillard, J. L. *Black English: Its History and Usage in the United States.* New York: Random House, 1972.

Gray, Barbara. "Dialect Interference in Writing: A Tripartite Analysis." *Journal of Basic Writing* l (Spring, 1975): 14–22.

Nattinger, James R. "Second Dialect and Second Language in the Composition Class." *TESOL Quarterly* 12 (March, 1978): 77–84.

Ohmann, Richard. "Reflections on Class and Language." *CE* 44 (1982): 1–17.

Shuy, Roger. *Discovering American Dialects.* Urbana, IL: NCTE, 1967.

Also see any issue of *Language in Society.*

Measuring Writing Skills

Diederich, Paul B. *Measuring Growth in English.* Urbana, IL: NCTE, 1974.

Faigley, Lester, Roger D. Cherry, David A. Jolliffe, and Anna M. Skinner. *Assessing Writers' Knowledge and Processes of Composing.* Norwood, NJ: Ablex, 1985.

Gere, Anne R. "Written Composition: Toward a Theory of Evaluation." *CE* 42 (1980): 44–58.

Mellon, John C. *National Assessment and the Teaching of English.* Urbana, IL: NCTE, 1975.

Myers, Miles. *A Procedure for Writing Assessment and Holistic Scoring.* Urbana, IL: NCTE, 1980.

Olson, Gary, Elizabeth Metzger, Evelyn Ashton-Jones. *Advanced Placement English: Theory, Politics, and Pedagogy.* Portsmouth, NH: Boynton/Cook, 1989.

Strategies For Basic Writing

Bartholomae, David. "The Study of Error." CCC 31 (1980): 253–69. Rpt. in *The Writing Teacher's Sourcebook* 303–17.

Carkeet, David. "Understanding Syntactic Errors in Remedial Writing." *CE,* 38 (1977): 682–86, 695.

Enos, Theresa, ed. *A Sourcebook for Basic Writing Teachers.* New York: Random House, 1987.

Rose, Mike. *Lives on the Boundary: The Struggles and Achievements of America's Underprepared.* New York: Free Press, 1989.

Rouse, John. "The Politics of Composition." *CE* 41 (1979): 1–12.

Weiner, Harvey S. *The Writing Room: A Resource Book for Teachers of English.* New York: Oxford University Press, 1981.

Also see any issue of *The Journal for Basic Writing.*

Chapter Five: Planning the Course

Institutional Perspectives

Applebee, Arthur N. *Writing in the Secondary School: English and the Content Areas.* Urbana, IL: NCTE, 1981.

Hillocks, George, Jr., ed. *The English Curriculum under Fire: What Are the Real Basics?* Urbana, IL: NCTE, 1982.

Martin, Nancy, Pat D'Arcy, Bryan Newton, Robert Parker. *Writing and Learning Across the Curriculum, 11–16.* Upper Montclair, NJ: Boynton/Cook. 1976.

Developing Writing Courses

Barr, Mary, Pat D'Arcy, Mary K. Healy. *What's Going On? Language/Learning Episodes in British and American Classrooms, Grades 4–13.* Portsmouth, NH: Boynton/Cook, 1982.

Carter, Candy, ed. *Structuring for Success in the English Classroom: Classroom Practices in Teaching English.* Urbana, IL: NCTE, 1982.

Hashimoto, Irvin Y. *Thirteen Weeks: A Guide to Teaching College Writing.* Portsmouth, NH: Boynton/Cook, 1990.

Irmscher, William F. *Teaching Expository Writing.* New York: Holt, Rinehart and Winston, 1979.

Johannessen, Larry R., Elizabeth A. Kahn, and Carolyn Calhoun Walter. *Designing and Sequencing Prewriting Activities.* Urbana, IL: NCTE, 1982.

Kirby, Dan, and Tom Liner. *Inside Out: Developmental Strategies for Teaching Writing.* 2nd ed. Portsmouth, NH: Boynton/Cook, 1988.

Moffett, James. *Active Voice: A Writing Program Across the Curriculum.* Portsmouth, NH: Boynton/Cook, 1982.

Stanford, Gene, ed. *Classroom Practices in Teaching English, 1979–80: How to Handle the Paper Load.* Urbana, IL: NCTE, 1980.

Developing Writing Assignments

Corbin, Richard with Jonathan Corbin. *Research Papers: A Guided Experience for Senior High School Students.* Second Revised Edition. Urbana, IL: NCTE, 1978.

Kiniry, Malcolm, and Ellen Strenski. "Sequencing Expository Writing: A Recursive Approach." CCC 36 (1985): 191–202.

Kraus, W. Keith. *Murder, Mischief, and Mayhem: A Process for Creative Research Papers.* Urbana, IL: NCTE, 1978.

Long, Littleton, ed. *Writing Exercises from "Exercise Exchange."* Urbana, IL: NCTE, 1976.

Grammar in the Writing Course

D'Eloia, Sarah. "The Uses—and Limits—of Grammar." *Journal of Basic Writing* 1 (1977): 1–20.

Elgin, Suzette Haden. *A Primer of Transformational Grammar: For Rank Beginners.* Urbana, IL: NCTE, 1975.

Harris, Muriel, and Katherine E. Rowan. "Explaining Grammatical Concepts." JBS 6 (Fall 1989): 21–41.

Loban, Walter. *Language Development: Kindergarten through Grade 12.* Urbana, IL: NCTE, 1976.

Weaver, Constance. *Grammar for Teachers: Perspectives and Definitions.* Urbana, IL: NCTE, 1979.

Chapter Six: Teaching the Course

Settings

Abercrombie, M. L. J. *Aims and Techniques of Group Teaching*, 3rd Ed. London: Society for Research Into Higher Education, 1974.

Beach, Richard. "Demonstrating Techniques for Assessing Writing in the Writing Conference." CCC 37 (1986): 56–65.

Calkins, Lucy McCormick. *The Art of Teaching Writing.* Portsmouth, NH: Heinemann, 1986.

Gall, Meredith D. and Joyce P. Gall. "The Discussion Method." In *The Psychology of Teaching Methods: The Seventy-fifth Yearbook of the National Society for the Study of Education.* Chicago: The University of Chicago Press, 1976.

Harris, Muriel. *Teaching One-to-One: The Writing Conference.* Urbana, IL: NCTE, 1986.

Hawkins, Thom. *Group Inquiry Techniques for Teaching Writing.* Urbana, IL: NCTE, 1976.

Seidner, Constance. "Teaching with Simulations and Games." In *The Psychology of Teaching Methods* 217–251.

Steiner, Karen. "A Selected Bibliography of Individualized Approaches to College Composition." CCC 28 (1977): 232–4.

Evaluating and Responding to Writing

Anson, Chris M. *Writing and Response: Theory, Practice, and Research.* Urbana, IL: NCTE, 1989.

Belanoff, Pat, and Peter Elbow. "Using Portfolios to Increase Collaboration and Community in a Writing Program." *Writing Program Administration* 9 (Spring 1986): 27–40.

Bolker, Joan L. "Reflections on Reading Student Writing." CE 40 (1978): 181–185.

Freedman, Sarah Warshauer. *Response to Student Writing.* Urbana, IL: NCTE, 1987.

Lotto, Edward, and Bruce Smith. "Making Grading Work." CE 41 (1979): 423–31.

Lynch, Catherine, and Patricia Klemans. "Evaluating Our Evaluations." CE 40 (1978): 166–180.

Sommers, Nancy. "Responding to Student Writing." CCC 33 (1982): 148–156.

Index

Abstraction, 17; generalization and, 91–92; progression to, 89

Abstractive distance, 87–92

Academic writing: cross-disciplinary, 173; inexperienced writers and, 172; purposes of, 170–71; vs. "real"-life writing, 168–69; transition to, 176

ACT English Usage tests: evaluating writing with, 143, 146: nonstandard English and, 128–31; skills tested by, 144–45

Aesthetic readings, 56

African-Americans. *See also* Black English; Minorities; college attendance of, 125–26

Aims of discourse, 96–103; constructionism and, 98–99 defined, 99; text and, 99

Analytic evaluation, of writing samples, 150, 152–55

Anthologies. *See also* Readings; noncontextual nature of, 186–87; writing instruction and, 184–88

Anthropology, 62, 74–75

Anti-foundationalism, 61, 97–98

Anxiety: in basic student writers, 161–63; feedback and, 213–14; in inexperienced writers, 171

Applebee, Arthur, 5

Aptitude tests, 128–131, 143–49

Aristotle, 23, 24, 86

Arrangement, rhetorical tradition and, 14

Assignments. *See* Writing assignments

Associationist psychology, 32

Audience. *See also* Readers addressed, 54–55; awareness of, 37, 175; categories of, 94–96; envisioning, 54–56; familiar, 54; inexperienced writers and, 175; internalized by writer, 54; one-to-one relationships and, 201; unknown, 54, 95–96; wider, 95–96; writer and, 33–35; writer as, 36

Author, implied, 53

Bain, Alexander, 32–33, 171

Bakhtin, M. M., 61, 63–64

Banking concept of education, 65, 195

Barthes, Roland, 68, 70

Bartholomae, David, 39, 76, 161–62

Basic student writers. *See also* Inexperienced writers; Students; Student writing anxiety of, 161–63; characteristics of, 158 defined, 155, 159; error-analysis strategies, 159; image of, 156–57; revising by, 159; teaching strategies for, 158–63

Basic writing: cognitive perspective on, 158–61; institutional perspective on, 161–63; programs in, 156–57

Beach, Richard, 32

Becker, A. L., 116–18, 120

Berger, Peter, 62

Berkenkotter, Carol, 208

Berlin, James, 61, 64

Bernstein, Basil, 72–73, 133

Berthoff, Ann, 26, 175, 184

Biadilectalism, 134–43

Bitzer, Lloyd, 14

Bizzell, Patricia, 162

Black, Edwin, 53

Black English, 133–43; analysis of, 141–42; aptitude testing and, 128 defined, 133–34; markers of, 134, 140–41; spoken and written forms of, 136–37; standardized tests and, 145–49

Bleich, David, 78

Brandt, Deborah, 127, 202

Brannon, Lil, 84, 200, 201

Brevity, in writing, 188

British Schools Council Project, 33

Britton, James, 21, 33–34, 36, 54, 83, 92–96, 100–102, 133, 148, 171, 188, 197, 200, 201

Brodkey, Linda, 186

Bruffee, Kenneth, 40, 52–53, 61, 77, 202, 203

Bruner, Jerome, 20, 24, 25, 40

Burke, Kenneth, 27–28, 82, 83, 84–87

Categorization, intellectual development and, 20

Chaika, Elaine, 182

Chomsky, Noam, 138
Christensen, Francis, 107–109, 113–16, 118, 120, 121
Christensen paragraph model, 105
Class. *See* Socioeconomic status
Classical rhetoric, 83
Classroom size, 194
Classroom writing instruction, 209–12
See also Writing instruction; advantages of, 210, 212; disadvantages of, 210; feedback and, 210; vs. individualized teaching, 193–96; inexperienced writers and, 211; retention in, 209
Clauses, in sentences, 108–109
CLEP composition tests, 146–47
Code: analysis, 132–33; class and, 132; research, 72–73
Cognitive construction, 3
Cognitive dissonance, 25
Cognitive egocentrism, 17
Cognitive growth stages, 15–17
Cognitive-process approach, 15–38; basic writing and, 161–63; composing and, 24; criticism of, 52–53; influence of, 23; invention strategies, 23–29; modal systems, 32–38; models, 20–23; pedagogy of, 49–53; process terminology, 49; revision and, 29–31; sentence combining and, 112; shift away from, 2; terminology, 49; theorists, 15–20; writer-based prose and schema, 31–32; writer/reader interaction and, 45–53; writing-and-reading process and, 47–49
Cognitive schema, 31–32
Coles, W. E., Jr., 210–11
Coles, William, 177
Collaborative learning: vs. individual instruction, 196; social construction and, 66, 75, 77–79; student writing groups and, 203–204; training students in, 204
Collaborative writing, 37, 38, 202–209; of drafts, 78
Collective knowledge-making, 202
Commission on the English Curriculum, 5
Committee of Ten Report, 2, 5
Commonplaces, 23, 24
Communal negotiation, 78
Communications triangle, 97–98
Community in writing, social construction and, 66, 75–78
Competence: in dialect, 228; in writing, 11, 84, 143–49;
Complex sentences, sentence combining and, 110–11

Composing. *See also* Writing; Writing instruction; cognitive psychology and, 24; as comprehension, 48–49; conceptual (preparatory) stage of, 20–21; contextual view of, 3; cultural relationships and, 63–64; defined, 1; developmental (incubation) stage of, 20–21; editing mechanics and, 9; examining process of, 185–86; expressive view of, 5; goal-directedness and, 48; incomplete nature of, 10; instrumental view of, 21; models of, 20–23, 24; as open capacity, 9–10; paradigm shift in, 2; as personal dialog, 51; production stage of, 20–21; reading as, 45; recursive view of, 21; relational view of, 3; revision and, 29–30; by students, 35–36; vs. syntax, 6; teaching, 167–68; verbal thinking (inner speech) and, 19; writing as, 45
Composition handbooks, 10–13, 170
Comprehension, as composing, 48–49
Comprone, Joseph, 168
Concept formation, 90
Conceptual patterns, of text, 96–97
Conceptual stage of composing, 20–21
Conceptual theories, of discourse systems, 103–107
Conceptual theory of the Rhetoric, A (D'Angelo), 103
Concrete logical operations period, 16
Conferencing, student-teacher, 198–200
Connors, Robert, 37–38, 171
Consensus: social constructionism and, 66; in student writing groups, 207
Construction: of readers by writers, 49; of texts by readers, 49
Constructionism. *See also* Social constructionism; cognitive, 3
Context, 45, 94–96, 178–80, 185
Context-dependent reading, 48–49
Context-dependent writing, 48–49
Contextual view of writing, 3, 38
Coordinate sequence, for paragraphs, 113–14
Creativity, discovery and, 26
Criterion-referenced tests, 150, 155
Cross-disciplinary writing, 173–74
Cues, in texts, 58
Culler, Jonathan, 186
Cultural literacy, 129–30
Cultural relationships, composing and, 63–64
Cumulative sentences, 108–109
Current-traditional writing handbooks, 10
D'Angelo, Frank, 83, 96–97, 103–107

Dartmouth Conference (1966), 36–37, 38, 171
de Beaugrande, Robert, 46
Decentering, 17, 18, 31, 38, 87, 89
Decoding, 48, 97–98
Deliberative oratory, 24
Derrida, Jacques, 70–71
de Saussure, Ferdinand, 68, 70
Description, 33
Developmental stage of composing, 20–21
Development of Writing Abilities, The (Britton), 54
Dewey, John, 38–39, 177, 209
Dialects: bidialectalism, 134–43; competence in, 228; defined, 132, 133; diversity and, 12–13; grammatical rules and, 12; nonstandard, 128–31, 226–33; prestige of, 226–27; reading ability and, 228–30; social class and, 232–33; standard, 227; "Students' Right to their Own Language" and, 135–43; 226–33; thinking ability and, 231–32; writing ability and, 230–31;
Dialogical discourse, 63–64
Dialogue, education as, 65
Différance, 70
Dillon, George, 58, 59
Discourse: aims of discourse theory and, 98; categorization of, 88; conventions of, individuality and, 67–68; defined, 82; as dynamic interaction, 87; ideology and, 63–64; interactive, 83; modes (forms) of, 32–33; political power of, 71; poststructuralist theory of, 68–71; static, 83
Discourse-centered paragraph rhetoric, 118
Discourse communities, 3, 69–70, 75–76
Discourse systems: categorical, 96–107; defined, 83; relational, 83–96; text-centered, 96–107; writing teachers and, 82–121
Discovery, 23. *See also* Invention creativity and, 26; dramatism approach to, 24, 27–28; overemphasis on, 27; prewriting approach to, 24, 28–29; problem-solving approach to, 24, 25–26; tagmemics approach to, 24, 26–27
Discussion leaders, in student writing groups, 206–207
Disequilibrium, 24
Dissensus, 207
Dissonance, 25
Diversity, in language, 63, 64
Dixon, John, 36–37

Documentation, 8
Drafts, 9. *See also* Editing; Revision; collectively written, 78; multiple, 30–31; teacher comments on, 212, 216
Dramatics, reading as, 186
Dramatism, 84–87; approach to discovery, 24, 27–28
Dyads, in student writing groups, 205
Ecological model of writing, 67
Ede, Lisa, 54, 59
Edited American English (EAE), 229–31
Editing. *See also* Drafts; Revision; composition and, 9; grammar instruction and, 182–84; handbooks and, 13; mechanics of, 7–8
Education: "banking" concept of, 65, 195; as dialogue, 65; "problem-posing," 65
Educational Testing Service (ETS), 129–31, 146
Efferent readings, 56
Egocentrism: vs. decentering, 17, 87; in speech, 18, 23, 31; in writing, 95
Eiseley, Loren, 91
Elbow, Peter, 40, 55, 175, 181, 184, 204, 205, 215
Embedding, 110
Emig, Janet, 32, 35
Empathy, 40, 198
Encoding, 97–98
English. *See also* Black English; dialects of, 12–13, 132–43, 226–33; educational policy for, 4–6; nonstandard, 128–31, 134–43; standard, 127–28, 133–43; usage testing, 144–45
English as a Second Language (ESL), 39
Errors: analysis of, 39, 159–60; basic writers and, 159–60; effective writing and, 8
Ethnography, 60, 74–75
Evaluation, 212–20. *See also* Feedback; Grading; Responses; Testing; analytic, 150, 152–55; defined, 212; direction of, 216–17; holistic, 150–52, 154; for placement or exemption, 150–53; portfolio system of, 219; primary trait scoring and, 155; for progress assessment, 153–55; for research purposes, 153–55; responses and, 213–14; standardized tests and, 35, 143–49; standards of, 217–20; student anxiety and, 213–14; timing of, 217; of writing samples, 149
Experience: construction of meaning and, 52; hierarchical categorization of, 20; student writing development and, 37–38

Exploratory discourse, 100
Exploratory (heuristic) methods, 8
Exposition, 33
Expressive discourse (Kinneavy),
  100–103
Expressive writing (Britton), 5, 34–36,
  54, 94, 96, 101–103
External speech, 18–19
Facilitating relationships, 40
Feedback. *See also* Evaluation; Grad-
  ing; Responses; in classroom, 210;
  direction of, 216–17; evaluation and,
  213–14; learning and, 196; peer vs.
  teacher, 214–16; in student-teacher
  writing conferences, 199–200; in stu-
  dent writing groups, 203, 208–209
Fields of discourse, 36
Fish, Stanley, 69
Flexibility, problem-solving and, 25
Flower, Linda, 21, 31, 48, 51–52, 55,
  175
Focused knowledge, 9
Forensic oratory, 24
Formalists, 53
Formal operations period, 17
Forms of discourse, 32–33
Foundationalism, 98–99
Freedom to Learn (Rogers), 40
Freewriting, revision and, 181
Freire, Paulo, 65, 195
Function categories for writing, 33–34
Garrison, Roger, 198
Geertz, Clifford, 62
Generalization, abstraction and, 91–92
Generative rhetoric: of paragraphs, 107,
  113–116; of sentences, 107–109
Genung, John Franklin, 33
Gere, Anne Ruggles, 203
Gibson, Walker, 54
Grading, 213. *See also* Evaluation;
  Feedback; standards of, 217–20
Grammar: dialect and, 12, 232–33;
  grapholect and, 183; rules of, 8, 11;
  social class and, 232–33; tagmemics
  and, 26; transformational, 11–12;
  writing skills and, 182–84
Grammar of Motives, A (Burke), 85, 86
Grammars (texts), 11. *See also* Hand-
  books
Grapholects, 137, 183
Group writing, 37, 40–41
Growth Through English (Dixon), 36
Haas, Christina, 51–52
Hairston, Maxine, 30
Handbooks, 10–13, 49–50, 178
Harris, Joseph, 76
Hartwell, Patrick, 11
Hawkins, Thom, 204, 205

Hayes, John, 21, 48
Heath, Shirley Brice, 74–75, 127
Hepburn, A. D., 33
Hesitation phenomena, 72–73
Heteroglossia, 63
Heuristics, 25–26; dramatism, 27–28;
  methods, 8; prewriting, 28–29; prob-
  lem-solving, 25–26; tagmemic,
  26–27; use of, 29
Hirsch, E. D., 12, 137
Holistic evaluation, 150–52, 154
Holistic revision, 29–30
Hunt, Kellogg, 110
Ideology, language and, 64–65
I-it scale, 87–91
Illiteracy, 127
Imagination, 26
Imagined readers, 49–51, 54–56, 58–59
Immense Journey, The (Eiseley), 91
Implied author, 53
Implied reader, 57
Impromptu writing, 181
Individual: discourse conventions and,
  67–68; language and, 66–67; social
  origins of development of, 22–23; tra-
  dition of, in writing, 44–59
Individualized writing instruction. *See
  also* Writing instruction; vs. class-
  room instruction, 193–96; through
  one-on-one relationships, 193–201
Inexperienced readers, construction of
  meaning by, 52
Inexperienced writers, 155. *See also*
  Basic student writers; awareness of
  audience by, 54–56; classroom writing instruction and, 211; difficulties
  of, 171, 172; error-analysis and, 39;
  one-on-one student-teacher relationships and, 201; personal writing and,
  171, 176; student writing groups and,
  205; understanding of revision by,
  182; writing assignments for, 176–80;
  writing groups and, 203, 204
Informative discourse, 100
Inner speech, 18–19, 31
Instrumental view of language, 3, 21
Intellectual growth: language and,
  15–20; Piaget's theory of, 15–17;
  social origins of, 22–23
Intentions: analysis of in reading, 186;
  in writing, 48, 168
Intertext, 70, 75
Invention: cognitive-process approach
  and, 24; rhetoric and, 14, 83; strate-
  gies for, 23–29
Iser, Wolfgang, 56–58, 59
I-you scale, 87–89
Jencks, Christopher, 131

Journal-keeping: as prewriting, 29; value of, 174

Judy, Stephen, 176

Katz, Marilyn, 176

Kent, Thomas, 77

Kernel sentences, 109–112

Kinneavy, James, 83, 96–103

Knoblauch, C. H., 62, 64, 84, 200, 201

Knowledge: focused, 9; personal, 8–9; tacit, 9, 11

Knowledge-making: collective, 202; social constructionism and, 61

Kuhn, Thomas, 2

Labov, William, 138

Language: constructionist view of, 3, 19; diversity in, 63, 64; ideology and, 64–65; individual control and, 66–67; instrumental view of, 3, 21; intellectual development and, 15–20; meaning and, 70–71; ornate view of, 3; poetic functions of, 92–96; power and, 5; recursive view of, 21; self-knowledge and, 62; self-presentation in, 6–7; social constructionism and, 61; social dialectics and, 63; thought and, 18–19; transactional functions of, 92–96

Language aptitude tests, 128–31, 143–49

Language deficiencies, 73–74

Language development: cognitive growth and, 16–17; ethnography and, 74–75; social class and, 72–73; social cohesion and, 74–75; sociology and, 72–74; theories of, 5

Language-fact exercises, 11

Leadership, in student writing groups, 206–207

Life-adjustment, language learning as, 5

Linguistics, 98

Listeners, as reactive, 53

Literacy: decline of, 125–32; definition of, 132; factors affecting, 156; liberation of the oppressed and, 65; minority students and, 125–32; standard English and, 127–28

Literary discourse, 100–102

Literary theory, 45, 56–58

Literature instruction, 5

Lunsford, Andrea, 54, 59, 160–61

Macrorie, Ken, 181

Marxism, social constructionism and, 64, 65

Meaning: construction of, 52; determinants of, 3; language and, 70–71; text(s) and, 56

Meditative writing, 29, 91

Mellon, John, 110

Micro-rhetorics. *See also* Rhetoric; defined, 82; of paragraphs, 112–21; of sentences, 107–12

Milic, Louis, 83

Miller, Susan, 184

Mind in Society (Vygotsky), 23

Minorities: college attendance and, 125–26; literacy and, 125–32; non-standard English and, 133–43; standardized tests and, 145–49

Mock readers, 54

Modal systems, 32–38

Models of writing behavior, 46

Moffett, James, 83, 87–92, 95, 96, 133, 183, 201

Murray, Donald, 31, 47, 182

Nader-Nairn report, 130–31

National Assessment of Educational Progress (NAEP), 35, 155

National Council of Teachers of English (NCTE), 135–36, 194; Commission on Composition, 37, 40, 223

New Criticism, 56

Newkirk, Thomas, 199, 214

Newsweek, 129

Noncontextual readings, 186–87

Nonstandard English, 134–43

Norm-referenced tests, 144, 150

North, Stephen, 53

Nystrand, Martin, 202

Ogbu, John, 127

O'Hare, Frank, 12, 183

Olson, Gary, 71

One-on-one instruction, 197–201; vs. classroom instruction, 193–96; conferencing, 198–200; criticism of, 198, 200–201

Ong, Walker, 54

Onore, Cynthia, 208

Open capacity, 7–8; composition as, 9–10; value of, 9

Oratory, 24

Ornate view of language, 3, 83–84

Orwell, George, 187

Outer speech, 18–19

Paradigmatic analysis, 105–107

Paradigm shift, 2

Paragraph structure, 112–21; coordinate sequence, 113–14; discourse-centered rhetoric, 118–21; micro-rhetorics of, 112–21; mixed sequence, 114–15; models of, 8; reader-centered, 120–21; sentence progression in, 105; subordinate sequence of, 113–14; tagmemic analysis of, 116–18; topic sentences and, 113, 115–16; TRI pattern of, 116–18

Park, Douglas, 55, 59, 175
Pascal, Blaise, 91
Passmore, John, 7
Pater, Walter, 119
Pedagogy of the Oppressed (Freire), 65
Peer groups. *See also* Student writing groups; review by, 202, 214–16
Pensées (Pascal), 91
Pentad of key terms (queries), 28, 85, 86
Perelman, Chaim, 15
Perl, Sondra, 29, 153
Personal knowledge, 8–9
Personal writing, 35, 37–38; criticism of, 171–72; inexperienced writers and, 171, 176; purposes of, 170–71; transition to academic writing from, 176; value of, 171–74
Persuasion, 33, 35, 100, 101, 103
Petrosky, Anthony, 162
Phelps, Louise Wetherbee, 47
Philosophy of Literary Form, The (Burke), 85
Piaget, Jean, 15–17, 19, 24, 25, 31, 38, 39, 55
Pike, Kenneth, 26
Plato, 3
Pluralism, 63, 64
Poetic writing, 34, 36; language functions and, 92–96; literary discourse and, 100–102
Polanyi, Michael, 8–9, 153, 168, 196
Politics, discourse and, 71
Polyphonic discourse, 63, 64
Portfolio system of evaluation, 219
Poststructuralism, 14, 66, 68–75; defined, 60, 68–69
Praxis, 2
Preoperational thought period, 16
Preparatory stage of composing, 20–21
Pretext, 30
Prewriting: discovery and, 24, 28–29; revision and, 180
Primary trait scoring, of writing samples, 155
Proactiveness: of readers, 45–46, 53; of speakers, 53–54; of writers, 45–46, 53
"Problem-posing education," 65
Problem-solving approach to discovery, 24, 25–26
Process-oriented textbooks, 49–50
Process-oriented writing, 50
Process view of writing. *See* Cognitive-process approach
Production stage of composing, 20–21
Progress assessment, 153–55. *See also* Evaluation
Progressivism, 5–6
Prose categories, 33

Protocols, 20, 32, 35
Proximal development, zone of, 23
Psycholinguists, 45–46
Published writing: examining composing methods with, 185–86; sources of, 186
Purposefulness: of reading, 48, 53; of writing, 48, 53, 168, 169
Race. *See* Minorities
Ratios, 28, 85
Reader-oriented paragraph structure, 120–21
Readers. *See also* Audience; Writer-reader; relationship; construction of texts by, 49; cues for, 55; early, 78; experienced, 52; imagined, 49–51, 54–56, 58–59; implied, 57; inexperienced, 52; mock, 54; as proactive, 45–46, 53; as reactive, 53; texts and, 56, 57, 58–59; writing for, 31
Reading: aesthetic, 56; attributes shared with writing, 47–49; as composing, 45; context-dependency of, 48–49; dialect and, 228–30; efferent, 56; as goal-driven, 48; as intentional, 47–48; teaching with writing, 184–88
Reading-and-writing process, 47. *See also* Writer-reader relationship
Reading communities, 78
Readings: anthologies, 186–88; examining composing methods with, 185–86; of published writings, 185–86; selection of, 184–88
Reading self, 51, 52, 185
Reality: aims of discourse theory and, 97–98; social construction of, 61–62
"Real-life" writing, vs. academic writing, 168–69
"Real world" writing, 179
Recursive view of writing, 21, 49; revision and, 29, 30
Reference discourse, 100, 101
Reflexive language, 36
Reinforcement, learning and, 196
Relational discourse theory, 3, 83–96
Remedial writing programs, 155–57. *See also* Basic student writers
Research papers, 177
Responses. *See also* Evaluation defined, 212; evaluation and, 213–14; to student writing, 212–20
Resymbolization, 78
Revision, 29–30. *See also* Drafts; Editing basic writers and, 159; benefits of, 30–31; freewriting and, 181; holistic, 29–30; prewriting and, 29–30; student understanding of, 29–30, 182; writing assignments and, 180–82

Rhetoric: classical, 83; conceptual the-
ory of, 103–107; defined, 85–86; gen-
erative, 107–109; ornate
interpretation of, 3; of paragraphs,
112–21; revival, 14; of sentences,
107–112; situational, 14; study of, 82;
theory of, 45, 52, 53, 58–59; tradition
of, 13–15; writer-reader relationship
and, 45, 52
Rhetorical distance, 87
Rhetoric of Motives, A (Burke), 86
Rodgers, Paul, 118–21
Rogers, Carl, 40, 198
Rohman, D. Gordon, 29
Romanticism, 5, 44
Rorty, Richard, 61, 62, 67
Rose, Mike, 158–59, 161
Rosenblatt, Louise, 56, 57, 59
Ryle, Gilbert, 168
SAT TSWE (Test of Standard Written
English), skills tested by, 144–45
SAT Verbal tests: literacy and, 156; non-
standard English and, 128–31; skills
tested by, 143, 144, 146
Schemas: context and, 48–49; defined,
46; establishment of, 175; for process-
ing information, 173–74; theory of,
31–32, 46
School-sponsored writing groups. *See*
Student writing groups
Scientific discourse, 100
Scribner, Sylvia, 127
Scripts, rhetorical theory and, 58
Self: as audience, 36; expressive dis-
course and, 102; social construction-
ism and, 65–66; writing for, 95
Self-awareness, learning and, 196
Self-directed speech, 18
Self-discovery, language learning as, 5
Self-knowledge, social construction
and, 62
Self-presentation, in language, 6–7
Semiosis, 16
Sensory-motor period, 16
Sentence combining, 109–112, 160–61
Sentences: cumulative, 108; kernel,
109–112; main clauses in, 108–109;
micro-rhetorics of, 107–112; progres-
sion of, 105–106; structure of,
109–112; topic, 113
Shaughnessy, Mina, 39, 157–61, 163,
171
Situational rhetoric, 14
Sledd, James, 12, 135, 141
Smith, Frank, 47, 48, 168
Social class. *See* Socioeconomic status
Social cohesion, language development
and, 74–75

Social constructionism, 3, 52–53; aims
of discourse theory and, 98–99; collaborative learning and, 202; community in writing and, 75–78; defined,
60; knowledge-making and, 61; language and, 19; learning and, 63; Marxism and, 64–65; mind and, 46–47;
self and, 65–66; writer-reader relationship and, 51–52, 60–68
Social dialectics, language and, 63
Socialized speech, 18
Socially constructed self, 62
Social view of writing: individual
development and, 22–23; pedagogy
of, 75–79; shift toward, 2; writer-
reader relationship and, 59–79
Socioeconomic status: code and, 132;
dialects and, 232–33; language development and, 72–73; standardized
tests and, 130–31
Sociology, language development and,
72–74
Sommers, Nancy, 29, 153, 159, 182, 216
Speakers, 53–54
Spear, Karen, 204
Spelling, 8
Spontaneous writing, 181
Standard English: Black English and,
133–43; literacy definitions and,
127–28; Standardized tests, 128–31,
143–149; Standard Written English,
144–45; Static characteristics of
texts, 83
Stimulus-response-reinforcement
(SRR) model, 195–196
Students: classroom writing instruction
and, 209–212; collaborative writing
by, 202–209; discourse communities
and, 76–77; expressive writing by,
35–36; interaction with teachers by,
38–40, 195; one-on-one relationships
with teachers by, 197–201, 209–212;
as passive recipients of knowledge,
195; relationships and writing development, 196; writing errors by, 39
"Students' Right to Their Own Language," 135–43, 226–33
Student-to-student relationships, 196,
202–209. *See also* Student writing
groups
Student writing. *See also* Basic student
writers; Inexperienced writers; attitudes toward, 38–41; audience
awareness and, 37; evaluation of,
212–20; responding to, 212–20; student experience and, 37–38; student
responses to, 214–15; teacher
responses to, 214–15

Student writing groups, 40–41; advantages of, 208–209; benefits of, 212; characteristics of, 205–206; consensus in, 207; dyads, 205; factors affecting success of, 203; feedback in, 208–209; forming, 203–205; interaction training for, 204–205; leadership in, 206–207; writing instruction through, 196, 202–209, 214–15
Style: in rhetoric, 14, 83; structure and, 106
Subordinate sequence, for paragraphs, 113–14
Syntactic maturity, 110
Syntagmatic analysis, 105–106
Syntax: composition and, 6, 11; transformational grammar and, 11–12
Tacit knowledge, 8–9, 11, 196; writing evaluation and, 153; writing process and, 168
Tagmemics: discovery and, 24, 26–27; paragraph analysis, 116–18
Tchudi, Stephen, 176
Teacherless writing classes, 205
Teachers: course loads for, 194; discourse systems and, 82–121; empathy of, 198; as facilitators, 195; NCTE position statement on, 224–25; process-orientation and, 50; responses by, 214–16; writing to please, 179, 181
Teacher-student relationships, 38–40, 195; one-on-one tutorials, 197–201, 209–212
"Teaching Composition: A Position Statement" (NCTE), 223–225
Teaching the Universe of Discourse (Moffett), 87, 133
Terminable (T) unit, 110
Testing. See also Evaluation; literacy and, 128–31; minority groups and, 128–31; standardized, 128–31, 143–49
Text-centered discourse systems, 96–107
Text (network of all texts), 70
Text(s): arrangement of, 104–107; cues in, 58; gaps in, 57; as intertextual, 70; meaning and, 56; New Criticism and, 56; paradigmatic analysis of, 105–107; poststructuralism and, 70; readers and, 49, 56, 57; rhetorical theory and, 58–59; syntagmatic analysis, 105–106; as Text, 70; writer-reader-text relationship, 56, 83–96
Theory of Discourse, A (Kinneavy), 97,103
Thought: conceptual theory of rhetoric and, 103–104; dialect and, 231–32; language and, 18–19; as social construct, 22, 46–47

Thought and Language (Vygotsky), 17–18, 22
Tompkins, Jane, 68, 69, 70
Topic sentences, paragraph structure and, 113, 115–16
Topics (topoi), 23–24; in rhetoric, 83; thought process and, 104; universal (common), 23–24
Transactional writing, 34, 36–37, 100, 101; conciseness of, 188; language functions and, 92–96
Transcendence, problem-solving and, 25
Transformational grammar, 11–12, 182; sentence combining and, 109–111
Trimbur, John, 64, 207
TRI pattern, of paragraph development, 116–118
Troyka, Lynn Q., 48
T-unit, 110
Tutorials, 197–201, 211–12. See also Writing instruction
Universal Grammar, 6, 138–39
Vocabulary testing, in SAT Verbal tests, 144
Vygotsky, L. S., 17–19, 22–23, 31, 38, 55, 63
Ways with Words (Heath), 74
Wiener, Harvey, 207
Woolf, Virginia, 44, 187
Writer-based prose, 31–32, 175, 178
Writer-reader relationship, 3, 7, 33–35, 59–79; abstractive distance in, 87–92; cognitive-process theory and, 45–53; constructionist perspective and, 51–52; context and, 94–96; consubstantiality and, 85–86; dialogical, 63–64; literary theory and, 45, 56–58; rhetorical theory and, 53–56, 87; social construction and, 60–68; text and, 56, 83–96; theories of, 45
Writer-reader-text relationship, 56, 83–96
Writers: imagining readers by, 49, 50–51, 54–56; as proactive, 45–46, 53
Writer-subject-audience relationship, 36
Writing. See also Academic writing; Composing; Personal writing; anxiety about, 161–63, 171, 213–14; attributes shared with reading, 47–49; beginning point of, 24; behavior models, 46; as cognitive process, 20, 45–46; as composing, 45; context-dependency of, 48–49; dialect and, 230–31; errors in, 8, 39, 159–160; function categories for, 33–34; as goal-driven, 48; individualist tradition, 44–59; inner speech and, 19; NCTE position statement on, 223–25;

Writing. (*cont.*)
  practical uses of, 172–73; purposefulness of, 47–48, 168, 169, 170–74;
  teacher-oriented, 178–79, 181
Writing-across-the-curriculum programs, 173–74
Writing assignments: attributes of,
  179–80; consequences of, 179; context and, 178–80; discipline and, 189;
  freedom in, 189; for inexperienced
  writers, 176–80; length of, 188; planning, 174–80; revision and, 180–82;
  series and sequences of, 177–78; significance of, 180
Writing competence: measurement of,
  11; NCTE definition of, 84; standardized tests of, 143–49
Writing conferences, 198–200
Writing evaluation. *See* Evaluation
Writing groups. *See* Student writing
  groups
Writing handbooks, 10–13
Writing instruction. *See also* Classroom
  writing instruction; One-on-one
  instruction; analyzing results of, 4;
  anthologies and, 184–88; for basic
  (remedial) writers, 158–63; classroom, 193–96; closed capacities and,
  7–8, 9; contract system, 190; course
  planning, 166–90; discourse communities and, 76–78; error analysis and,

159–60; grammar instruction and,
  182–84; individual, 163, 197–201,
  211–12; issues in, 167–69; NCTE
  position statement on, 225; open,
  7–8, 9, 190; pacing of, 188–90; place
  in English education, 5–6; planning
  questions in, 169–90; sentence
  combining and, 160–61; as service
  course, 172–73; student anxiety and,
  161–163, 171, 213–14; student-to-
  student, 196, 202–209; teacher-to-
  student, 38–40, 195, 197–201,
  209–212; teaching reading with,
  184–88; theories of, 2–10; writing
  purposes and contexts in, 170–74
Writing labs, 40–41
Writing process. *See* Cognitive-process
  approach
Writing relationships one-on-one,
  193–201; student-to-student, 196,
  202–209; teacher-to-student, 38–40,
  195, 197–201, 209–212
Writing self, 51, 185
Writing teachers. *See* Teachers
Writing textbooks: handbooks, 10–13;
  lack of context in, 178; process-oriented, 49–50
Written language, normative function
  of, 12
Young, Richard, 2
Zone of proximal development, 23